AF614906

Praise for *All Things Catholic*

"Mr. Shaun McAfee has put together a great and easy resource for learning more about the Catholic Faith. Whether you have been Catholic your whole life or are simply curious about becoming one, this book is one to have on your shelf and read."

—Archbishop Gregory Aymond, Archdiocese if New Orleans

"When I saw this book's title, I presumed Shaun McAfee had produced an updated version of a classic Catholic dictionary, such as those by Donald Attwater, Fr. John Hardon, and Fr. Peter M. J. Stravinskas. Not so. McAfee's offering makes no attempt, as the others did, to be comprehensive. It aims to be captivating—and it is. It's an eclectic, idiosyncratic, and delightful compendium of nearly 250 definitions and explanations, with many topics not found in any other Catholic dictionary."

—Karl Keating, author of *1054 and All That* and twenty other books

"As a convert, I discovered the Catholic Church to be a very big place with a huge and rich jumble of jargon, furniture, bric-a-brac, customs, tribes, tongues, philosophies, mystical beliefs, theological terms, saints, sinners, foundational principles, peculiar legends, jargon, odd quirks, richly nourishing sacraments, intensely attractive (and deeply alienating) people, offices, departments, societies, and all manner of other stuff—all centered on the Person and work of Jesus Christ, fully present in the Eucharist. When you go to a country you've never visited, having a guidebook to help you navigate it all is awfully handy. Shaun McAfee's *All Things Catholic: A Guide from A to Z* is that guidebook. Good for both deep diving and random reading, it will help not just converts but native-born Catholics learn what's what in this rich, wonderful, globe-spanning stew of many ingredients that is the Catholic Faith."

—Mark P. Shea, author of *The Church's Best-Kept Secret: A Primer on Catholic Social Teaching*

"The Catholic Faith is so deeply rich in words, symbols, and history that even cradle Catholics can find themselves stumped when asked about a particular Catholic belief, tradition, or aspect. In this book, Shaun McAfee has done the Church a service by succinctly capturing the meaning and importance of nearly every major Catholic concept. McAfee gives just enough description to cover each topic while avoiding getting bogged down in minute details. He sprinkles in practical observations and tips throughout the book that provide helpful insights and interest."

—- Devin Rose, author of *The Protestant's Dilemma*

"Remember everything you never learned or you forgot in Catholic school? Are you a new discoverer of the Catholic Church and eager to learn the A-to-Zs of the Catholic Faith? Well,

Shaun McAfee has made it as easy as ABC. With his guide, *All Things Catholic*, information on the Faith is only a page flip away. It is an easy-to-read, engaging book with pithy articles on topics from abortion to zeal and everything in between. Well documented and full of apologetical and theological tips, it is rooted in Scripture and the *Catechism of the Catholic Church*. Read the whole book, an article or two a day, or simply use it as a reference when a topic comes up. Keep this book on your desk—you will use it often."

—Steve Ray, CatholicConvert.com

"Shaun McAfee has created what might be the most original Catholic book in a generation! Compact yet wide-ranging, timeless and timely, it is a massive accomplishment and the work of a truly apostolic soul."

—Shane Kapler, author of *The Biblical Roots of Marian Consecration*

"*All Things Catholic: A Guide from A to Z* is a chest of Catholic treasures. Every Catholic home needs a handy resource to help family members understand the morals, ethics, doctrines, and devotional details of the Catholic life. Shaun McAfee's book is pithy, punchy, effective, and accessible. It provides quick answers and helpful advice for apologists, catechists, religion teachers, parents, and pastors. Buy it, use it, share it!"

—Fr Dwight Longenecker, author of *Beheading Hydra* and *Immortal Combat*

"What's a 'kerygma'? After two thousand years, the Catholic Faith has no shortage of terms. Cradle Catholics and converts alike will benefit from Shaun McAfee's clear, concise explanations of expressions we hear often but of which we may not have a solid grasp. Keep it close at hand and set yourself free from Google!"

—Christopher Check, President of Catholic Answers

All Things Catholic

Cover design by LUCAS Art & Design / Jenison, MI.

Cover images (1446619544) © Vector Tradition / Shutterstock.

Sophia Institute Press
Box 5284, Manchester, NH 03108
1-800-888-9344

www.SophiaInstitute.com

Sophia Institute Press® is a registered trademark of Sophia Institute.

hardcover ISBN 979-8-88911-162-7
ebook ISBN 979-8-88911-163-4

Library of Congress Control Number: 2024934421

First printing

ALL THINGS CATHOLIC

A GUIDE FROM A TO Z

Shaun McAfee

SOPHIA INSTITUTE PRESS
Manchester, New Hampshire

Cover design by LUCAS Art & Design / Jenison, MI.

Cover images (1446619544) © Vector Tradition / Shutterstock.

Sophia Institute Press
Box 5284, Manchester, NH 03108
1-800-888-9344

www.SophiaInstitute.com

Sophia Institute Press® is a registered trademark of Sophia Institute.

paperback ISBN 979-8-88911-162-7
ebook ISBN 979-8-88911-163-4

Library of Congress Control Number: 2024934421

First printing

This book is dedicated to Fr. Stephen Ingram, a.k.a. "Fr. Trekkie," and Fr. Mike Palmer, CSC. Thank you for your priesthood and your friendship.

Contents

C

D

E

I

J

K

L

M

N

O

P

R

S

T

U

Introduction

The task of evangelizing all people constitutes the essential mission of the Church.... She exists in order to evangelize.

—Pope St. Paul VI, *Evangelii Nuntiandi*, no. 14

I absolutely love the Catholic Church. There is nothing that gives me such stalwart confidence and hope for my salvation. In response to this love, I have made it my mission to dialogue with Catholics all over the world, and what I've discovered is that many Catholics want to know more about their faith but have no idea where to begin. On the other hand, I've also heard countless times, "I was in Catholic school for twelve years. I know what the Catholic Church teaches." (This statement, in all honesty, is perhaps the quickest indicator that the individual has no idea what he or she is talking about.) Both of these situations speak to an important point: Catholics must continue to learn about the Faith throughout their lives. Why? Because all Catholics are called to evangelize. As Pope St. Paul VI wrote, "Those who have received the Good News and who have been gathered by it into the community of salvation can and must communicate and spread it."[1]

Yes, all Catholics must be evangelists, especially today! We take certain intellectual nuances for granted in our time. We expect people to be well informed about ideas they hold, especially when they make arguments for those ideas—although social media has made it abundantly clear that this expectation is not grounded in reality. Those of us in the West also assume that people around us hold general Christian beliefs or at least understand what Christians believe. But many moderns in the formerly Christian West are looking to Confucius for spirituality, not to the crucifix. Perhaps more prevalent are those whose spiritual interests (even moral interests) can be reduced to "Meh."

Catholics in the twenty-first century have more factors working against them now than others had during many of the most challenging periods in the Church's history. In order to fulfill our calling to evangelize in these difficult times, we must learn about our Faith. We can't preach until we learn. St. Ignatius of Loyola put it this way: "He who goes about to reform the world must begin with himself, or he loses his labor."

That's where this book comes in. Take this book as a hybrid of an encyclopedia and a user's guide. In these pages, I define Catholic terms, explain concepts, and show how these things are important in the lives of Catholics. I clear up fables and defend misunderstandings about Catholic teaching. This book offers Catholics more than an internet site or forum can present in such a compact volume: it provides you with the ability to understand and practice the Catholic Faith, plenty of tips to show others how to do the same, and guidance for defending the Faith.

As you proceed, you should know that this book covers a wide variety of Catholic topics, including doctrine, people, practices, and more. Given the wide scope of information, rather than reading the book cover to cover (though you're welcome to do so), you might find it suits you best to move from topic to topic based on your needs. Use the A-to-Z setup for easy reference, and keep in mind that I also provide a generous number of book recommendations and other resources on many topics. This book is here to be consulted as you need it, to give you concise information on many aspects of the Catholic Faith, and to point you to other sources of information so you can keep learning, growing in, and sharing your faith.

A note on abbreviations in this book:

+ CCC refers to the *Catechism of the Catholic Church*, 2nd edition (see "**Catechism**").
+ CIC refers to the Code of Canon Law for the Latin Church, *Codex Iuris Canonici* (see "**Canon Law**").

Abortion

Induced termination of a pregnancy before the fetus is capable of surviving outside the womb.

This definition of "abortion" is also known as a "direct" or "artificial" abortion, since there are abortions that occur naturally by conditions beyond human control (such as miscarriages). A direct and intentional abortion is always a serious sin forbidden by the law of God because it is the killing of an innocent person.[2]

Abortion is addressed as a serious sin in the Old Testament, warranting serious punishment (Exod. 21:22–25). Of course, the punishments for certain offenses are not the same under the New Covenant as they were under the Old Covenant. Nevertheless, abortion contradicts Christian teaching on the value and dignity of human life, which starts from the moment of conception and continues until natural death. The *Catechism of the Catholic Church* says: "Human life must be respected and protected absolutely from the moment of conception. From the first moment of his existence, a human being must be recognized as having the rights of a person—among which is the inviolable right of every innocent being to life" (2270). Therefore, the Catholic Church opposes all actions that are directly intended to terminate a pregnancy, whether as an end in itself or as a means.

Further reading on the subject of abortion should begin with the Catechism of the Catholic Church *paragraphs 2270–2275. For concise and useful arguments regarding abortion, read* Persuasive Pro-Life: How to Talk About Our Culture's Toughest Issue, *by Trent Horn.*

Abstinence

Temporarily refraining from food or types of food.

This action is also known as "penitential abstinence." As a precept of the Catholic Church (see "**Precepts of the Church**"), abstinence refers specifically to the consumption of meat—the flesh and organs of mammals and fowl. On the regulated days of abstinence in the Church (for Roman Catholics in the United States, Ash Wednesday and all Fridays in Lent), Catholics are obliged to fast and abstain from meat. Abstinence is meant to help Catholics keep the memory of the death of Our Lord. The rules about abstinence from meat are binding upon Catholics (in the Roman Rite) from age fourteen onward.

The Church also teaches that in memory of the Lord's Passion, all Fridays are days of penance, and abstinence is the preferred form of penance, although in the United States it is permissible to choose another form of penance on Fridays outside of Lent.

Absolution

The remission of sin, or of the punishment due to sin, granted by the Church through the sacrament of Reconciliation.

Absolution is a juridical act of the priest. "Juridical" refers to the administration of the sacrament according to Canon Law and published rituals, with the juridical act being expressive of the priest's authority. Therefore, absolution of some sins is reserved for a bishop or the Holy See.

Absolution is administered by a validly ordained priest and received by a penitent. In order to grant absolution, the minister must be validly ordained

CATHOLIC TIP

A frequent challenge to absolution is: "I don't need a priest to forgive me. I can go to God alone." On its face, the challenge is correct: the Church, too, teaches that only God has the authority to forgive sins (see Mark 2:5–12). A priest is merely a man, not God, and therefore it would seem he should not have this authority.

The words of John 20:23, however ("If you forgive the sins of any, they are forgiven; if you retain the sins of any, they are retained") have to be read precisely, not as an announcement of the Gospel but as an action: *you* forgive; *you* retain. This authority was given to the apostles after they received an outpouring of the Holy Spirit. This same authority is prefigured in Peter's proclamation of Jesus as the Son of God (Matt. 16:18–19) and later addressed to the rest of the apostles (Matt. 18:18). Paul's words to the Corinthians vividly acknowledge this idea: "All this is from God, who through Christ reconciled us to himself and gave us the ministry of reconciliation" (2 Cor. 5:18). Jesus, who alone possessed the power to forgive sins, entrusted the Church He founded to Peter and the apostles, and He gave the Church the ability to continue ministering to mankind the graces necessary to obtain holiness and salvation. Jesus gave to the bishops and priests of the Church a special participation in His authority to forgive sins as a participation in His priesthood (John 20:21–23, James 5:14–17). Accordingly, when we refer to a priest forgiving sins, we mean the priest ministers on the authority of Christ Himself.

with competent authority over the person receiving the sacrament (for example, some priests are limited in faculties to practice sacraments outside of a bishop's direction or diocesan boundaries). To receive absolution, the penitent must have contrition, confess his sins, and be prepared to make satisfaction. A priest may also provide "general absolution" to a group of people who are not able to make a Confession, such as soldiers entering battle or those in other dire emergencies.

The principal source for absolution in the Bible is John 20:22–23: "And when he had said this, he breathed on them, and said to them, 'Receive the Holy Spirit. If you forgive the sins of any, they are forgiven; if you retain the sins of any, they are retained.'" We read about the power of "binding and loosing" sins in Matthew 16:19, in which Jesus appoints Peter as supreme minister of the sacrament.

A confessional, used for the sacrament of Reconciliation

In Matthew 18:18, He also grants the power to the remaining apostles, in communion with Peter. (See also 2 Corinthians 5:18 and James 5:14–17.) Early Christian writings and authors that defend absolution include *The Shepherd of Hermas*, Ignatius of Antioch, John Chrysostom, Clement of Alexandria, Tertullian, Origen, Athanasius, Cyprian, and Basil.

God's forgiveness is the grace that accompanies absolution, but His forgiveness is not limited to absolution.

Adoration

A sign or act of devotion, prayer, and worship given to God alone.

The word "adore" comes from the Latin *adoratio*, meaning the homage or worship given to a person or thing. The *Catechism of the Catholic Church* tells us,

> Adoration is the first attitude of man acknowledging that he is a creature before his Creator. It exalts the greatness of the Lord who made us and the almighty power of the Savior who sets us free from evil. Adoration is homage of the spirit to the "King of Glory," respectful silence in the presence of the "ever greater" God. Adoration of the thrice-holy and sovereign God of love blends with humility and gives assurance to our supplications. (CCC 2628)

Adoration of the Magi, by Giotto, Scrovegni Chapel, Padua.

Adoration is reserved for God alone: "You shall worship no other god, for the Lord, whose name is

CATHOLIC TIP

When Catholics say they are "going to adoration," they are referring to Eucharistic Adoration. Catholics believe that Jesus is truly present—Body, Blood, Soul, and Divinity—in the Eucharist under the appearances of bread and wine (see "**Eucharist**" for more). Although Eucharistic Adoration is not explicitly present in Sacred Scripture, we do find glimpses of it in the teachings of Jesus. In the Bread of Life Discourse in John 6, Jesus says to the Jews, "For the bread of God is that which comes down from Heaven, and gives life to the world. . . . I am the bread of life; he who comes to me shall not hunger, and he who believes in me shall never thirst" (John 6:33, 35). When you go to Eucharistic Adoration, simply try to contemplate the mystery of the Eucharist set before you. Pray, think joyful, holy thoughts, have peace, and take time to be with Jesus, who is truly present in the Blessed Sacrament.

Jealous, is a jealous God" (Exod. 34:14). As a result, Catholics do not worship Mary or any other saint. Mary is not a goddess, and none of the saints are regarded as minor gods. Rather, the honor Catholics give to Mary and the saints is veneration, the act of showing special reverence for their life, service, and love of Christ. In venerating the saints, Catholics wish to imitate them and so to grow closer to Christ.

Since the Middle Ages, theologians have used the Greek term *latria* to describe adoration, the worship given to God alone. Theologians use the Greek word *dulia* to describe the honor we show to the saints. The honor we show to Mary alone is called *hyperdulia*, since Mary is held in special regard above all other followers of Christ.

Advent

The liturgical season of the year during which the Church prepares for the solemn celebration of Christmas. The first Sunday of the Advent season marks the start of the liturgical calendar year.

Advent is one of the Western Church's two penitential seasons; Lent is the other. For Latin (or Western) Catholics, Advent begins four Sundays before Christmas and ends on Christmas Eve. The name "Advent" comes from the Latin word *advenire*, meaning "to arrive," thus appropriately marking the season as one of expectation and preparation for the arrival of Christ, both in the liturgical sense and in the eschatological sense: His Second Coming (see "**Parousia**").

Advent wreath

Countries throughout the world have various norms and traditions for observing Advent. Universally, the liturgical color of the Advent season is purple, or violet. This tradition is in part because of the penitential focus of the season, as already mentioned, but also because we are looking forward to the coming of Christ, our King, and the traditional color of royalty is purple. This double meaning therefore gives Advent a special appreciation for Christ's coming and for His role as King.

During Advent, we mark the passing of the weeks with an Advent wreath—an evergreen wreath with four candles, each of which is lit in succession on the four Sundays of Advent. The lights represent our hope in the Messiah, but each of the four candles also has a traditional meaning. The first Sunday symbolizes hope, with the "Prophet's Candle" reminding us that the Savior is coming. The second Sunday signifies faith, with the "Bethlehem Candle" reminding us of Mary and Joseph's journey to Bethlehem. The third Sunday symbolizes joy, with a rose-colored "Shepherd's Candle" reminding us of the joy the world experienced when Christ was born. Finally, the fourth Sunday symbolizes peace, with the "Angel's Candle" reminding us of the message delivered by the angels: "Peace on earth, good will toward men" (see Luke 2:14). Some Advent wreaths also include a white candle that is lit on Christmas day. The USCCB's *Catholic Household Blessings and Prayers* provides a blessing for a wreath at home, as well as prayers to be recited at the candle-lighting each evening.

Almsgiving

The giving of money or material goods to those in need.

Almsgiving is a corporal work of mercy (see "**Works of Mercy**"), "a work of justice pleasing to God" (CCC

2462). It is one of the three main expressions of interior penance (see CCC 1434) and is thus highly recommended as a practice during Lent, along with fasting and prayer (see "**Fasting**" and "**Prayer**").

Almsgiving also stands as one of the points of merit in the Last Judgment and as a commandment in the law of charity: "Then he will answer them, 'Truly, I say to you, as you did it not to one of the least of these, you did it not to me.' And they will go away into eternal punishment, but the righteous into eternal life" (Matt. 25:45–46). As Christians, we are expected to give according to our means (see 2 Cor. 8:1–15).

Because almsgiving is a special work of mercy, the merits gained from it may be applied to the souls in Purgatory (see "**Purgatory**"). Quoting St. John Chrysostom, the *Catechism* explains, "Let us help and commemorate them. If Job's sons were purified by their father's sacrifice, why would we doubt that our offerings for the dead bring them some consolation? Let us not hesitate to help those who have died and to offer our prayers for them" (CCC 1032).

Almsgiving adds to merit, but it does not directly affect salvation, meaning nobody can buy their way into Heaven. Having pity on the poor is commendable, but we don't give alms because we want to make the world better; we give alms out of love for God and neighbor.

Angels

Purely spiritual beings with intelligence and will, who were created before humans and who greatly assist mankind in the struggle for salvation (see Heb. 1:14).

The word "angel" is derived from the Greek word *angelos*, and *angelos* is in turn a translation of the Hebrew word *mal'akh*, which means "messenger." Angels are found in the Bible and affirmed unanimously in Tradition.

The study of angels (angelology) generally classifies the angels into nine "choirs": seraphim, cherubim, thrones, dominions, virtues, powers, archangels, principalities, and common angels. Each choir of angels has its own unique task, ranging from warriors, to guardians, to those whose sole purpose is to glorify God.

According to St. Augustine, the name "angel" refers to their office, not their nature (which is spiritual). Angels are depicted in artwork based on descriptions found in biblical accounts, but they are ordinarily invisible to human beings. All angels belong to Christ because they were created through

Tobias and the Archangel Raphael, by Davide Ghirlandaio

Him and for Him (Col. 1:16). In their service to Christ, the angels aid the Church "on her earthly pilgrimage and protect every human being" (CCC 352). In Heaven, the faithful praise and glorify God along with the angels.

The Bible mentions only three angels by name: Michael, Gabriel, and Raphael, who serve God faithfully (Rev. 12, Luke 1, John 5, respectively); and also Lucifer, though not directly named, who became Satan when he refused to serve God (Is. 14). We also know that there are fallen angels with Satan in Hell (see "**Demons**"). The world is filled with a superabundance of these beings, who are countless and unseen.

CATHOLIC TIP

The prayer to St. Michael is a powerful protection for the Church. Many parishes in the United States and abroad include this after the final blessing at Mass, and the prayer is used in private devotion universally among Eastern Churches too. The prayer, which may be used against all forces of evil and temptation, can be said alone, at the end of a Rosary, and in many other settings.

> *St. Michael, the Archangel, defend us in battle. Be our protection against the wickedness and snares of the devil. May God rebuke him, we humbly pray, and do thou, O Prince of the heavenly host, by the power of God, cast into Hell Satan and all evil spirits who prowl about the world seeking the ruin of souls. Amen.*

But despite the presence of these demons, we are not left alone in our spiritual battles. Indeed, Tradition and many of the saints teach that each person is given an angel as protector and aid for our whole lives (CCC 336). These are the guardian angels (see "**Guardian Angel**" for more).

Annulment

The unofficial term for the declaration by a Church tribunal that "a marriage thought to be valid according to Church law actually fell short of at least one of the essential elements required for a binding union."[3]

This declaration by the Church is not "Catholic divorce" (see "**Divorce**") or the termination of a valid marriage but a judicial recognition that the marriage never existed in the first place, regardless of appearances, such as the externally correct celebration of a wedding.

A valid marriage under the Church's law includes the following essential elements:

1. At least one of the spouses is a baptized Catholic.
2. The wedding must be celebrated in a Catholic church in the presence of a Catholic priest, deacon, or bishop as well as two other witnesses.
3. The two spouses must be free to be married (for example, no prior valid marriages or any other vow that would impede the spouses fulfilling their commitment to marriage).
4. The two must be psychologically mature and capable of consenting to the marriage.
5. The two must each understand the nature of marriage (that it is exclusive, permanent, and open to having children).

If a marriage lacks any one of these essential elements, it constitutes an invalid marriage.

Because the Church reveres the sanctity of marriage and must discover all of the facts and circumstances present, the process to obtain a decree of nullity is extensive. The annulment process starts with a petition for annulment being accepted by a Church tribunal. This petition is only accepted if there is some "semblance" of marriage—that is, if a wedding or marriage ceremony has taken place but there is doubt that all conditions for valid marriage have been met or fulfilled. When the process to determine the validity of the marriage is complete, the judgment is pronounced with the traditional "nullity *is* [(or) *is not*] established."

Anointing of the Sick

One of the seven sacraments (see "Sacraments") that brings spiritual help—and sometimes physical healing—to those who are seriously ill, in danger of death, or elderly.

Anointing of the Sick is also known as Extreme Unction, and it is also sometimes called the Sacrament of the Sick. The main purpose of this sacrament is to prepare a person for death and, if possible, restore the sick person to health. "Through the sacrament of Anointing, the Church supports the sick in their struggle against illness and continues Christ's messianic work of healing."[4] We have a great need for this sacrament because Jesus, who continues to heal the sick, desires the health of our body and spirit and for us to experience a holy death.

There are three integral aspects to the administration of this sacrament: a prayer of faith, the laying on of hands, and the anointing with oil. The oil used in this sacrament is called the Oil of the Sick, which bears the initials O. I. (*Oleum Infirmorum*) and is found with the other oils in each church's ambry. We can receive the Anointing of the Sick within the context of a Mass or outside of a Mass in a home, a hospital, a church, or a chapel. This sacrament may be received multiple times, particularly for those suffering from grave chronic illness or for the elderly, and it may be repeated if the person anointed recovers and later becomes sick again, or if, during the same illness, the conditions become more serious.

Detail of a stained-glass window in St. Patrick's Cathedral, Armagh, Northern Ireland, showing St. Malachy being anointed

Sometimes, when a person receives the Anointing of the Sick at the end of life, the Eucharist will also be administered. This reception of the Eucharist is known as "Viaticum" (Latin for "provision for a journey"). Viaticum is distinctive from ordinary reception of the Eucharist, as the recipient renews his or her Baptismal profession of the Faith before receiving the Eucharist.

Physical healing is always hoped for from the Anointing of the Sick, but the primary effect is spiritual healing and the Holy Spirit's gifts of peace and strength to endure the difficulties and sufferings of illness and old age. Other effects of the sacrament as preparation for the final journey in this life are a special union with Christ's suffering, the strength to endure, and the forgiveness of sins.

Apologetics

The theological discipline that is primarily concerned with the explanation and defense of the Christian Faith.

The term "apologetics" is derived from the Greek term *apologia*, which broadly means to make a defense, as one might do when accused of

St. Catherine among the Philosophers,
by Scarsellino

a crime. Recall that from the earliest days of the Church, Christianity has often been outlawed, which has necessitated the development of sound arguments and proofs for the Faith that not only serve to justify Christian beliefs but also to convince and inspire potential converts. Apologetics is also rooted in the Bible, as we are instructed, "Always be prepared to make a defense to anyone who calls you to account for the hope that is in you, yet do it with gentleness and reverence" (1 Pet. 3:15).

The history of apologetics can generally be organized by the various intellectual struggles the Church has faced:

1. The twofold struggle of Christianity with Judaism and with paganism (roughly A.D. 33 to the collapse of the Western Roman Empire in 476).
2. The struggle of Christianity against heresies rooted in pagan philosophy, against Islam, and against the internal strife within the Church that eventually led to the Protestant Reformation (A.D. 476 to 1517).
3. The struggle between Catholicism and Protestantism (1517 to the mid-seventeenth century).
4. The struggle between the Church (and Christianity generally) and Deism, Pantheism, Materialism, Agnosticism, and Naturalism (mid-seventeenth century to the present day).

Although it may initially appear as a fixed study, the development of apologetics has never and will never cease. Because of the fallen human inclination to sin, there will always be attempts to corrupt Catholic teaching and usher in worldviews, morals, and ideals that conflict with the natural law and good governance. Apologetics is therefore not substantially separated from systematic theology (see "**Theology**"), in which proper defense of the Faith is methodically created with retrospective and retrodictive arguments that build on one another in order to form an intelligent and persuasive argument. Today, we find that effective Catholic apologetics requires a fourfold application of biblical studies, logic, history, and the testimonies of the Church Fathers.

Further reading: Avery Cardinal Dulles, A History of Apologetics; *James Cardinal Gibbons,* The Faith of Our Fathers; *St. John Henry Newman,* An Essay on the Development of Christian Doctrine; *and G. K. Chesterton,* Orthodoxy.

Apostle

One of the twelve specially chosen followers of Christ who were given the mission and authority to convert the world with the message of the Gospel.

The word "apostle" is derived from the Greek *apostello*, which literally means "to send forth" and is

Christ and the Twelve Apostles, by Taddeo di Bartolo

typically applied to a messenger (*apostolos*). By the first century A.D., this Greek word was equated with the Aramaic word *seliah*, which denoted not just a messenger but a delegate who was entrusted with a mission.

"Apostle" refers first of all to one of Jesus' twelve followers whom He chose to be witnesses of His Resurrection. St. Paul is also an apostle, uniquely so, since Jesus revealed Himself to him and because he also delivered apostolic teachings (cf. 1 Cor. 9:1, 11:23). The successors to the apostles—Matthias, for example—are not referred to as apostles but are given apostolic authority (more on this in "**Apostolic Succession**"). These successors, the bishops of the Church today, follow the mission of converting the whole world with the same command and duty given by Christ.

The apostles were given the authority of Christ to preach, teach, and heal. Christ told the Twelve, His inner circle, "He who receives you receives me, and he who receives me receives him who sent me" (Matt. 10:40). After Peter declared that Jesus was the Messiah, Jesus gave him the power to bind and loose: to make decisions on behalf of the entire Church. The same authority, in a collective sense and in communion with Peter's authority, was given to the twelve apostles in Matthew 18:18: "Truly, I say to you, whatever you bind on earth shall be bound in Heaven, and whatever you loose on earth shall be loosed in Heaven." We see the authority of Christ given to the apostles to forgive sins (John 20:22–23), to baptize (Matt. 28:19), and to confirm (Acts 8:14–17).

Apostolic Succession

A term in Catholic doctrine used to describe the historical continuity between the present Church and its origins in the college of apostles.

This article of faith refers to two related concepts. First, it means that the bishops of the Catholic Church today are direct successors of the apostles. Second, it refers to the authority vested in these ecclesiastical offices as uninterrupted, present, and continuous. As the apostles were given authority over the Church and their respective episcopal sees, so today's bishops and patriarchs are given the same authority. Such succession also implies that along with the inheritance of authority, that of revelation, tradition, and doctrine is also preserved.

We observe apostolic succession in the Bible in the authority given to Matthias, who was chosen to replace Judas Iscariot (Acts 1:26). Other biblical characters bearing witness to apostolic succession are Timothy and Titus, who received their bishopric (meaning they became bishops and were shepherds over a regional diocese; see "**Bishops**") and were thus successors to the apostles, and who also received the apostolic traditions from Paul in his letters to them and in their in-person interactions with him (see 2 Tim. 2:2).

In the writings of the Church Fathers (see "**Fathers of the Church**"), we also see apostolic succession as a teaching and a practice. Ignatius of Antioch wrote, "See that you all follow the bishop, even as Jesus Christ does the Father, and the presbytery as you would the apostles."[5] Clement—who became bishop of Rome—wrote, "Our apostles ...

appointed those [ministers] already mentioned, and afterwards gave instructions, that when these should fall asleep, other approved men should succeed them in their ministry."[6] Polycarp, Irenaeus, Tertullian, Origen, Cyprian, and several other reliable, early Christian authors also tell us of this teaching.

An objection that regularly surfaces with regards to Apostolic Succession in the Bible has to do with the case of Paul, who writes, "For I would have you know, brethren, that the gospel which was preached by me is not man's gospel. For I did not receive it from man, nor was I taught it, but it came through a revelation of Jesus Christ" (Gal. 1:11–12). Anti-Catholics use this verse to argue that Paul needed no succession of authority for apostleship because the revelation he received from Jesus was sufficient. The answer is that there is no disagreement with the way Paul presents himself: All apostles are sent by Christ. The fundamental principle is that all apostles recognize a consistent faith and authority.

Our Lady of Lourdes, by Virgilio Tojetti

Even after Paul's revelation, he went to Jerusalem to confirm the event and his teachings (Gal 1:11–2:2), and he defends his own apostolicity (1 Cor 9:1–2) and the preaching of others (15:11).

CATHOLIC TIP

Apparitions can be an invitation to piety and devotion. Approved apparitions are understood as aids to the worship of God, from whom all such supernatural graces are derived. It is important to note that *genuine apparitions and visitations always emphasize an aspect of public revelation.* They do not provide unique formulas for getting to Heaven or secret recipes for holiness, nor are they reserved for the very holy or the very intelligent. Private revelation is always an encouragement to increase one's devotion to God.

Apparitions

The supernatural event of an appearance or vision of a person (or persons) not ordinarily accessible to the senses.

Apparitions include appearances of angels, saints, the Virgin Mary, and Jesus, though many of the most well-known apparitions have been of the Virgin Mary. Other than the apparitions described in the Bible (1 Sam. 28:12–14, Ezek. 40:3–4, Dan. 10:4–7, Matt. 17:3–4, Acts 16:9), these visitations and visions are considered private revelation and private experience. While the Church has declared that many apparitions are worthy of belief, they do not alter divine revelation (see "**Revelation**"), and Catholics are not bound to believe in them.

Famous apparitions include appearances of Mary in Guadalupe, Mexico; in Fatima, Portugal; and in Lourdes, France; and apparitions of Jesus to St. Margaret Mary and St. Faustina. The Church generally reserves judgment on these apparitions. Often, the local Catholic Magisterium (see "**Magisterium**"), under the leadership of the bishop, tests the claims and responds to reports of apparitions. That an event is supernatural in origin is not to be presumed; rather, it must be proved.

Ascension

The biblical event of Jesus being "carried up into Heaven" (Luke 24:51).

Traditionally, it is believed that the Ascension event took place on the Mount of Olives. The interpretation of this event is not that Jesus was symbolically transported to Heaven but that His whole Body was "lifted up" (CCC 662) forty days after the Resurrection, as witnessed by the apostles (Acts 1:9). The Solemnity of the Ascension of the Lord is celebrated in some dioceses on the fortieth day after Easter, a Thursday, although many episcopal sees have transferred it to the following Sunday.

The Ascension is a fundamental part of the raising of Jesus to "the right hand of the Father" (Mark 16:19), where He exercises power over the whole universe. The Ascension of Jesus began the period of the apostolic delegation to the Church on earth, with the promise of the Holy Spirit to come at Pentecost. Consequently, following the Ascension, the Church became the visible presence of Christ's authority. Paul highlights this reality: "But God, who is rich in mercy, out of the great love with which he loved us, even when we were dead through our trespasses, made us alive together with Christ (by grace you have been saved), and raised us up with him, and made us sit with him in the heavenly places in Christ Jesus" (Eph. 2:4–6). Even now, our participation with Christ seats us in the heavens.

CATHOLIC TIP

Christ's Ascension is celebrated on the Feast of the Ascension, forty days after Easter Sunday, in keeping with the biblical narrative. "To them he presented himself alive after his passion by many proofs, appearing to them during forty days" (Acts 1:3). Currently, the United States Conference of Catholic Bishops (USCCB) has permanently transferred the observation of this feast to the next Sunday as a norm, but some dioceses still observe Ascension on Thursday.

Altarpiece depicting the Ascension of Christ, by Martin Schongauer

The term *ascension* also applies to the faithful. Prefigured in Baptism, as Christ is raised from the dead, so the Ascension is the guarantee of our destiny to eternal happiness in the beatific vision (see "**Beatific Vision**"). Paul tells the Thessalonians: "And the dead in Christ will rise first; then we who are alive, who are left, shall be caught up together with them in the clouds to meet the Lord in the air; and so we shall always be with the Lord. Therefore comfort one another with these words" (1 Thess. 4:16–18).

Asceticism

The pursuit of spiritual perfection through the practice of devotions and exercises.

The word "asceticism" comes from the Greek word *askesis*, which referred to the practice of athletic training. Early Christians adopted the term and applied it to those practices that would bring forth the fruit of moral and spiritual virtues.

An ascetic Christian does not have to scourge himself for sanctification or to gain virtue. However, it is normal for those who wish to develop good spiritual habits to practice mortification and physically demanding exercises as well, such as fasting, weight lifting, distance walking, endurance training, cold showers, and abstaining from certain activities. We see asceticism illuminated in the writing of St. Paul: "Do you not know that in a race all the runners compete, but only one receives the prize? So run that you may obtain it. Every athlete exercises self-control in all things. They do it to receive a perishable wreath, but we an imperishable" (1 Cor. 9:24–25).

Those who wish to live an ascetic life, or incorporate some ascetic practices into their spiritual devotions, ought to keep in mind that it is a gift of grace to practice asceticism; it is not our own efforts and strivings that dispose us to it. Hence, it is not the ascetic practice itself that makes us holy, but it disposes us to be further open to grace, which leads to our sanctification.

Assumption

Mary's passage, body and soul, into Heaven when she had completed the course of her earthly life.

The Assumption of Mary is not found in the Bible, but it is a dogma of the Church (see "**Dogma**"). This

CATHOLIC TIP

Asceticism is a time-honored means of spiritual growth. We see it especially in the lives of the saints, and the practice is encouraged for all Christians. Still, it is important not to give in to the temptation to view the flesh as the complete cause of our failure to live up to a Christian ideal. "The spirit is willing, but the flesh is weak" (Matt. 26:41) is not a teaching that condemns our flesh as a source or thing of evil (a misunderstanding that has been at the root of a number of great heresies). The reverse is also true: Paul tells of those who fall into sin by way of their weak consciences (1 Cor. 8). God wants our body and spirit to be healthy and happy, and that comes from balanced foods, exercise, and spiritual practices such as regular prayer. Paul, writing as a spiritual coach to Timothy, says, "Train yourself in godliness; for while bodily training is of some value, godliness is of value in every way, as it holds promise for the present life and also for the life to come" (1 Tim. 4:7–8).

The Assumption of Mary, by Guido Reni

doctrine was defined by Pope Pius XII on November 1, 1950, in the apostolic constitution *Munificentissimus Deus*: the Virgin Mary, "having completed the course of her earthly life, was assumed body and soul into heavenly glory."[7]

Our belief in the Assumption is based on Apostolic Tradition (see "**Tradition**" for more). Although Mary's Assumption is not drawn from the Bible, the "taking up" of certain individuals into Heaven is biblical, such as the assumption of Elijah (2 Kings 2), and Jewish tradition supplies assumptions for Moses, Isaiah, and other prophets. It may be said, then, that the Apostolic Tradition of the Assumption of Mary is credited in light of her unique position as Mother of Christ, her Immaculate Conception, and her complete and total fidelity to God.

Several ancient writers witness to this tradition, including Jerome, Augustine, Gregory of Tours, and John Damascene (or John of Damascus), who gave a homily on the Roman tradition of Mary's Assumption into Heaven: "St. Juvenal, Bishop of Jerusalem, at the Council of Chalcedon (A.D. 451), made known to the Emperor Marcian and Pulcheria, who wished to possess the body of the Mother of God, that Mary died in the presence of all the apostles, but that her tomb, when opened, upon the request of St. Thomas, was found empty; wherefrom the apostles concluded that the body was taken up to Heaven."

The Feast of the Assumption is liturgically celebrated on August 15. The earliest records of the feast come from the fifth century, in which it was called the feast of Theotokos (Greek for "God-bearer"—see the "**Theotokos**" entry for more). Focus was soon put on the Dormition of Mary, her "falling asleep," and around the seventh century, it became known as the Feast of the Assumption. The Eastern Church still celebrates August 15 as the Feast of the Dormition of the Mother of God.

B

Baptism

The principal Sacrament of Initiation in the Church, in which a person is cleansed of all sin, made a member of the mystical body of Christ, and charged with the Christian mission.

Baptism is "the basis of the whole Christian life, the gateway to life in the Spirit, and the door which gives access to the other sacraments" (CCC 1213). The sacrament is called "Baptism" after the Greek word *baptizein*, meaning to "plunge" in water. It symbolizes the person's burial into Christ's death, from which he rises up with Christ in His Resurrection, regenerated as a new creature.

We find an abundance of foreshadowing of this sacrament in the Old Testament, from the very beginning, when God's presence above the waters gave sanctification and life to the world (Gen. 1:2), to the great flood that cleansed the world from sin (Gen. 6–7), to Moses emancipating God's people from oppression and slavery by crossing the Red Sea (Exod. 14).

Baptismal font in the baptistery of San Giovanni Battista, Volterra, Italy

In the New Testament, John the Baptist used baptism as a sign of repentance. Christ Himself was baptized by John (Matt. 3:16) and taught that no one can enter Heaven without being "born of water and the Spirit" (John 3:5). Therefore, we find urgency in Baptism as an immediate and initiatory sacrament in the biblical accounts (see Acts 2:38, 8:36–38).

The Rite of Baptism includes a reading, prayers, a simple exorcism (three in the Extraordinary Form), anointing with chrism, and the pouring of water over the head with the words, "[Name], I baptize you in the name of the Father and of the Son and of the Holy Spirit." The newly baptized person receives a white garment that symbolizes that he or she has "put on Christ" and a candle signifying the enlightenment of Christ.

The ordinary minister of the sacrament of Baptism is a validly ordained minister (a deacon, priest, or bishop). However, in an emergency, anyone may baptize with the proper form ("[Name], I baptize you in the name of the Father, and of the Son, and of the Holy Spirit,") and matter (the pouring of water over the head of the person to be baptized).

In the Catholic Church, adults and infants may be baptized. While some Protestant Christian denominations do not allow for infant Baptism, the Church teaches that this practice is not only implied in Scripture (see Acts 2:39 and 16:33) but is also accounted for by several Church Fathers (see "**Fathers of the Church**").

The Church continues to teach that Baptism is required for salvation (CCC 1257). But if a person cannot be baptized with water, he may receive a "Baptism of blood" through martyrdom, or a

"Baptism of desire" emanating from perfect contrition and a desire to follow God.

Beatific Vision

Immediate knowledge of God enjoyed by the blessed in Heaven.

The term "Beatific Vision" is often used in theology to emphasize *how we will be* rather than *where we will be*. Therefore, it is sometimes used interchangeably with Heaven: "When we get to the Beatific Vision" or "The saints are rewarded for their fasting with glimpses of the Beatific Vision."

Knowledge of God is obtainable during life on earth, but only mediate knowledge, limited knowledge or understanding of ideas obtained by inference and extrapolation. In Heaven, however, the knowledge the blessed have of God is immediate and complete. As Paul teaches in his letter to the Corinthians: "For our knowledge is imperfect and our prophecy is imperfect; but when the perfect comes, the imperfect will pass away.... For now we see in a mirror dimly, but then face to face. Now I know in part; then I shall understand fully, even as I have been fully understood" (1 Cor 13:9–10, 12).

Beatitudes

Promises "at the heart of Jesus' preaching" (CCC 1716) *that describe Christian blessedness or happiness and "express the vocation of the faithful"* (CCC 1717).

The most well-known list of the Beatitudes comes from Matthew's Gospel:

> Blessed are the poor in spirit, for theirs is the Kingdom of Heaven.
>
> Blessed are those who mourn, for they shall be comforted.
>
> Blessed are the meek, for they shall inherit the earth.
>
> Blessed are those who hunger and thirst for righteousness, for they shall be satisfied.
>
> Blessed are the merciful, for they shall obtain mercy.
>
> Blessed are the pure in heart, for they shall see God.
>
> Blessed are the peacemakers, for they shall be called sons of God.
>
> Blessed are those who are persecuted for righteousness' sake, for theirs is the kingdom of Heaven.
>
> Blessed are you when men revile you and persecute you and utter all kinds of evil against you falsely on my account. (Matt. 5:3–11)

The Sermon on the Mount, by Ivan Makarov

Matthew states the Beatitudes in the third person, which emphasizes their moral aspect. The Catholic Church has traditionally numbered these Beatitudes as eight, combining the final two (in Matt. 5:10–11) since they both deal with persecution.

Luke's Gospel lists four Beatitudes and four opposed "woes":

> Blessed are you poor, for yours is the kingdom of God.
>
> Blessed are you that hunger now, for you shall be satisfied.
>
> Blessed are you that weep now, for you shall laugh.
>
> Blessed are you when men hate you, and when they exclude you and revile you, and cast out your name as evil, on account of the Son of man! Rejoice in that day and leap for joy, for behold, your reward is great in Heaven; for so their fathers did to the prophets.
>
> But woe to you that are rich, for you have received your consolation.
>
> Woe to you that are full now, for you shall hunger.
>
> Woe to you that laugh now, for you shall mourn and weep.
>
> Woe to you, when all men speak well of you, for so their fathers did to the false prophets. (Luke 6:20–26)

Luke wrote his Beatitudes in the second person, emphasizing their social application.

In both accounts, the Beatitudes are described in an eschatological context: they point to eternal happiness, our everlasting satisfaction in Heaven. Other Beatitudes are found throughout Scripture, for example in the Psalms (1:1, 32:1–2) and in Revelation (1:3; 14:13; 16:15; 19:9; 20:6; 22:7; 22:14). (See also "**Happiness**" in this book to learn more about the function of the Beatitudes in happiness.)

Further reading: Much loved books on the Beatitudes include Fulton Sheen's The Cross and the Beatitudes *and Chris Ruff's* Blessed Are You.

Bible

The inspired, written Word of God, also known as Sacred Scripture and Holy Writ.

The word "Bible" comes from the Greek word *biblia*, meaning "books." The collection of writings in the Bible is known as the canon of Scripture (see "**Canon of Scripture**" for more detail). The Catholic Church has approved forty-six books for the Old Testament and twenty-seven for the New Testament: "For Holy Mother Church, relying on the faith of the apostolic age, accepts as sacred and canonical the books of the Old and the New Testaments, whole and entire, with all their parts, on the grounds that, written under the inspiration of the Holy Spirit, they have God as their author and have been handed on as such to the Church herself" (CCC 105).

Christians believe the Bible to be the story of God's love for His people and the steady unfolding of His plan to reunite us to Him forever. The Old Testament includes the Pentateuch (the five books of Moses), the historical books, the wisdom books, and the prophets. The New Testament then completes the story of the Old: as St. Paul writes,

CATHOLIC TIP

It is important for all Catholics to read and apply the Bible to their everyday lives. Each Sunday at Mass, Catholics listen to readings from Scripture, but it is in private that we grow our appetite for and knowledge of God's Word. Novices need look only to a short reading during the week to get started—reading cover-to-cover is not always recommended. Preparing for the upcoming Sunday Mass by reading the readings *ahead of time* (or reading the readings for daily Mass during the week) keeps us in tune with the Church's liturgy and gives us the opportunity to learn in a proven structure, connecting the Old and New Testaments throughout the year so we see one complete story of God's pursuit of mankind.

"For whatever was written in former days was written for our instruction, that by steadfastness and by the encouragement of the scriptures we might have hope" (Rom. 15:4). This hope is consummated and revealed in the person of Jesus Christ. The New Testament therefore focuses on the Gospels, eyewitness accounts of Christ's life and teachings. It also includes the history and tradition of the early Church: the Acts of the Apostles, letters from the apostles, and John's Revelation. Most of the Old Testament was originally written in Hebrew; small parts were written in Aramaic. The New Testament was written in Greek.

The ultimate author of the Bible is God, but the books were written by human authors under the inspiration of the Holy Spirit. These human authors gave their total consent, employing their own talents and understanding. Under the Holy Spirit's inspiration, they wrote only what He wanted written, and no more (CCC 105–106). What is written in the Bible is complete, whole, and entire; it cannot be added to nor subtracted from (see Deut. 4:2; Rev. 22:18).

The inspired books of the Bible teach the truth about faith, morals, and divine revelation. *Dei Verbum*, the Dogmatic Constitution on Divine Revelation, tells us, "Since therefore all that the inspired authors or sacred writers affirm should be regarded as affirmed by the Holy Spirit, we must acknowledge that the books of Scripture firmly, faithfully, and without error teach that truth which God, for the sake of our salvation, wished to see confided to the Sacred Scriptures."[8] As Paul tells us, "All scripture is inspired by God and profitable for teaching, for reproof, for correction, and for training in righteousness" (2 Tim. 3:16).

Two common misconceptions are, at best, that Catholics devalue the Bible, and at worst, that they believe the pope and the Church have a higher authority than Scripture. These ideas are wildly inconsistent with the treatment of and service to the Sacred Scriptures in all epochs of the Church's history. *Dei Verbum* confirms the Church's view of the authority of the Bible with precise and unambiguous language: "The Church has always venerated the divine Scriptures just as she venerates the body of the Lord. . . . She has always maintained them, and continues to do so, together with sacred tradition, as the supreme rule of faith."[9]

Further reading: For those looking for more in-depth studies, I wholly recommend The Bible Timeline *studies and resources,* Understanding the Bible *by Fr. Jeffrey Kirby, and just about anything from acclaimed Scripture scholar Scott Hahn.*

Bishop

The successor to the apostles who holds administrative and spiritual authority over a specific territory (see "Apostolic Succession") and the fullness of the sacrament of Holy Orders.

The word "bishop" is derived from the Greek *episkopos*, meaning "overseer." The territory over which a bishop has authority is known as the episcopal see or diocese. As a shepherd is responsible for his flock, so a bishop exercises special temporal and spiritual power over his diocese—his ecclesiastical authority—and is responsible before God for the souls entrusted to his care. All valid bishops are appointed by the pope, and therefore all bishops are subject to the supreme authority of the Bishop of Rome, the Holy See.

We find the office of bishop in the New Testament. Paul writes of the *episkopos* in 1 Timothy 3:1–7 and Titus 1:7–11, and he describes the bishop as "God's steward" (Titus 1:7). Clerical hierarchy and the authority of the bishop were then firmly in place as early as the close of the first century (as evidenced by the writing of St. Ignatius of Antioch).

There are varying degrees of ecclesiastical authority of a bishop. Diocesan bishops exercise authority over a diocese. An archbishop is the head of a larger, metropolitan area. A titular bishop is a non-residential bishop who is assigned a "titular see." This type of see is usually the name of a city or area that used to be the seat of a once-thriving diocese but whose see is no longer functioning as such and, therefore, has no functioning authority over that area. Auxiliary bishops serve in full-time assistance to a diocesan bishop. Auxiliary bishops are sometimes titular bishops without the right of succession, in which case their diocese can be reactivated or reused without a continuous line of bishops. A coadjutor bishop is given the special right of succession, normally seen as a means of providing for continuity of Church leadership. Finally, Catholics use the title "Bishop Emeritus" when referring to a bishop retired from service.

Head of a Bishop, by Gaetano Gandolfi

Canon Law

The formal body of laws, regulations, and guidance made and enforced by ecclesiastical authority for the governance of the Church.

The *Code of Canon Law* (in Latin, *Codex Iuris Canonici*), is the official compilation of ecclesiastical law promulgated by the Vatican in 1917 and revised most recently in 1983 by Pope St. John Paul II. It applies to Catholics of the Latin Church. The Code applies to Catholics of Eastern churches only when it specifically refers to them or clearly applies to all the faithful. There also exists the Code of Canons of the Eastern churches which exclusively govern the twenty-three autonomous Eastern churches.

In a fundamental and historical sense, the law follows ancient Roman civil law, enunciating general principles and hard decrees on matters relevant to the life and practice of Catholics. It remains legislatively stable, requiring some reasonable malleability in application, but it also provides for dispensation by competent authorities when necessary.

You can read the full text of the Code of Canon Law in English at Vatican.va. Newadvent.org also has plenty of helpful information on the Code of Canon Law.

Canon of Scripture

The approved list of sacred books that the Church has determined are truly divinely inspired.

The word "canon" is derived from the Greek *kanōn* (in Hebrew, *qaneh*), which signifies a "reed" or "measuring stick." In antiquity, *kanōn* was a subtle term for a rule of law as a measurement, but it was quickly adopted by Christian writers and administrators within the Church.

The Catholic Church treats the Canon of Scripture as final and closed; it can never be added to nor removed from (see Deut. 4:2; Rev. 22:18). In the Catholic Church, the Canon of Scripture is made up of forty-six books in the Old Testament and twenty-seven in the New Testament. All of the New Testament books are accepted by all Christian denominations, though their translations vary. Protestant translations of the Bible omit seven books from the Old Testament, however: Tobit, Judith, 1 and 2 Maccabees, Wisdom, Sirach, and Baruch, as well as a few chapters from the book of Daniel. These books are sometimes called the "Apocrypha" ("hidden") or, more popularly in Catholic academic circles, the "deuterocanonical books." "Hidden" here means that they are found in the Old Testament Latin Vulgate translation, but not in the Hebrew bible. The Old Testament books accepted by all Christians are referred to as the protocanonical books. This difference is not to suggest that there are two distinct lists but rather that the protocanonical list includes those books that have always been received by Christians without dispute.

The Old Testament, called the Hebrew scriptures, is generally agreed to have been established by the second century B.C. The most widely accepted collection and translation of the Hebrew scriptures is known as the Septuagint, a Greek translation of the Bible used by Greek academics as well as by the Jews. The deuterocanonical books were included in the Septuagint. Approximately two-thirds of the Old Testament passages quoted in the New Testament are from the Septuagint.

CATHOLIC TIP

It must be clarified that the Church's ability to determine the Canon of Scripture does not mean that the Church has a higher authority than Scripture. The Second Vatican Council says it best:

> This teaching office is not above the Word of God, but serves it, teaching only what has been handed on, listening to it devoutly, guarding it scrupulously and explaining it faithfully in accord with a divine commission and with the help of the Holy Spirit, it draws from this one deposit of faith everything which it presents for belief as divinely revealed. (*Dei Verbum*, no. 10)

Around the third century A.D., Christians began debating about which books were truly authoritative, canonical, and inspired. Particularly, they wished to agree on which books could be read in Mass. Although multiple Church Fathers and other eminent writers opined—St. Athanasius in A.D. 367 gives a complete list of books of those he considered canonical—the final Canon of Scripture was promulgated by Pope Damasus I at the synod of Rome in 382, and it was again later defined at the Council of Hippo (393) and the Councils of Carthage in 397 and 419. These councils produced lists that included the seventy-three books now found in Catholic Bibles. The Council of Trent (1545–1563) reaffirmed the books included in the Bible.

Further reading: Why Catholic Bibles Are Bigger, *by Gary Michuta, excellently explains the composition of the Canon of Scripture.*

Canonization

The solemn proclamation of the pope that a person lived a life of heroic virtue and is now a saint in Heaven.

Canonized saints are included in the official list of persons accepted and recognized by the Church as saints. Their names are included in the General Roman Calendar for universal celebration and veneration, and they enjoy universal veneration.

In the Church's early history, deceased Christians were proclaimed saints by popular acclamation. Starting in the sixth century, local bishops were responsible for canonizations. The first saint to be officially canonized by a pope was St. Ulrich, bishop of Augsburg, who was canonized by Pope John XV in 993 at the Lateran Council. Pope Alexander III (1159–1181) began to reserve the causes of canonization to the Holy See, and this became general law under Gregory IX (1227–1241). Several centuries later, Pope Sixtus V (1585–1590) obligated that the Congregation of Rites, part of the Roman Curia, had the duty of managing the processes of beatification and canonization. Following this, Pope Urban VIII banned the communal cult of any person not yet beatified or canonized by the Church. An exception was granted for those whose cult persisted from time immemorial or for at least one hundred years.

Norms for canonization developed in the centuries that followed, and in 1738, *De Servorum Dei Beatificatione et Beatorum Canonizatione* ("The Office of the Canonization and Beatification of the Blessed") was written by Pope Benedict XIV and was included in part in the Code of Canon Law of 1917. This was the norm until the "New Laws for the Causes of the Saints" was published in Rome in 1983. Today, the laws for approval are still shifting: a change by John Paul II reduced the number of

Crowds at the canonization of Bl. Pope John XXIII and Bl. Pope John Paul II, April 27, 2014

miracles required to two, in place of the longstanding requirement for three.

Canonization begins at least five years after a person's death. The process starts with a "cause," which is a petition to the papal Curia to recognize the life of the person as deserving of recognition and veneration. The bishop of the diocese in which the individual died petitions the Holy See to allow the initialization of a Cause for Beatification and Canonization. If there is no objection, the Congregation for the Doctrine of the Faith issues the *nihil obstat* ("nothing stands in the way"). The individual is then called a "Servant of God."

Writings, statements, testimonies, and all related facts, known as the *acta*, are compiled and provided to a diocesan tribunal, collected for the bishop's ultimate decision to proceed with the cause. Next, a college of theologians with the Congregation for the Causes of Saints votes on the cause, and if the decision is affirmative, the recommendation of a Decree of Heroic Virtues is sent to the Holy Father, whose judgment is final. If the cause is approved by the pope, the individual is given the title of Venerable, or Blessed if the cause was approved for martyrdom.

There must be a verified miracle attributed to the venerable's intercession before the person can be beatified, however no miracle is required for an approved martyr to be beatified. If the miracle occurs outside of the diocese of the cause, it is brought forth for investigation in the diocese where it is alleged to have occurred. This decision is then sent to the Holy See. The Congregation then makes an arduous and comprehensive investigation of the proposed miracle, and the decision is forwarded to the Supreme Pontiff. If a miracle is approved by the pope, the title of "Blessed" is given. "Blesseds" may by publicly venerated at the local or regional level. This restriction in the veneration is a disciplinary norm because beatification is not considered an infallible papal act, and so it is not yet appropriate that the entire Church give liturgical veneration to the blessed.

Before a blessed can be named a saint, there must be another miracle attributed to his intercession, and the miracle must undergo the same intensive process. If it is approved, the blessed may be canonized. Once a person is canonized, universal veneration is authorized, and Masses, offices of prayer, and other acts of veneration may now be offered throughout the universal Church.

Capital Punishment

The death penalty as punishment for crime, typically reserved for the most heinous crimes, such as murder.

Capital punishment is a topic of growing interest to modern Catholics due to the progression of systems and technology for detaining and treating criminals as well as the advancement of moral arguments on the dignity of life.

In the Bible, capital punishment is a permissible punishment of the law: "Whoever sheds the blood of man, by man shall his blood be shed; for God made man in his own image" (Gen. 9:6); "Your eye shall not pity; it shall be life for life, eye for eye, tooth for tooth, hand for hand, foot for foot" (Deut. 19:21); "For rulers are not a terror to good conduct, but to bad ... he is God's servant for your good. But if you do wrong, be afraid, for he does not bear the sword in vain; he is the servant of God to execute his wrath on the wrongdoer" (Rom. 13:3–4).

Scholars and moral theologians today, however, often disagree on the treatment of criminals and authorization to inflict capital punishment. Those in favor of capital punishment argue that it is proper to the responsibility of a state to protect the well-being (and life) of its citizens, and that the severe retribution achieved by capital punishment holds individuals responsible for their actions and demands that they face their consequences. St. Thomas Aquinas, medieval theologian and Doctor of the Church, agreed with this view, arguing that "to kill a man who retains his natural dignity is intrinsically evil," but that those who commit horrible sins against the community have deviated so far from rational, human behavior that they forfeit human dignity.[10] But he also maintained that the punishment inflicted must not be done in a vindictive spirit nor hatred.[11]

Following more recent moral arguments, however, in 2018 Pope Francis made a revision to paragraph 2267 of the *Catechism*. It now reads:

> Recourse to the death penalty on the part of legitimate authority, following a fair trial, was long considered an appropriate response to the gravity of certain crimes and an acceptable, albeit extreme, means of safeguarding the common good.
>
> Today, however, there is an increasing awareness that the dignity of the person is not lost even after the commission of very serious crimes. In addition, a new understanding has emerged of the significance of penal sanctions imposed by the state. Lastly, more effective systems of detention have been developed, which ensure the due protection of citizens but, at the same time, do not definitively deprive the guilty of the possibility of redemption.
>
> Consequently, the Church teaches, in the light of the Gospel, that "the death penalty is inadmissible because it is an attack on the inviolability and dignity of the person," and she works with determination for its abolition worldwide.

Helpful reading on capital punishment includes Fratelli Tutti *by Pope Francis, and* By Man Shall His Blood Be Shed *by Edward Feser and Joseph M. Bessette.*

Capital Sins

Seven principal tendencies of fallen human nature that are the source of all sins.

Also known as the seven deadly sins or vices, the capital sins are: pride, avarice, lust, anger, gluttony, envy, and sloth (or acedia).

1. *Pride*, known as the chief sin, is the turning away from God as the sovereign Lord. It leads to an over-confidence in oneself and self-centeredness.
2. *Avarice* is greed, the insatiable desire to possess something, normally wealth, and is rooted in a lack of trust in God's providence.
3. *Lust* is an excessive appetite for sexual pleasure, rooted in the lack of respect for true intimacy, union, and love.
4. *Anger*, sometimes called wrath, is the disproportionate response to a perceived injustice, leading to resentment, hate, or withholding true justice and forgiveness.
5. *Gluttony* is the over-indulgence in food and drink.
6. *Envy* is the begrudging of or sadness because of another's good, which can manifest as desire for another's possessions, status, or their life in general.
7. *Sloth*, also called acedia, is not simply general laziness; it is indifference toward one's obligations to God or a general apathy regarding the spiritual life and guiding principles of Christian truth.

All sins that we commit flow from these capital sins, which take root in our hearts and become habits if we do not take care to weed them out.

Further reading: The Seven Deadly Sins: A Thomistic Guide to Vanquishing Vice and Sin *by Kevin Vost and* Dark Night of the Soul *by St. John of the Cross.*

Cardinal Virtues

The four primary virtues, from which all other virtues flow.

The word "cardinal" developed through the Church's use of the Latin word *cardinalis*, which referred to all priests permanently attached to a church. Prior to the Middle Ages, though, the word signified only those attached to an ecclesiastical group; *cardo*, meaning "hinge" in Latin, indicated an attached member. And so because all other virtues hinge on these virtues, they became known as "cardinal" virtues.

Wrath and Sloth, in *Les Péchées Capitaux* (The deadly sins; ca. 1620), illustration by Jacques Callot

Illustration of the four cardinal virtues in *La Somme le roi*, by Dominican Laurent d'Orléans

The *Catechism* says that virtues are "firm attitudes, stable dispositions, habitual perfections of intellect and will that govern our actions, order our passions, and guide our conduct according to reason and faith. They make possible ease, self-mastery, and joy in leading a morally good life" (CCC 1804).

The four cardinal virtues are prudence, justice, fortitude, and temperance.

1. *Prudence* is the virtue that disposes practical reason to discern our true good in every circumstance and to choose the right means of achieving it (CCC 1806).
2. *Justice* is the constant and firm will to give God and neighbor what is due to them. It disposes one to respect the rights of others and to establish in human relationships the harmony that promotes equity with regard to persons and to the common good (CCC 1807).
3. *Fortitude* ensures firmness in difficulties and constancy in the pursuit of the good. It may also lead to self-sacrifice for a just cause and to face the trials of persecution (CCC 1808).
4. *Temperance* moderates the attraction of pleasures and provides balance in the use of created goods, helping a person to master their will and desires (CCC 1809).

Catechesis

Instruction in the Christian Faith, particularly for those preparing for the sacraments of Baptism or Confirmation.

The word "catechesis" comes from the Greek word *katechein*, meaning "to echo." Pope St. John Paul II wrote, "Catechesis is an education of children, young people, and adults in the faith, which includes especially the teaching of Christian doctrine imparted, generally speaking, in an organic and systematic way, with a view to initiating the hearers into the fullness of Christian life."[12] The primary goal of catechesis is to promote the conversion. Such growth is manifested in the Christian life and witness of the believer.

It may seem that catechesis is the responsibility of clergy, Catholic school teachers, or religious education teachers, but the Church says that parents are the primary educators in faith, morals, and virtue.[13] All the same, the primary catechist in the diocese is the bishop; the bishops are the successors to the apostles, and so it is through their authority that Christianity is preached. Throughout history, in fact, no one could preach without the consent and delegation of the bishop. Today, this hasn't necessarily changed—the bishop remains the principal catechist—but the growing initiatives of bishops and popes allow priests, religious, and even laity to

The Catechism Lesson, by Jules-Alexis Muenier

participate in catechesis. In 2021, Pope Francis instituted the ministry of the lay catechist, providing leadership and direction for episcopal conferences to form the criteria and processes for admission into this ministry.

Catechism

A concise, written resource that summarizes Christian doctrine and acts as a manual for instruction on faith and morals.

The *Didache*, an early Christian document of the first or second century, is recognized as the first written catechism, and some early Church leaders were persuaded that it should be included in the Canon of Scripture (see "**Canon of Scripture**"). Catechisms were prominently used (and needed) after the invention of the printing press. Popular catechisms of this time included the *Bellarmine Catechism*, proposed as the model for the current *Catechism of the Catholic Church*, and the *Catechism of the Council of Trent*. In the United States, the *Catechism of the Third Plenary Council of Baltimore* (1885), also known as the "Baltimore Catechism," was the standard guidebook of Catholic doctrine for about seventy-five years.

Although they were robust and useful for teaching, none of these catechisms contained the fullness that the fathers of the Council of Trent hoped for when they called for the creation of a new catechism for universal use in the Catholic Church. This hope was finally realized in the *Catechism of the Catholic Church*, promulgated in 1993. Written in narrative form, the *Catechism* has four main parts: the Apostles' Creed (as faith professed); the sacraments (as faith celebrated); virtues, Beatitudes, and commandments (as faith lived); and prayer, particularly the Lord's Prayer (as faith prayed).

Further reading: A favorite of many is the Living the Catechism of the Catholic Church *series by Christoph Schönborn, a collection of commentaries on Christian living in light of the* Catechism *for the entire year.*

Catholic Social Teaching

The Church's teachings related to life in society.

The basic Catholic social teaching is the propagation of a virtuous society that cares for the poor, the imprisoned, laborers, the sick, and the family, and that promotes the common good.

Catholic social teaching is not based in any particular political party or economic construct or other agenda. These versions of the "common good" are often directed toward the exclusive and particular good of sections of society, despite what their platform talking points may say. True Catholic social justice is built upon an authentic appreciation for life and human dignity and the proper understanding and application of mercy, justice, and love of neighbor. It takes into account the financial, judicial, moral, religious, and life-centric issues that impact society.

Because society is composed of individuals, Catholic social teaching has at its core the dignity of the human person. From working conditions

Pope Leo XIII (ca. 1878), who wrote *Rerum Novarum*, one of the most famous Church documents related to social issues

and wealth distribution to religious freedom and protection of the unborn, the immutable basis of Catholic social teaching is the belief that all people are created equally in the image of God. Therefore, the Catholic Church proclaims that human life is sacred and that the dignity of the human person is the basis of God's plan for society.

The *Catechism of the Catholic Church* puts it this way: "The Church receives from the Gospel the full revelation of the truth about man. When she fulfills her mission of proclaiming the Gospel, she bears witness to man, in the name of Christ, to his dignity and his vocation to the communion of persons. She teaches him the demands of justice and peace in conformity with divine wisdom" (CCC 2419).

Jesus' concept of social doctrine went beyond society's rubrics. He demonstrated and emphasized a radical approach to service, social equity, and personal economics. He made the poor His own identity (Matt. 25:40–45). He condemned social hypocrisy (Mark 12:38–40). He made an example of ethnic bigotry (the parable of the Good Samaritan, Luke 10:25–37). And He commended giving generously no matter the amount (Mark 12:41–40), while acknowledging that mankind cannot rid the earth of circumstantial inequalities (see Mark 14:7, Luke 12:48).

Further reading: The Catechism of the Catholic Church *2423–2425, Pope Leo XIII's* Rerum Novarum, *and Pope John Paul II's* Centesimus Annus, *which brings the central topics presented by Leo XIII up to speed with the current milieu.*

Celibacy

The state of being unmarried and sexually abstinent.

In the New Testament, celibacy was highly advised for Christians, as Paul proposes: "Now concerning the unmarried, I have no command of the Lord, but I give my opinion as one who by the Lord's mercy is trustworthy.... Are you free from a wife? Do not seek marriage" (1 Cor 7:25, 27). For the first four centuries of the Church, celibacy was advised but not required. By the sixth century, with the authoritative decree of Pope Gregory VII, priestly celibacy became a regular discipline in the Western Church. The First and Second Lateran Councils forbade clerical marriages.

Today, clergy of the Latin Church accept the obligation of celibacy in the strictest form upon their ordination to the transitional diaconate. The practice of celibacy is not immutable but is a matter of discipline, and priests and bishops in the Roman Catholic Church accept it willingly.

Priests of the Eastern churches may marry, but the ideal discipline is to remain free from the bonds of marriage in order to serve the Church more completely. Entering into marriage *after* ordination is not a general practice, and all bishops are chosen from among the celibates or widowers.

Charisms

Extraordinary gifts of the Holy Spirit granted to individuals for the sanctification of others rather than for themselves (see CCC 800).

In addition to the seven gifts of the Holy Spirit, which each person receives at Baptism (see "**Gifts of the Holy Spirit**"), Christians receive special gifts called charisms to build up the Church. St. Paul wrote, "To each is given the manifestation of the Spirit for the common good" (1 Cor. 12:7). St. Paul names some of these gifts in Romans 12:6–8 and in 1 Corinthians 12. Among other charisms, he lists prophecy, service, teaching, exhortation, liberality, and acts of mercy, but there are countless charisms.

Protestant denominations will sometimes judge a person's Christian authenticity by his ability to demonstrate these charisms. But in the lives of the saints and the teachings of great theologians—indeed, in our own experiences and in the application of reason—we can see that this judgment is not a fair or suitable measure of one's personal faith or sanctity. The charisms are not always active, and they are not "unlocked" by a certain act or level of piety; instead, they are gifts freely given by God's grace or concealed by His authority: "All these are inspired by one and the same Spirit, who apportions to each one individually as he wills" (1 Cor. 12:11). *Lumen Gentium* wisely reminds the faithful that "These charisms, whether they be the more outstanding or the more simple and widely diffused, are to be received with thanksgiving and consolation for they are perfectly suited to and useful for the needs of the Church."[14]

"It is in this sense that discernment of charisms is always necessary. No charism is exempt from being referred and submitted to the Church's shepherds" (CCC 801). If a charism is believed to be present or encountered in an individual, it should be confirmed by a responsible and knowledgeable source, such as a priest, pastor, spiritual director, or, if necessary, a bishop.

Chastity

The virtue of temperance by which one regulates his or her sexual appetites according to his or her state in life.

Sexuality is a gift. True sexual happiness is only in the context of a marriage between a man and a woman, when the sexual relationship is freely given, lifelong, and mutual. Because sexuality is a gift, chastity is also a gift when one maintains the integrity of God's purpose of life and love (cf. CCC 2337–2338). As Pope St. John Paul II wrote, "Therefore, only a chaste woman and a chaste man are capable of true love."[15]

Chastity is a moral virtue that applies to all Christians, married and unmarried alike, albeit differently. For the married, a chaste life implies the fecundities of sexuality and the relative restraint of unlawful sexual gratification proper to the bonds of marriage. For single people, a chaste life implies absolute restraint from any sexual activity. The *Catechism* lists and describes important offenses against chastity, including lust, masturbation, fornication, pornography, prostitution, and rape (CCC 2351–2356).

All baptized persons are called to observe a life of chastity, with Christ as their model (CCC 2348). Those in religious life make a vow of chastity by which they promise to God a deliberate observance of a chaste life as an evangelical counsel (see "**Evangelical Counsels**"), under the pain of sin, for a time or perpetually, according to the terms of their particular profession.

Chrism

A mixture of olive oil and balsam, consecrated by a bishop to be used in liturgical functions and sacraments.

The oil is traditionally consecrated by the bishop on Holy Thursday, after which it is dispersed to all parish churches in the diocese. Churches store the chrism in an ambry, a box specially designated to

Vessel for sacred chrism, Patriarchal Residence, Moscow

hold the three sacramental oils. The chrism oil jar is marked with the letters "S.C." for *Sanctum Chrisma* ("Holy Chrism"), and it is used for the sacraments of Baptism and Confirmation as well as for Holy Orders when a priest or bishop is ordained. It is also used in liturgical functions, such as the consecration of churches, chalices, patens, altar stones, and church bells, and in the blessing of baptismal fonts.

Christmas

The celebration of the birth of Jesus Christ in Bethlehem.

The feast of the Nativity is celebrated on December 25. Christmas is an octave within the liturgical calendar, and the Christmas season lasts until the feast of the Baptism of Our Lord.

Celebrations of the birth of Christ were not common in early lists of Christian feasts, although there is evidence of various dates in the year prescribed for the celebration, mostly throughout Egypt. Around the end of the fourth century, however, the Church firmly established the celebration of the feast to be on December 25 throughout Christendom. Why December 25? Unfortunately, we don't really know: given the wide array of contemporaneous accounts, quotations, and testimonies examining possible origins in astronomy or the Christianization of pagan winter festivals, the evidence is simply inconclusive.

Christmas is one of the holy days of obligation in the Church (see "**Holy Days of Obligation**"), which means that Catholics are obligated to attend Mass on Christmas. Traditionally, there are four Masses of Christmas: the Vigil Mass, celebrated on Christmas Eve, the Midnight Mass, the Mass at dawn, and the Mass during the day. A typical parish will offer one or more of these, if not all four. Catholics may choose from any one of these Masses to fulfill the obligation.

Nativity scenes (also called "cribs," "creche," or "presepe") are a tradition credited to St. Francis of

Nativity Scene, altarpiece in the church of Saint Matthew in Stitar, Croatia

> **CATHOLIC TIP**
>
> Christmas is a Holy Day of Obligation, meaning that Catholics must attend one of the Christmas Masses. This obligation holds true even if it happens that Christmas Day falls in close proximity to a Sunday. In this situation, the two Masses are not the same but constitute two separate obligations. Parishes are fairly good at publishing a Christmas Mass schedule to make it easy to avoid an unintentional mistake. Be sure to give those publications and announcements a good look when making Christmas plans.

Assisi in the thirteenth century. Many parishes and families will wait until Christmas morning to place their statue of Baby Jesus (or a real infant) in the crib and will wait to bring out the accompanying Magi until Epiphany (traditionally on January 6).

Among the most popular of Christmas traditions is hanging wreaths and laurels and decorating an evergreen tree. Along with this tradition comes a recurring attack against the Church: that Christians have adopted Christmas from pagan ritual, that the idea was stolen from the celebration of the pagan god Sol Invictus. The fact is that we can observe in extant histories that the two celebrations—Christmas and various mid-winter pagan celebrations—were concurrently present. The Church also has the ability to Christianize people and celebrations alike. Light overcame darkness at the celebration of Sol Invictus, and in celebrating the birth of Christ, we celebrate the ultimate defeat of darkness by the Light of the World. Paganism had a hint, a riddle of the truth, but Christianity became the fulfillment.

A custom more closely connected to the ancient Church is the use of evergreen wreaths. Anti-Catholics will often say that the tradition comes from the pagan Roman celebration of Saturnalia, but the theologian Tertullian wrote as early as A.D. 190–220 that Christians hung more "wreaths and laurels" than the pagans (who would hang it for the "gate gods") at their doors. In his letter, Tertullian condemned placing hope in the wreath as the pagans did with their temples; rather Christians must put their hope in Jesus, who is the true Light who illumines the actual temples of the Spirit: us. He ends with, "You are a light of the world, and a tree ever green. If you have renounced temples, make not your own gate a temple."[16]

Clergy

Ordained ministers in the Church.

A member of the clergy is called a "cleric," which in general refers to those who have received the power of Holy Orders. All clergy belong to the hierarchical leadership of the Church as members of the diaconate (deacons), the presbyterate (priests), or the episcopate (bishops).

College of Cardinals

The sacred corporation of the cardinals of the Catholic Church.

As a unified body, the cardinals exist to assist the pope with counsel, administrative duties, and the overall government of the Church. Sometimes called "princes" of the Church, cardinals must at least be ordained priests, in accordance with Canon Law (351, no. 1). Since 1179, their appointment has been solely reserved to the pope. There are some two hundred cardinals that make up the college, and outside of their duties to support various offices of the Church, their main purpose is to elect the pope. Scarlet garments identify a cardinal, representing the blood of the martyrs, a symbol of their willingness to die for the Faith.

In rare circumstances in the Church's history, cardinals were not bishops, and some were not previously clergy. Their only canonical requirement was the reception of the tonsure. However, this practice was abandoned in 1972 by the reforms of Pope Paul VI.

Communion of Saints

"The communion of saints is the Church" (CCC 946).

The term "Communion of Saints," which appears in the Apostle's Creed—"I believe in the Holy Spirit, the Holy Catholic Church, the Communion of Saints"—comes from the Latin *communio sanctorum*, and it indicates two things: first, a sharing of our faith, the sacraments, holy charisms, our goods, and charity among God's holy people (CCC 949–953); and second, a communion "among holy persons" (CCC 948).

The Communion of Saints binds all Christians, both in this life and the next: the saints in Heaven (the church victorious/triumphant; see "**Beatific Vision**"); the souls on earth (the church militant); and the souls bound for Heaven but enduring Purgatory (the church suffering/penitent; see "**Purgatory**"). The Communion of Saints is therefore the unity of the mystical body of Christ, and this unity transcends death. We participate in this communion during the course of our earthly life especially in the sharing of prayers and acts of mercy for the mutual assistance and benefit of all members.

Further reading: Any Friend of God's Is a Friend of Mine: A Biblical and Historical Explanation of the Catholic Doctrine of the Communion of Saints *by Patrick Madrid.*

Concupiscence

An inclination to sin that remains even after Baptism as a result of the stain of Original Sin.

Because of Original Sin (see "**Original Sin**"), the *Catechism* explains: "human nature is weakened in its powers; subject to ignorance, suffering, and the domination of death; and inclined to sin" (CCC 418).

The Forerunners of Christ with Saints and Martyrs, by Bl. Fra Angelico

Concupiscence does not mean that our human nature is entirely corrupted, as several Protestant Reformation theologians would have it, but that human nature is weakened, susceptible, and even attracted to sin. Man's concupiscence is not limited to physical cravings for pleasure, such as lust, but includes a tendency to desire things that are contrary to the will of God. What's important to bear in mind is that concupiscence is not sinful in itself. It inclines our appetites to move us against our reason, but it cannot force us to sin, and the work of "manfully resisting" concupiscence in our lives is an important aspect of the Christian life (see CCC 1264).

The Sacrament of Confirmation, by Pietro Longhi. In conferring the sacrament of Confirmation, the bishop anoints the person with chrism.

Confirmation

Sacrament of Initiation in which an individual receives the Holy Spirit through the imposition of hands and anointing with chrism.

Confirmation is one of the three Sacraments of Initiation, along with Baptism and the Eucharist (see "**Baptism**" and "**Eucharist**"). According to the norms of each episcopal see and the decision of each bishop, Confirmation is sometimes the final Sacrament of Initiation, completing a person's entry into the fullness of communion with the Catholic Church, or it may be given on the same occasion as Baptism and first Eucharist for adults. The bishop, therefore, is the ordinary minister of this sacrament, but it may be delegated to a priest as an extraordinary minister, depending upon the pastoral needs within the parish and the diocese.

A Confirmation candidate is invited to investigate and choose the name of a saint as a Confirmation name. This name is imposed by the bishop in conferring the sacrament. The chosen saint should exude virtues that the candidate intends to imitate and petition for intercession. A candidate must also have a sponsor, either a close friend in the Church who has led the candidate along his or her journey or an individual provided by an OCIA parish program (see "OCIA") who will help guide the candidate through his or her formation.

With the gift of the Holy Spirit, Confirmation imparts a seal or character on the soul and strengthens actual grace in a person so that he or she may profess the Faith, persevere in the toils of life, and fight temptation.

Contraception

The intentional prevention of conception from sexual intercourse, also known as birth control.

Contraception can take place hormonally, artificially with chemicals, or physically by blockage apparatuses and medical procedures. Common forms of contraception include oral drugs, condoms, vaginal rings, and surgical procedures like vasectomies and tubal ligations.

The Church teaches that the practice of contraception is evil: "'Every action which, whether in anticipation of the conjugal act, or in its accomplishment, or in the development of its natural consequences, proposes, whether as an end or as a means, to render procreation impossible' is intrinsically evil" (CCC 2370). Catholic moral teaching preserves the conjugal act as procreative and unitive, meaning the couple is open to life and that the marital act is always mutual. Thus, contraception is a self-seeking act that denies true conjugal love, arising from an unwillingness to be open to life, and leads to using another person as an object for sexual pleasure. With many technologies, too, contraception does not simply prevent conception but, should fertilization unintentionally occur, aborts the newly conceived child. Sadly, contraception remains a common practice in the modern world.

While the Church does not condone the practice of contraception, it does support families in responsibly discerning children and family size by using self-observation and fertility period monitoring (see "**Natural Family Planning**"). Natural Family Planning vastly differs from contraception in that it not only remains open to life but encourages a married couple to grow in love, conversation, and trust.

Further reading: The encyclical Humanae Vitae *by Pope St. Paul VI and apostolic exhortation* Familiaris Consortio *by Pope St. John Paul II offer strong arguments and insight regarding the Church's treatment of contraception.*

Contrition

Heartfelt sorrow and aversion for sin committed along with the intention of sinning no more.[17]

When man becomes aware of his sin and senses regret, shame, and a resolve to turn away from sin, his heart is contrite. The Church describes two types of contrition: perfect and imperfect. Perfect contrition is sorrow for sin out of love for God, and this contrition can remit venial sins and even mortal sins, provided the penitent resolves to go to Confession as soon as possible (see CCC 1452). Imperfect contrition is sorrow for sin for a reason other than love of God, often due to fear of eternal punishment. Although not as meritorious as perfect contrition, imperfect contrition moves the sinner to seek forgiveness through sacramental Confession, and over time it greatly adds to awareness of one's sin and gratitude for God's mercy. Contrition, whether perfect or imperfect, is always supernatural—a gift from God, prompted by the Holy Spirit—because it orients the heart to God.

CATHOLIC TIP

While imperfect contrition is sufficient, we should seek and pray for perfect contrition. When we pray the Act of Contrition, we express the desire for a perfectly contrite heart:

> *O my God, I am heartily sorry for having offended You, because I detest the loss of Heaven and the pains of Hell, but also because You, my Lord, are deserving of all my love. I firmly resolve with the help of Your grace to amend my life, to seek penance, and to avoid whatever causes me to sin. Amen.*

Conversion

The turning of the heart to God.

Conversion comes from the Latin *conversio*, meaning "turning around." The Greek writers of the New Testament used the word *metanoia*, meaning "a change of heart and mind," particularly toward repentance. Conversion involves both turning away from a past life and turning toward God, resulting in an interior transformation of the person.

Conversion often refers to a person's initial turning toward Christ, whether away from a life of sin or from another faith to the fullness of Christian truth in communion with the Catholic Church. Yet conversion is a continuous part of the Christian life and is something every follower of Christ must bear in mind throughout his or her earthly life. While a person's initial conversion is important and unique for each individual, it is just a milestone in one's journey to Heaven. The Christian life requires continual conversion of the heart, soul, mind, and strength (see Mark 12:30). We are not just called to turn around and face the way of safety and peace but to continually "sweeten" our faith to provide flavor, enhancement, and improvement.

The Conversion of St. Paul,
by Spinello Aretino

CATHOLIC TIP

Conversion is the central aim of all evangelization. And conversion is for everyone: Christians and non-Christians. The ignorant require education; the baptized require further catechesis; and the believer must constantly look to the perfection demanded by the Gospel. We are also called to help others convert. It's not up to clergy or published authors to do this important work; evangelizing and thus accompanying others in their own conversion is accomplished by Christians with all sorts of backgrounds and all levels of education.

Most of the time, good evangelization is a simple matter of sharing your own testimony. Your testimony is your story. It is how you came to know your faith, believe in God, and accept Christ as your Savior. People identify with stories. Yours might include any number of elements, whether pain and struggles, disaster, illness, or any other themes. Whatever it was, however you got there, your story should always arrive at the foot the Cross: how you came to understand Christ and the Church. Then, develop the *why I'm Catholic* aspect of your story. Life is better and is given meaning when we find freedom and consolation in the life of Christ and the mysteries of the sacraments.

Sharing your testimony can be a scary prospect. Unwrapping painful memories and unhinging your life's most personal details is a daunting task for many, and understandably so. But nothing is as worthwhile as moving someone closer to their own conversion and pursuit of life in Christ.

Covenant

A binding agreement between two people or between God and human beings.

Our word "covenant" is the English translation of the Hebrew word *bĕrît* and Greek *diathēkē*, which both refer to a relationship of obligation, oftentimes mutual but sometimes unilateral. Sacred Scripture details the history of God's relationship with His people in a series of covenants. Normally, when we speak of covenants, we are referring to the Old Covenant (described in the Old Testament—"testament" being another word for "covenant") and the New Covenant (described in the New Testament).

The Old Covenant was between God and Israel and was a *series* of covenants rather than one single contract between God and His people. In the Old Testament, we read of the covenants between God and Noah (Gen. 9:8–17), between God and Abraham (Gen. 17:2–14), and between God and the people of Israel through the mediation of Moses (Exod. 19–24). The Old Covenant is generally understood as the laws that Yahweh (God) provided to the people of Israel as a means of living, governance, celebration, and priestly sacrifice (see **"Yahweh"**).

The New Covenant was once and final. It was established by Jesus Christ, who is God, and it fulfills the prior covenant. It began at the Last Supper, Jesus' celebration of the Passover meal, when Jesus announced that He would become the unblemished sacrifice—the Passover lamb—spilling His blood so that it would no longer be necessary for animals to be sacrificed to renew or fulfill the covenant. The New Covenant was then fully established through Jesus' death and Resurrection.

The New Covenant is definitive and will last forever. *Dei Verbum* explains that "The Christian dispensation, therefore, as the new and definitive covenant, will never pass away and we now await no further new public revelation before the glorious manifestation of our Lord Jesus Christ."[18]

Agnus Dei (Lamb of God), by Francisco de Zurbarán

Creed

A statement of faith composed of several articles that contains the beliefs central to the Christian religion.

The word "creed" comes from the Latin *credo*, which means "I believe"—the first words of both the Apostles' Creed and the Nicene Creed. The creed is both a profession of faith and a prayer.

The earliest Christian creeds were simple, such as "Jesus is Lord," but with the development of the Christian community, the creed transitioned into a broader statement of faith. When new converts were instructed and presented for Baptism, they would be questioned on matters of Christian doctrine to ensure they were in full communion with apostolic teaching. Soon these items formed the content in a general and universal statement of faith.

The common understanding is that the Apostles' Creed was probably the early baptismal creed of Rome that was then used as a profession of faith before Sacred Scripture was copied, used for teaching, and canonically approved by the Church. Some formulation of the creed is believed to have been used in the Church as early as the beginning of the second century, and possibly much earlier.[19] Early in the Church, creeds might have also served to test the faith of those accused of heresy. A creed would detail items of the Faith but not define them—this process was saved for various ecumenical councils. Over time, through the scholarship of theologians and apologists, examination of issues, and promulgation of documents, local synods and ecumenical councils defined Christian articles of faith in detail. At some points, these definitions were summarized and adopted into a new creed, particularly the Athanasian Creed and the Nicene Creed (which we pray at Mass).

Cross

The primary symbol of our salvation and the most recognized symbol of Christianity.

A Christian cross is the symbol of two transverse beams and is made to represent the Cross upon which Christ was crucified. A crucifix always contains a cross, but it also includes the image of Jesus being crucified. Both are sacramentals (see "**Sacramental**" for more).

The image of Christ on the Cross is one of the most important symbols of the Christian Faith. A crucifix is required in every Catholic church and is also placed on or over the altar, acknowledging both the great suffering poured out on our behalf as well as the fact that Christ became our sacrificial Lamb. Catholics are also encouraged to keep crucifixes in their homes. Above the head of every crucifix are the letters I. N. R. I., which stand for *Iesus Nazarenus, Rex Iudaeorum*, "Jesus of Nazareth, King of the Jews," the words that Pontius Pilate had ordered to be placed over the Cross of Jesus (John 19:19).

Different from a crucifix, an ordinary cross does not contain an image or figure of Christ crucified. Crosses without an image of the crucified Jesus are also considered sacramentals—indeed, they both have ancient origins. Recognizable variations are the Tau cross, St. Andrew's cross, the Greek cross, the Maltese cross, and the Celtic cross. An ordinary cross, such as the traditional shape of the cross in Jesus' Crucifixion, is the "crux capitata," or headed cross, also known as a Latin cross.

Crucifixion

A form of capital punishment used in the Roman Empire; the method used to kill Jesus.

Pontius Pilate had no legal cause to crucify Jesus Christ, as he himself admitted, "I find no crime in him" (John 19:4). Crucifixion was reserved for enemies of the state, murderers, and slaves. Unique in its brutality, it was an occasion for public humiliation and punishment and was meant to deter people from crimes against the Empire. But it was the method of execution chosen and demanded by the Jews. Thereafter, crucifixion became a common method of execution in Christian martyrdom, and Christians themselves were often notably moved to accept this punishment due to their reading of the words of Christ: "If any man would come after me, let him deny himself and take up his cross and follow me" (Matt. 16: 24).

Ordinarily, to avoid expenses or logistical challenges, a Roman crucifixion might make use of a tree or a simple plank of wood. Nails, which had to be crafted by hand, were not often used unless the criminal was a person of some specific fame or repute; ordinarily, the victim was simply tied to the cross. A victim might hang on the cross for several days for people to mock or observe, and he usually died of exhaustion or asphyxiation.

Crucifixion was outlawed in the Roman Empire by the first Christian emperor, Constantine, in A.D. 337, out of admiration for Christ as its most famous victim.

Deacon

The third degree of the sacrament of Holy Orders.

Our word "deacon" comes from the Greek word *diakonos*, which indicated a servant. The origination of the diaconate is found in the Bible:

> [The apostles] summoned the body of the disciples and said, "It is not right that we should give up preaching the word of God to serve tables. Therefore, brethren, pick out from among you seven men of good repute, full of the Spirit and of wisdom, whom we may appoint to this duty. But we will devote ourselves to prayer and to the ministry of the word." And what they said pleased the whole multitude, and they chose Stephen [and six others]. (Acts 6:2–5)

St. Lawrence Enthroned with Saints and Donors, by Fra Filippo Lippi. St. Lawrence was a third-century deacon and martyr.

The very word (*diákonos* or "deacon") used at the time the New Testament was written literally meant to "serve tables."

There are two types of deacons: transitional and permanent. Both fall under the sacrament of Holy Orders (see **"Holy Orders"**). Transitional deacons are those men who, prior to becoming ordained as priests, are first ordained as deacons. Ordinarily this period is for a year, after which the bishop or religious authority (such as a prior of a monastery) may "transition" the deacon through ordination into the priesthood. A permanent deacon, however, is a layman, and he may be married or widowed. He is a deacon for life, and he promises service to a bishop and diocese.

As the name suggests, the deacon's chief function is to assist the bishop and priests in ministry, especially at Mass and by performing Baptisms, weddings, and certain other liturgical services. A deacon can always be distinguished from a priest by the way he wears the stole diagonally from shoulder to the hip. A priest wears the stole across both shoulders.

Death and Burial

A universal consequence of Original Sin and the natural end of a human life on earth.

After the sin of Adam and Eve, death entered the world (see Gen. 2:17, 3:19; Rom. 5:12–21). This consequence included both physical death and spiritual death—the loss of the life of grace. "God

Mourner at a cemetery

did not make death" (Wisd. 1:13). As believers in the Resurrection of Christ, Christians profess that Jesus "defeated death," meaning that life with God is restored in our being new creations through the sacrament of Baptism. Although we still die—a continuation of the effects of Original Sin (see "**Original Sin**")—we may continue toward the perfection of our holiness with the help of sanctifying grace from the sacraments in the hope that we will share in the Resurrection and be raised on the final day (see "**Resurrection of the Dead**").

As Christians, we believe that death is not the end but the transition to the afterlife, and it is a particularly important moment that deserves consideration and preparation. St. Robert Bellarmine preached that Christians should aim to die well. He did not mean one should try to die in an easy or painless way or that we should be happy about our death—death is an evil that entered the world as the result of sin—but that we must prepare ourselves to die in a state of grace, built upon merit, ready for eternal life with Christ. Because Christ died for us and rose again, we do not need to fear death, but we do need to prepare for it.

Death's foremost consequence is the separation of the soul from the body. The Church teaches that when we die, our soul is separated from our flesh until the Resurrection of the Dead, when we will receive a body again (CCC 990). The Church does not profess to know with exactitude the composition of this body, but we will be reunited with a body, nonetheless. Because of this critical teaching, the Church shows the utmost respect for the body even after death (see "**Resurrection of the Dead**").

Burial in the Catholic Church demonstrates the dignity in which the human body is held. The burial process also provides a sense of closure and healing when the death of a loved one may leave a sting. The *Catechism* says, "The bodies of the dead must be treated with respect and charity, in faith and hope of the Resurrection. The burial of the dead is a corporal work of mercy; it honors the children of God, who are temples of the Holy Spirit" (CCC 2300). Although the preference for treatment of human remains is a full-body burial, the Church does permit cremation in the event that it does not demonstrate a denial of faith in the resurrection of the body.

Demons

Fallen angels who were created by God but who later freely rejected God and His reign and were thus banished from Heaven (see CCC 414).

The fall of the angels occurred before man committed the first sin. In their rebellion against God, which is a final and eternal decision of their free will, the fallen angels endeavor to coax men to take part in their plan by tempting, corrupting, and tormenting us, and they seek our damnation. They want human beings to share in their eternal separation from God.

These spirits who roam the world, serving Satan and tempting man, are to be avoided and combatted through prayer, steadfast discipline of the body, and works of charity and justice. A stern warning of active preparation can be taken from Paul's letter to the Ephesians:

> Put on the whole armor of God, that you may be able to stand against the wiles of the devil. For we are not contending against flesh and blood, but against the principalities, against the powers, against the world rulers of this present darkness, against the spiritual hosts of wickedness in the heavenly places. (Eph. 6:11–12)

Deposit of Faith

The total sum of the divine truths revealed by Christ, witnessed in Sacred Scripture and Tradition, and taught by the Church.

The entirety of the teachings of Christ was entrusted to the apostles and their successors. Since this fullness of the Faith has not all been located in the Scriptures, as attested by John the Evangelist (see John 21:25), it is clear that the deposit is a combination of the Scriptures and Sacred Tradition. The Catholic Church is charged with guarding the deposit of faith, which is fulfilled in every age through the guidance and protection of the Holy Spirit. "Mindful of Christ's words to his apostles: 'He who hears you, hears me,' the faithful receive with docility the teachings and directives that their pastors give them in different forms" (CCC 87). The words of Christ reflect great credibility on this powerful image: "But the Counselor, the Holy Spirit, whom the Father will send in my name, he will teach you all things, and bring to your remembrance all that I have said to you" (John 14:26).

The wisdom and counsel of *Dei Verbum* accurately articulates the Church's position on this deposit:

> Sacred tradition and Sacred Scripture form one sacred deposit of the word of God, committed to the Church.... But the task of authentically interpreting the word of God, whether written or handed on, has been entrusted exclusively to the living teaching office of the Church ... guarding it scrupulously and explaining it faithfully in accord with a divine commission and with the help of the Holy Spirit, it draws from this one deposit of faith everything which it presents for belief as divinely revealed.[20]

Development of Doctrine

The careful process whereby the Church has interpreted God's revelation over the course of time to form the official teaching of the Church.

"Doctrine" is the teaching of the Catholic Church. "Development," in this sense, does not mean that the teachings change but that the Church grows in her understanding of what God has revealed. In order for an idea to be taught, it first has to be understood, and in order for an idea to be understood, it first must be revealed. This revelation, in the context of Christian teaching, doesn't necessarily happen through being told but also through experience: what God says and does. For example, God established a covenant involving sacrifice and observance of the law in the Old Testament. But in the person, teachings, and actions of Christ in the New Testament, we have come to understand that Christ did not change the Old Covenant but fulfilled it so we could live it more perfectly through union with Him. In a similar manner, as teaching and understanding develop, the doctrine of the Church develops.

Some doctrine is developed in a linear, logical fashion. Our understanding of the human will of Christ is a perfect example. Christ was revealed as both fully God and fully man, which means He must have possessed a human will that assented to the divine will. Other developments of doctrine are less straightforward, such as our definition of the Holy Trinity. The word "Trinity" does not appear in Scripture, but the reality is visible in Sacred Scripture (see the section on "**Trinity**" for a fuller examination of this idea).

The development of doctrine is often likened to a rose. In the morning, the flowers are so tightly compacted that one can only see the bud. As the sun shines and warms the garden, however, the rose buds slowly open, revealing the full glory of the flowers. So it is with the truth—as the fullness of time proceeds, we see it the more. We must remember, though, that just as the rose was always a rose, and the truth is always the truth; it is always what it was.

Likewise, the infant has the soul, senses, powers, and passions capable of being a fully functioning adult, but he lacks maturity. The Church from her infancy has revealed firm truths, but she has come to understand these truths through inquiry, testing, contemplation, and observing God's will.

The Church cannot change her doctrine, because truth itself is unchangeable. But as the Church continues to examine what has been revealed and endures every society and age, the content of her doctrines will grow to address different questions and human problems.

Devil

Satan, the enemy of God and chief opponent of man's salvation.

The Church teaches that Satan was once the angel Lucifer (meaning "bearer of light"). Yet Lucifer rejected God, and because of his angelic nature as a created spirit, his was a final and unchangeable choice.

The name "devil" comes from the Latin *diabolus*, meaning "slanderer" or "accuser." The devil is known in the Bible as "the enemy" (Matt. 13:39), a "murderer ... liar and the father of lies" (John 8:44), the "god of this world" (2 Cor. 4:4), and a "roaring lion, seeking someone to devour" (1 Pet. 5:8). Eschatological language in Revelation piles up

The fall of Lucifer, illustration by Gustave Doré in John Milton's *Paradise Lost*

several more titles for the devil: "The great dragon was thrown down, the ancient serpent, who is called the devil and Satan, the deceiver of the whole world" (Rev. 12:9).

What led to the fall of Satan and his followers? We can't know for sure, but some theologians have conjectured that the angels in Heaven were told of God's plan to create man in His own image and to become man Himself in the Incarnation. In his pride, the devil could not bear that a lower nature than his would be thus elevated, and so he rejected God and was cast out of Heaven. It is out of this envy that the devil spreads lies, accuses man, and attempts to corrupt souls to join him in Hell forever (see Wisd. 2:24).

Further reading: Catechism *paragraphs 391–395.*

Devotions

External practices of piety whereby a person of faith expresses his love for God and his desire to live a holy life.

Devotions (also known as "popular devotions") include prayers, supplications, or readings, or the devout following and imitation of a saint or a particular cause. Popular devotions include the Sacred Heart of Jesus, the Immaculate Heart of Mary, the Holy Family, the rules or teachings of various saints, specific apparitions of the Blessed Mother, works of mercy, praying the mysteries of the Rosary (see "**Rosary**"), and the Divine Mercy (see "**Divine Mercy**").

The practice of a devotion usually indicates an intentional offering or act of some sort. Devotions are important to the life of a believer because they keep us focused on Christ through study, imitation, prayer, spiritual exercises, and meditation. Devotions should always draw us closer to union with Christ and render our hearts more open to the work of the Holy Spirit. Fortunately for us, many of the saints and other scholars have written instruction on the practical methods of and approaches to devotion. Some of the most popular saints who wrote on the practices of devotion are St. Francis de Sales, St. Louis de Montfort, Bl. Pier Giorgio Frassati, and St. Ignatius of Loyola.

Praying the Rosary is a popular devotion.

A "devotional" is a book that assists someone in the practice of a devotion. Devotionals include readings, points for meditation, and prayers.

Further reading: Exceptional books on devotions include the Compendium of Marian Devotions *by Fr. Ed Broom and* Catholic Prayers for All Occasions, *edited by Jacquelyn Lindsey.*

Diocese

A bishop's geographical boundary of authority.

All dioceses are governed by a bishop, but some dioceses may have multiple types of bishops depending on the ministerial needs of that diocese (see "**Bishop**"). An archbishop is the head of an archdiocese, which usually comprises the metropolitan see. An archdiocese either reports directly to the Holy See in Rome or to another ecclesial province. When the archdiocese is the ecclesial province, there are suffragan dioceses that operate under the leadership and authority of the archbishop.

CATHOLIC TIP

All Catholics should make a good faith effort to attend the parish within whose boundaries they reside. If someone chooses otherwise, they should have an honest and meaningful reason and should fully commit themselves wherever they go. Visiting another parish can be a wonderful means of growing in faith or seeing the splendor of a church. But practices like "parish hopping" can be pitfalls for individuals and the diocese alike.

Likewise, following a much-loved priest to his new parish when he is reassigned by the bishop also circumvents the intentions of the bishop and takes away from the existing Catholic community at a parish. By attending your local parish, you have the opportunity to build up the faithful, grow with your peers, develop a relationship with clergy, and also open yourself to the possibility of having a stable confessor.

A diocese is further broken into parish church boundaries. A parish is a Catholic church within a diocese. These parishes are identified areas where the diocese attempts to plant a church that will minister to local Catholics. A bishop's discretion for parish boundaries is important from an administrative point of view, but also from a sacramental one. A bishop's decisions on parish boundaries also involve his decisions on where he will staff his priests, addressing numerous pastoral needs of the faithful.

Discernment

The prayerful process of determining God's will for us, both in particular situations and for our whole life.

The word "discernment" comes from the Latin *discernere*, meaning "to divide, to separate." Therefore, discernment is a process, not a one-time event. Catholics often use the word "discern" to describe the process by which a person makes a vocational choice, such as to become a priest, get married, or live the consecrated life. This kind of discernment, which pertains to one's entire life, is best completed under the guidance of a spiritual director. Priests—who undergo constant discernment as part of their formation—usually complete coursework to become spiritual directors in order to further their ability to discern their own vocation as well as to help others.

Discernment is an ongoing process. When discerning an important decision, the following

St. Ignatius of Loyola

practical steps are recommended by St. Ignatius of Loyola: take your time, spend time alone and in silence, be honest, tell God "Thy will be done, not mine," and then make your decision and commit. Let us emphasize that first part of his instructions: the process of discernment requires *as much time as necessary* to determine the presence of God in a decision.

Even in day-to-day life, discernment plays an important role. Devoting oneself to prayer each day, taking time to be silent and listen, journaling thoughts and events, and consistently taking time to assess and test events of the past are solid starting points for any Christian.

"Discernment of spirits" refers to the movements of the human will, and in order to accurately discern, training is recommended. Here the goal is to discover and confirm where such a "spirit"—a movement of the will—is leading as opposed to determining the origin of a spirit as a motive, or spiritual issue.

Further reading: The Imitation of Christ *by Thomas à Kempis is among the most treasured Catholic writings of all time and has proven especially useful in discernment.*

Disciple

A follower of Christ.

The word "disciple" comes from the Latin *discipulus*, meaning "follower" or "student." To be a disciple of Jesus means deliberately allowing Christ to teach, lead, and transform our lives.

The term "disciple" appears more than two hundred and fifty times in the Gospels and the Acts of the Apostles, but it is nowhere else in the New Testament. It first appears in Matthew's account of the Sermon on the Mount (Matt. 5:1), when, after calling the Twelve, Jesus sat down with His disciples (followers) and began to teach them. We see, from here, the essence of Christian discipleship. More than mere admirers, these were men and women who hoped to be instructed by and to imitate Christ: they followed Him into Baptism; they confessed Him as Lord and Savior; they were sure to obey His commands; and they consumed His Body and Blood as the meal of salvation.

To do the spiritual work of discipleship means to guide another into this intimate following of Christ as God and King, as ruler of one's entire life. But whether we work in discipling others in the apostolate or a ministry, or not, we are all called to be disciples of Christ. Remember that in the New Testament He called the Twelve to be His closest followers, but a great multitude followed Him. The universal call to discipleship involves knowing God, loving God, and serving God.

Further reading: Forming Intentional Disciples: The Path to Knowing and Following Jesus, *by Sherry A. Weddell, is a superb resource for learning more about transforming ourselves, our parish community, and the Church into true disciples of Jesus.*

Divine Law

The law of God that was made known to man through divine revelation and examination of the natural law; also known as the eternal law.

The Old Law, contained in the Pentateuch (the first five books of the Bible), was comprised of civil, ceremonial, and moral rules for God's people. It paved the way for the New Law of Christ, which is contained in the New Testament. This new law is focused on morals and charity, the offering of Christ as the paschal sacrifice, and the reception of the sacraments. It is this New Law, then, that Christians are concerned with in respect to observing the Divine Law, particularly the moral aspects.

The New Law of Jesus Christ fulfills and perfects the Old Law. Divine Law does not change, but man's ability to receive it has changed as a result of Christ's redeeming work. The Old Law was a necessary path given to aid man in understanding sin, both personally and socially, as well as redemption. As St. Paul writes, "What then shall we say? That the law is sin? By no means! Yet, if it had not been for the law, I should not have known sin. I should not have known what it is to covet if the law had not said, 'You shall not covet'" (Rom. 7:7). In a similar way, the Old Law prepared mankind to worship Christ as the ultimate sacrifice and gave mankind a rhythm and liturgical means of living that coincides with our desire to express true life and communion in Christ.

Divine Mercy

God's perfect compassion poured out in a continuous act of grace.

Modern use of the word "mercy" usually denotes judicial pardon or mere pity. But God's mercy is more than Him feeling sorry for us or excusing our sins in a juridical act. Divine Mercy specifies God's prodigious concern and empathy for man's plight, weakness, and frailty. St. Thomas Aquinas defines mercy as grief for another's distress and the greatest of the virtues.[21] For a perfect, infinite, unchangeable God—a God who is, then, perfectly, infinitely, and unchangeably merciful—mercy is the chief motive of every act: "Hence mercy is accounted as being proper to God: and therein His omnipotence is declared to be chiefly manifested," says St. Thomas.[22] "The Lord is merciful and gracious, slow to anger and abounding in steadfast love" (Ps. 103:8).

For Catholics, the Divine Mercy is recognized as a specific devotion to Jesus Christ that was received in a private revelation (see "**Revelation**") by St. Faustina Kowalska. This devotion was then promoted by Pope St. John Paul II, who authorized it to be celebrated in the General Calendar of the Roman Catholic Church when he created the Feast

Divine Mercy image, by Eugeniusz Kazimirowski

of the Divine Mercy (or "Divine Mercy Sunday"), which falls on the first Sunday after Easter. Divine Mercy Sunday is of course a day of obligation like all Sundays of the year, but we have an enhanced cause to celebrate this feast, since it was written in St. Faustina's private diary that Jesus proclaimed that "whoever shall come to the Fount of Life on that day shall be granted full remission of sins and punishment."[23]

CATHOLIC TIP

The Divine Mercy Chaplet is a popular prayer that Jesus taught to St. Faustina and encouraged the faithful to pray. The chaplet is said using rosary beads, and the faithful are encouraged to pray it especially on Divine Mercy Sunday and on Fridays at 3:00 p.m., "the hour of great mercy" when Jesus died. It is a very simple prayer and can be memorized with some practice:

1. Sign of the Cross
2. Optional opening prayer: "O Blood and Water, which gushed forth from the Heart of Jesus as a fount of mercy for us, I trust in You!" (Repeat three times.)
3. Our Father
4. Hail Mary
5. Apostles' Creed
6. On the Our Father bead: "Eternal Father, I offer You the Body and Blood, Soul and Divinity of Your Dearly Beloved Son, Our Lord, Jesus Christ, in atonement for our sins and those of the whole world."
7. On the ten smaller beads: "For the sake of His sorrowful Passion, have mercy on us and on the whole world." (Repeat ten times.)
   Repeat numbers 6 and 7 for all five decades.
8. "Holy God, Holy Mighty One, Holy Immortal One, have mercy on us and on the whole world." (Repeat three times.)
9. Optional closing prayer: Eternal God, in whom mercy is endless and the treasury of compassion inexhaustible, look kindly upon us and increase Your mercy in us, that in difficult moments we might not despair nor become despondent, but with great confidence submit ourselves to Your holy will, which is Love and Mercy itself.

Divine Office

The daily liturgical prayer of the Church.

The purpose of the Divine Office is to sanctify the day, to commemorate saints and feasts, and to intercede for the salvation of souls. It is also known as the Canonical Hours or the Liturgy of the Hours, since it is separated into several prayers throughout the day.

The Office grew over time from the Hebrew tradition of prayerfully repeating the psalms and other readings, and so this liturgy predominantly consists of psalms, canticles, and other readings from Sacred Scripture, readings from the saints and Church documents, and intercessory petitions. The traditional "hours" are Matins (traditionally prayed in the middle of the night, now called the Office of Readings), Lauds (dawn), Prime (morning, though following The Second Vatican Council, this hour has been removed), Terce (mid-morning), Sext (midday), None (mid-afternoon), Vespers (evening), and Compline (night). The Office is prayed throughout the liturgical year, inviting deeper reflection in each season: Advent, Christmas, Ordinary Time, Lent, and Easter.

CATHOLIC TIP

There are many versions of the Divine Office to choose from. The full version is offered by Catholic Book Publishing Company, and an authorized version with interlinear Latin and English and with the layout of the hours as they were prior to the reforms, the *Roman Breviary*, is distributed by Baronius Press. More concise Hours are also useful: *Little Office of the Blessed Virgin Mary*, the *Shorter Christian Prayer*, and *The Little Office of Baltimore*.

Praying the Divine Office is certainly an intimidating venture for many, no matter which version you choose. But it doesn't have to be. If the general layout and ribbon-keeping is too complicated, there are apps that are updated each day with all hours.

But if time, concentration, and habit are the concern, it helps to get started in small increments. First, start with only the Office of Readings. After a while, add night prayer (Compline), since it is the shortest of all, and we usually have personal time to carve out before sleep. After this routine takes firm root, add morning prayer (Lauds). Proceed from there if you wish to pray the rest of the hours. As an added bonus, try browsing the other offices included in your book or app, such as the Office of the Dead, the Seven Penitential Psalms, and the Litany of the Saints. These prove useful on special occasions throughout the year, and throughout life.

Priests, religious, and some tertiary orders pray the Office daily, either in whole or in part. But one does not have to be consecrated or religious to pray the Office (or parts of the Office). The Fathers of The Second Vatican Council invited all the faithful to join in this chorus, since it is the prayer of the Church: "And the laity, too, are encouraged to recite the Divine Office, either with the priests, or among themselves, or even individually."[24]

Divorce

Legal separation of married persons.

In civil law, divorce is the public, legal recognition of a couple's separation. The Catholic Church teaches that, as a sacrament, marriage is indissoluble—meaning it cannot be ended, broken, or parted by any means as long as both spouses are living. In instituting marriage as a sacrament, Jesus taught, "So they [husband and wife] are no longer two but one flesh. What therefore God has joined together, let not man put asunder" (Matt. 19:6). When asked why Moses allowed divorce, Jesus answered: "For your hardness of heart Moses allowed you to divorce your wives, but from the beginning it was not so. And I say to you: whoever divorces his wife, except for unchastity, and marries another, commits adultery; and he who marries a divorced woman, commits adultery" (Matt. 19:8–9). Sadly, today all major Christian denominations in the West accept divorce except the Catholic Church.

The *Catechism of the Catholic Church* straightforwardly teaches that "Divorce is a grave offense against the natural law. It claims to break the contract, to which the spouses freely consented, to live with each other till death. Divorce does injury to the covenant of salvation, of which sacramental marriage is the sign" (CCC 2384). Canon Law asserts: "A marriage that is *ratum et consummatum* [certain and consummated] can be dissolved by no human power and by no cause, except death" (CIC 1141). Divorce brings grave harm and disorder to the family, society, and particularly the children of divorced families, making it "truly a plague on society" (CCC 2385).

Although the teaching of the Catholic Church on divorce is immutable, there are cases when a civil divorce is permissible. The *Catechism* teaches that, "If civil divorce remains the only possible way of ensuring certain legal rights, the care of the children, or the protection of inheritance, it can be tolerated and does not constitute a moral offense" (CCC 2383), and "It can happen that one of the spouses is the innocent victim of a divorce decreed by civil law; this spouse therefore has not contravened the moral law" (CCC 2386). A Catholic who is civilly divorced is *not* free to remarry, however, as legal divorce does not dissolve the marriage bond. (For more on a related topic, see "**Annulment**.")

Further reading: Readers are encouraged to read the Catechism's *section on divorce and remarriage, paragraphs 2382–2386.*

St. Augustine of Hippo, attributed to Gerard Seghers

Doctor of the Church

A title conferred by the Church on a saint whose writing or preaching on the Faith has proven impactful for the Church throughout the ages.

This title—in Latin, *Doctor Ecclesiae Universalis*—is usually conferred by a pope. Pope Boniface VIII is usually recognized as the first to confer the title, when he named Sts. Gregory the Great, Ambrose, Augustine, and Jerome as Doctors of the Church in the thirteenth century. Since Boniface VIII to the present day, popes of the Catholic Church have designated thirty-seven male and female saints as Doctors of the Church. In all cases, the designation comes sometime after canonization.

These saints who are recognized as Doctors can be likened to the doctors designated for their academic achievement. Doctors of the Church are distinguished for their significant contributions to a particular area of study, the development of Christian doctrine, and the deepening of faith and holiness throughout the Church.

Dogma

A truth that has been revealed by God, authoritatively declared by the Church, and binding on all the faithful.

All dogma is revealed by God; it is not simply a matter of the opinion of a pope or the consensus of bishops. Some dogma may be a written solemn judgment by a pope (for more on this, see "**Infallibility**") or communicated through the ordinary Magisterium (see "**Magisterium**").

The teaching of the Immaculate Conception, declared by Pope Pius IX in 1854, provides an example of the formula for dogmatic teaching:

> We declare, pronounce, and define that the doctrine which holds that the most Blessed Virgin Mary, in the first instance of her conception, by a singular grace

> and privilege granted by Almighty God, in view of the merits of Jesus Christ, the Savior of the human race, was preserved free from all stain of Original Sin, is a doctrine revealed by God and therefore to be believed firmly and constantly by all the faithful.[25]

There is also a concept known as dogmatic fact, which is a teaching or concept so closely related to dogmatic truth that it is necessary to preserve in theological teaching. These may also be proclaimed infallibly. Common examples include the validity of an elected pope, the actuality of the presence of a saint in Heaven, or the legitimacy of an ecumenical council.

Domestic Church

A term that refers to the family.

Taken from the Second Vatican Council document *Lumen Gentium*, the term "Domestic Church" elucidates the special place of the family in the catechesis and religious development of children. "In what might be regarded as the domestic Church, the parents, by word and example, are the first heralds of the faith with regard to their children."[26]

The *Catechism* puts this image into profound context:

> Christ chose to be born and grow up in the bosom of the holy family of Joseph and Mary. The Church is nothing other than "the family of God." … Families are of primary importance as centers of living, radiant faith. For this reason the Second Vatican Council, using an ancient expression, calls the family the *Ecclesia domestica*. (CCC 1655–1656)

A dedicated prayer corner or home altar provides a center for the family's prayer and devotion.

Following the example of the Church at large, Catholic families are encouraged to pray daily, participate in the sacraments (especially the Eucharist and Confession), read Scripture, live according to the liturgical calendar as a source of structure throughout the seasons, and observe the moral life. In order to build up their domestic churches, families might also consider hanging religious imagery throughout their homes and participating in certain devotions together, such as a family Rosary. All of these, when put together, make for a robust domestic catechesis that lays the foundations of faith in the hearts and minds of our children, who are the future of the Church.

Easter

The feast of the Resurrection of Christ.

Easter Sunday is the feast that commemorates the triumphant Resurrection of Christ from the dead—the most important event in the Church's liturgy. This feast was among the earliest of Christian celebrations. Easter recalls the proof of Christ's divinity and His triumph over death. Easter is also a liturgical season that lasts fifty days and is represented by the liturgical color white. As the most special of the liturgical seasons, Easter surpasses Christmas, Lent, and Advent in length of time.

In the West, Easter is a "movable feast," meaning the feast may be celebrated on varying dates year to year, but it always lands on a Sunday between March 22 and April 25. Indeed, all other movable feasts are set based on when Easter is celebrated in a particular year. The specific formula to determine the date each year is somewhat complex, but in short, it places Easter Sunday on the first Sunday following the Paschal moon, which is the full moon that occurs on or just after the ecclesiastical spring equinox on March 21. In the East, for the most part, Easter's date is fixed to lunar cycles, resulting in the celebration of Easter sometimes falling on a day other than Sunday. This difference as to when Easter should be celebrated caused much consternation between bishops in the second century and still leads to confusion today. The date of Easter was one of the major decrees of the Council of Nicaea in A.D. 325.

Stained-glass window depicting the Resurrection of Christ, St. Patrick Church, Troy, Ohio

The "Easter Duty," as it is often called, refers to one of the precepts of the Catholic Church (see "**Precepts of the Church**"): the faithful are obligated to receive Holy Communion during the Easter period, ordinarily between Easter Sunday and Pentecost.

Eastern Catholic Churches

The twenty-three autonomous Catholic churches that are in communion with the Holy See.

Also referred to (commonly, though incorrectly) as "Eastern Rite Catholicism," the Eastern Catholic Churches are *sui iuris* (meaning autonomous) churches with their own rituals, canon law, ceremonies, organizational structure, and liturgy. They are in full communion with the Holy See and recognize the Bishop of Rome as the earthly head of the universal Catholic Church. They profess the Catholic Faith and observe the same seven sacraments as the Latin Church. These churches are different from Eastern Orthodox churches, which are discussed more in "**Orthodox Churches**."

There are twenty-three Eastern Catholic Churches, and they are generally grouped into five liturgical traditions:

+ Alexandrian Rites, originating in Egypt:
  Coptic Catholic Church (Coptic Rites)
  Eritrean Catholic Church (Ge'ez Rites)
  Ethiopian Catholic Church (Ge'ez Rites)
+ West Syriac Rite, drawing from Antioch and West Syria:
  Maronite Church
  Syrian Catholic Church
  Syro-Malankara Catholic Church
+ Armenian Rite, containing only the Armenian Catholic Church
+ Chaldean or East Syrian Rite, originating in Mesopotamia
  Chaldean Catholic Church
  Syro-Malabar Church
+ Byzantine or Constantinopolitan Rite, the largest of the Eastern Catholic Churches, which originated in Constantinople:
  Albanian Catholic Church
  Belarusian Catholic Church
  Bulgarian Catholic Church
  Croatian Byzantine Catholic Church (or Croatian Greek Catholic Church)
  Greek Catholic Church
  Hungarian Catholic Church
  Italo-Albanian Catholic Church
  Macedonian Catholic Church

Holy Resurrection Melkite Church, Columbus, Ohio

Melkite Greek Catholic Church
Romanian Church United with Rome
Russian Catholic Church
Ruthenian Catholic Church
Slovak Catholic Church
Ukrainian Greek Catholic Church

Further reading: the Second Vatican Council's Decree on the Catholic Churches of the Eastern Rite.

Ecumenical Councils

Joint assemblies of bishops from around the globe, presided over by the pope or his legate.

Ecumenical councils bring together the bishops from around the world to discuss particular topics of concern and elucidate the Church's teaching on various subjects. Only the pope can call together a general ecumenical council, and he must also approve any documents resulting from the council.

These ecumenical councils sprang forth from the tradition of early councils or meetings of Church bishops and leaders, the first of which is known as the Council of Jerusalem (though not between East and West as we observed them in later centuries), recorded in Acts 15 in the New Testament. A controversy had arisen around the topic of circumcision, so "The apostles and the elders were gathered together to consider this matter. And after there had been much debate," Peter offered his guidance, as did the other apostles. In the end, the entire assembly agreed to a solution and sent a letter with instructions with Paul and Barnabas (Acts 15:1–23).

What we observe in Acts supports the communion of authority established in the Gospel of Matthew. First, Jesus said to Peter, "I will give you the keys of the kingdom of heaven, and whatever you bind on earth shall be bound in heaven, and whatever you loose on earth shall be loosed in heaven" (Matt. 16:19). Later He gave authority to all the apostles when He said, "Truly, I say to you, whatever you bind on earth shall be bound in heaven, and whatever you loose on earth shall be loosed in heaven" (Matt. 18:18).

Although the councils of the first three centuries were ecumenical in context, historians generally classify the ecumenical councils to begin with Nicaea (A.D. 325). The main goal of these councils was to reach some point of orthodoxy in the universal Church regarding a certain subject or to reach consensus on a specific item of heresy.

Today, ecumenical councils invite attendance and participation from bishops from every corner of the world, as well as abbots and superiors of religious orders, canonists, and theologians of proper and relevant training. Another important role in an ecumenical council is that of a peritus, an individual theologian of particular repute or use to the presiding council fathers. To date, there have been twenty-one general ecumenical councils, most recently, the Second Vatican Council.

Ecumenism

Actions and dialogue that promote and enhance unity among Christians.

Ecumenism is the central aim in the Catholic Church for the conversion and salvation of the world. Unity is one of the marks of the Church and is mentioned in the Nicene Creed: "I believe in *one*, holy, catholic and apostolic church" (emphasis added; see "**Four Marks of the Church**"). *The Catechism of the Catholic Church* defines and presents the importance of ecumenism:

> "Christ bestowed unity on his Church from the beginning. This unity, we believe, subsists in the Catholic Church as something she can never lose, and we hope that it will continue to increase until the end of time." Christ always gives his Church the gift of unity, but the Church

> must always pray and work to maintain, reinforce, and perfect the unity that Christ wills for her. (CCC 820)

This unity is what Jesus asked for in His prayer to the Father before suffering His Passion: "I do not pray for these only, but also for those who believe in me through their word, that they may all be one; even as thou, Father, art in me, and I in thee, that they also may be in us, so that the world may believe that thou hast sent me" (John 17:20–21). Recovering the unity of all Christians is the will of Christ and a chief work of the Holy Spirit.

Further reading: Ecclesiam Suam *by Pope St. Paul VI, the Second Vatican Council's* Unitatis Redintegratio *(The Decree on Ecumenism), and the encyclical* Ut Unum Sint *by Pope St. John Paul II.*

Encyclical

A letter written by the pope to the Church on a specific concern or matter of doctrine.

An encyclical letter is usually written first in Latin; official translations are then made into other languages. Latin is the official language of the Catholic Church, but historically, a limited number of encyclicals have been written in the language of the intended audience. For example, Pius X wrote *Une Fois Encore* (1907) only for the clergy of France; therefore the encyclical itself was originally written only in Latin.

An encyclical's title is typically taken from the first words of the document in Latin. For example, Pope Paul VI's *Humanae Vitae* ("Of Human Life") is from the opening sentence, *Humanae vitae tradendae munus gravissimum* ... ("The transmission *of human life* is a most serious role ..."). Popes use these letters to discuss a wide variety of topics, issuing instruction, communicating their vision, and imparting their wisdom. Encyclicals are considered part of the ordinary Magisterium and should communicate continuity with previous popes (see "**Magisterium**"), but they are not infallible. Encyclicals aim to correct errors that threaten faith and morals. Therefore, they should be read with openness and sincerity of heart.

CATHOLIC TIP

Encyclicals are much more than run-of-the-mill documents that a pope is expected to release in order to gain political clout or any other poor intention. They are truly a pulse check on the Church's ability to remain relevant, consistent, and pastoral on various topics of faith and morals. Popes have released encyclicals on everything from condemning the practice of dueling (*Pastoralis Officii*) to employers being ethical in their work conditions and terms of employment (*Rerum Novarum*).

Although encyclicals are not infallible and should be read with an open heart, some Catholics become alarmed when they see that an encyclical challenges their moral and social beliefs. They wonder where—in their efforts to be good Catholics—the consistency is. It's important in these situations to remain steadfast: It is not in the purview of any pope to innovate in or tamper with the Faith. A pope and his advisors, indeed the document editors and drafters, understand that it is their solemn duty to safeguard and preserve the Catholic Faith. Accordingly, it benefits everyone to remain patient, ask for clarification, study diligently, remain resolute in faith, and be charitable when navigating challenging encyclicals.

End-of-Life Care

The care given to a person nearing death, and the moral obligations and other considerations associated with that circumstance.

The Catholic Church teaches that all human life is precious and must be treated with dignity from conception to natural death. Christian belief that "the human person has been willed for its own sake in the image and likeness of the living and holy God" (CCC 2319) forms the bedrock of this teaching. The Church therefore requires that we provide dignified end-of-life care to everyone to the greatest extent possible, regardless of the burden.

The fifth commandment, "You shall not kill," precludes euthanasia or "mercy killing," and the *Catechism* describes this practice as "morally unacceptable" (CCC 2277). God is the author of life, and He alone may determine when life ends. Care for someone at the end of life may include the use of painkillers to reduce suffering (CCC 2279), and it is allowable to refuse "'over-zealous' treatment" (CCC 2278). Palliative care is encouraged (CCC 2279), and those on the brink of death should be given appropriate care to ensure dignity and peace in their last moments (2299).

In the mission of the Church to win all souls for Christ, a special emphasis is paid to maintaining these end-of-life teachings no matter the opposition or ever-changing, ever-evolving morality of the world around us (see the related topics "**Death and Burial**" and "**Euthanasia**").

Further reading: Because of the importance of these topics and their frequent disagreement with public policy and modern ethics, readers are encouraged to read the Catechism *paragraphs 2276–2301 thoroughly.*

Environment

The whole of creation, but especially the natural ecosystem in which we live, labor, and operate.

Maintaining the environment is an enduring work of God's people, and it is rooted in the Great Commandment given by Jesus: "You shall love your neighbor as yourself" (Mark 12:31). The *Catechism*

God calls mankind to be stewards of His creation.

acknowledges: "Man must therefore respect the particular goodness of every creature, to avoid any disordered use of things which would be in contempt of the Creator and would bring disastrous consequences for human beings and their environment" (CCC 339).

It may seem like an emerging topic only recently acknowledged by the Church due to social and economic movements, but the concept of caring for the environment—protecting resources, safeguarding water and food in impoverished areas, combatting consumerism, and exercising general stewardship of the planet for future generations—is not new, though it has become a more urgent issue in recent decades. Recent popes have spoken out on the environment:

> Pope St. John Paul II: "We cannot interfere in one area of the ecosystem without paying due attention to both the consequences of such interference in other areas and to the well-being of future generations."[27]
>
> Pope Benedict XVI: "Environmental degradation makes the life of the poor intolerable. In dialogue with Christians of different denominations, we need to commit ourselves to caring for creation, without squandering its resources, but instead sharing in them in a collaborative way."[28]
>
> Pope Francis: "Instead of resolving the problems of the poor and thinking of how the world can be different, some can only propose a reduction in the birth rate.... To blame population growth instead of extreme and selective consumerism on the part of some, is one way of refusing to face the issues."[29]

Regardless of political developments and economic interests, Christians preserve the notion that God created the world, and man is subject to sustaining it: "And God blessed them, and God said to them, 'Be fruitful and multiply, and fill the earth and subdue it'" (Gen. 1:28). This subduing is God's wise command—for the benefit of mankind to be happy and healthy—to be merciful stewards of the Earth through respect for creation, safeguarding of resources, and love of our neighbors.

Eternity

A state of being with no beginning and no end.

God lives and operates from eternity: "Before the mountains were brought forth, or ever thou hadst formed the earth and the world, from everlasting to everlasting thou art God" (Ps. 90:2). God exists outside of space and time, and He wills for us to spend the rest of this eternity with Him. But the rejection of God also results in the eternal separation from our Creator, as the *Catechism* confirms (CCC 1035).

Man is captivated with the concept of eternity, but it remains an enigma to us, as the wise writer of Ecclesiastes says: "He has made everything beautiful in its time; also he has put eternity into man's mind, yet so that he cannot find out what God has done from the beginning to the end" (Eccl. 3:11). As a mystery and an object of hope, eternity is also relative to the believer, since the promise of Christ is eternal life with God: "For God so loved the world that he gave his only Son, that whoever believes in him should not perish but have eternal life" (John 3:16).

Eucharist

The sacrament of the New Covenant, in which Jesus Christ offers us His Body, Blood, Soul, and Divinity under the appearances of bread and wine.

The word "eucharist" comes from the Greek word *eukharistia*, meaning "thanksgiving." The term is reminiscent of Christ's words at the Last Supper: "And he took a cup, and when he had *given thanks*

Disputation of the Holy Sacrament, by Raphael

he gave it to them, and they all drank of it" (Mark 14:23, emphasis added). In the original Greek, that emphasized word is *eukharistia*, which is also the same word used to describe Paul's consecration of bread during a storm: "And when he had said this, he took bread, and *giving thanks* to God in the presence of all he broke it and began to eat" (Acts 27:35, emphasis added).

In the Holy Sacrifice of the Mass, the Eucharist becomes the meal of our salvation that Jesus promised to the multitude (John 6:47–51). Outside of Mass, Catholics give the Eucharist special veneration in Eucharistic Adoration, where the consecrated host is displayed for worship. On special occasions the Eucharist is also honored in a Eucharistic procession.

Catholics believe in the Real Presence of Christ in the Eucharist, which means that we believe that Christ is truly and substantially present under the appearance of bread and wine, and we also believe that eating this bread and wine—the Body and Blood of Christ—gives spiritual nourishment to our souls. When the bread and wine are consecrated, the accidents (the taste, smell, and other physical characteristics) of bread and wine remain, but the *substance* of them changes into the actual Body and Blood of Jesus. The theological term for this process is transubstantiation (see "**Transubstantiation**").

Sadly, some Catholics doubt the truth of the Eucharist. An alarming study from 2019 reported that some two-thirds of Catholics do not believe in the Real Presence of Christ in the Eucharist. Most of these people seem to question what Jesus really meant when He said, "This is my body.... This cup which is poured out for you is the new covenant in my blood ... do this in remembrance of me." But there are several encouraging aspects to search and contemplate the truth of the Eucharist and to discuss it with those who have difficulty believing.

First, let us consider the scriptural sources. As we see above, the word *Eucharist* is biblical and used multiple times in the New Testament; it's not a fancy word from medieval Catholic theologians. Jesus presents this teaching directly to the multitude of followers in John 6. Even as they attempt to clarify that Christ can't possibly mean His words literally, He verifies that He truly intends for His followers to consume His flesh. He uses graphic language to teach that they will "chew" His flesh and "drink" His blood (John 6:52–59). Christ provides the most glaring response to their doubt about His meaning: "For my flesh is food indeed, and my blood is drink indeed" (John 6:55).

Another strongly worded and persuasive biblical passage on the Eucharist is in the First Letter of St. Paul to the Corinthians. As Paul addresses various behavioral matters that seem to derive from the Corinthians' disbelief, he explains the reality of the Eucharistic meal: "The cup of blessing which we bless, is it not a participation in the blood of Christ? The bread which we break, is it not a participation in the body of Christ?" (1 Cor. 10:16). This "participation" Paul mentions is the Greek word *koinonia*, which indicates the most intimate privilege of reception, the same intimate communion shared in the reality of the sacrament of holy matrimony with the two becoming "one flesh." Paul also reprimands those who consume the Eucharist and refuse to believe: "For anyone who eats and drinks without discerning the body eats and drinks judgment upon himself" (1 Cor. 11:29).

Next, the historicity of the Eucharist is rich: The Real Presence of Jesus in the Eucharist is a long-standing teaching, virtually unchallenged for Christianity's first 1,500 years until the time of the Protestant Reformation. And in fact, many of the first Protestant Revolutionaries, such as Martin Luther, believed in the Real Presence. Indeed, folks will search in vain for a substantive, orthodox source that challenges the Church's teaching on the Eucharist.

Finally, there have been many Eucharistic miracles that offer further proof of the truth of the Real Presence, which we shall discuss in the next entry ("**Eucharistic Miracles**").

The Eucharist is truly the "source and summit" of our Christian life (CCC 1324). All of the teachings of Christ point to this sacrifice and our participation in consuming it as a valid and efficacious sacrament. It is the singular aspect of our Faith that unites us and sustains us.

Further reading: The Lamb's Supper *by Scott Hahn is a well-presented study on the celebration of Mass and the Holy Eucharist.*

Eucharistic Miracles

Observable events involving the Real Presence of Christ in the Eucharist that contravene natural laws.

Eucharistic miracles abound in history and continue to this day. They are not a matter of divine revelation but are considered private revelation and therefore do not require our assent or belief. Nevertheless, these miracles achieve three general purposes: to confirm the Real Presence; to cause or increase the faith of believers; and to demonstrate the power of God in the Eucharist. Insofar as they confirm the presence of Christ in the Eucharist, they propagate the teachings of divine revelation (see "**Revelation**"). These events offer confirmation for many that Jesus is truly present in the sacrament and that the species truly change into the Body and Blood of Christ.

Famous Eucharistic miracles include the altar corporal of Bolsena, Italy, which was stained when

Eucharistic miracle of Lanciano, Italy

an unbelieving Bohemian priest witnessed his consecrated host bleeding in his hands. The corporal is still on display in Orvieto. Other "bleeding hosts" have occurred in Lanciano, Italy, and Santarém, Portugal, which also remain displayed for pilgrims to see. Another famous miracle involves St. Clare of Assisi, who drove away the armies of Frederick II with a monstrance containing a Host. And in 1370, a man in Cimballa tried to desecrate a Host by stabbing it, and blood spewed out onto the altar linens.

Eucharistic miracles remain some of the most fascinating events in Church history. They are stunning stories, and to this day, science cannot explain (though it sometimes confirms) the phenomena behind the events. They help to increase our faith and affirm the doctrine of the Real Presence of Christ in the Eucharist.

Further reading: A Cardiologist Examines Jesus: The Stunning Science Behind Eucharistic Miracles *by Franco Serafini, not only looks at the history and stories behind various Eucharistic Miracles across the globe but also presents the science confirming a link between all of these miracles.*

Euthanasia

The practice of putting someone to death in order to end physical or mental suffering.

The word "euthanasia" comes from the Greek word meaning "good death," but this etymology does not reflect the true reality of euthanasia. The substance of the act of euthanasia remains the intentional death of the handicapped, terminally or mentally ill, or dying; and so while it is portrayed as "mercy killing," the action itself is never merciful and constitutes a gravely immoral act. The *Catechism* teaches that euthanasia is "an act or omission which, of itself or by intention, causes death in order to eliminate suffering" and that it "constitutes a murder gravely contrary to the dignity of the human person and to the respect due to the living God, his Creator" (CCC 2277). And so, regardless of the perceived mercy, the intentions do not justify the act.

Catholic teaching confirms that euthanasia is contrary to the natural law, and it also contradicts authentic medical care. The correct response to human suffering is to cure the sick through morally acceptable solutions, and if someone cannot be cured, the dignified approach is to comfort the afflicted. Comfort may take the form of palliative care, in which the symptoms of suffering are cared for without providing a solution to the cause of suffering.

Suffering can also be a superior opportunity to understand and identify oneself with the sufferings of Christ, who did not deserve the wrath of His persecutors and the agony of His Passion. With God's grace, we can meritoriously endure, and we also can make sense of suffering in a way that is meaningful to our spiritual well-being.

Further reading: For more on death and the Church's pastoral approach to caring for persons who are suffering at the end of life, read the Catechism *paragraphs 2276–2279.*

Evangelical Counsels

Voluntary poverty, chastity, and obedience, by which a person seeks to grow in holiness and achieve spiritual perfection.

When one professes to take up the evangelical counsels as a permanent state of life, the Church recognizes this as a life consecrated to God. "Christ's faithful, moved by the Holy Spirit, propose to follow Christ more nearly, to give themselves to God who is loved above all and, pursuing the perfection of charity in the service of the Kingdom, to signify and proclaim in the Church the glory of the world to come" (CCC 916).

St. Francis of Assisi, by Francisco Pacheco. St. Francis embraced the evangelical counsels.

The evangelical counsels come from Matthew 19:16–30, in which a wealthy man asks Jesus about the requirements to be "perfect." Jesus answers first by stating that complete obedience and conformity to the commandments is absolutely necessary. But when the man says he lacks nothing in observing the commandments, Jesus tells him to sell everything he owns and give the money to the poor.

Although the man asked what "good deed" he must do to have eternal life, Jesus' counsels are a point of continuous perfection and are not obligatory conditions for salvation. Rather, they are known as "acts of supererogation" that exceed the minimum duty required by the commandments. The evangelical counsels, then, are not limited to those in the consecrated life but are, as the *Catechism* says, proposed by Christ to every disciple (CCC 915). Every Catholic can observe the evangelical counsels in a general sense through practical applications to their daily life such as modest spending and generous giving, observation of the supreme law of love, and the pursuit of self-mastery and discipline of the carnal appetites.

Evangelization

Proclaiming the gospel, the good news of salvation in Christ.

At its core, evangelization is the very reason for the existence of the Church, which aims to witness to others the life-giving message of Jesus Christ through our life as an example and through our spoken testimony. Evangelization is closely related to the *kerygma* (see "**Kerygma**"), which is the announcing of the good news—the gospel—in the world. Evangelization might take place through missionary activities or in the daily interactions of the laity in the world with unbelievers and those who are in need of further spiritual development.

In the Bible, we find that evangelization is not limited to the special work of priests and pastors but is a universal mission of all Christians: "Go therefore and make disciples of all nations, baptizing them in the name of the Father and of the Son and of the Holy Spirit, teaching them to observe all that I have commanded you" (Matt. 28:19–20). This command to evangelize is also known as the Great Commission, the final and enduring instructions given to the apostles (and to all Christians) by Christ before His Ascension (see "**Ascension**").

Pope St. Paul VI's encyclical *Evangelii Nuntiandi* provides three primary rudiments to the work of evangelization. First, the faithful must bear witness that God, revealed by His Son, Jesus Christ, in the Holy Spirit, has loved the world and called men to eternal life with Him. Second, we must make a clear proclamation that Jesus Christ, the Son of God, died and rose from the grave, and in Him salvation is offered to all men as a free gift of God's grace and mercy. Third, we must preach the promises made by God in the New Covenant of Jesus Christ: forgiveness of sins, peace, sanctification, and eternal happiness.[30]

Further reading: George Weigel's Evangelical Catholicism *is an illuminating examination of Catholic evangelization in the current age.*

Evil

Impairing or corrupting of a good or perfection in an act, thing, or person.

Two general types of evils are recognized: physical, which is the deprivation of a physical good, such as the lack of sight in a blind person; and moral, the deprivation of a moral good, such as the lack of truth in a lie. Evil is not a thing in and of itself but is the absence of a good. St. Thomas Aquinas famously remarked: "One opposite is known through the other, as darkness is known through light. Hence also what evil is must be known from the nature of good."[31]

Evolution

Gradual changes and development in the biology of living things through various demands in the environment, genetic variations, or mutations in DNA.

Theories of evolution begin with Jean Baptiste Lamarck, a French scientist and deist who first constructed an evolution theory that complex species derive organs from less complex or simple organs, forming the critical arguments for "use and disuse" of traits and characteristics being passed from generation to generation. Charles Darwin later became the most influential and articulate evolutionist. The most notable of his numerous publications is the famous *Origin of Species*. His theory of evolution through natural selection was groundbreaking and still influences modern scientists.

Notwithstanding the limitations of science and not having access to all the facts, the Church does not oppose evolution. Therefore, Catholics are free to consider evolutionary theories that provide for a Creator as the ultimate cause of all things, including evolutionary change. The items Catholics must uphold are: the soul is not subject to evolution but is created immediately upon conception by God; and even if God used an animal to create humankind (the idea of "common descent" of humans and animals), man is not the son of that animal but is specially created and purposed by God. Pope Pius XII adds in *Humani Generis* that the faithful cannot embrace an opinion that maintains that after Adam, there existed men who did not take their origin through him as from the first parent of all, nor that Adam represents a certain number of first parents.[32] The Biblical Theological Commission also concludes that Catholics must uphold that the first woman was made from the first man.

There is a common misconception that the Catholic Church is "anti-science" and that Catholics cannot believe modern scientific theories. All truth, however, comes from God, the author of

Fr. Gregor Mendel, the father of modern genetics

truth, and so the truth of the Church and true scientific knowledge must be compatible. Indeed, some of the most popular and influential Creation and scientific theories have been supported and developed by some of history's greatest Catholic minds. Belgian priest Fr. Georges Lemaître is the father of the Big Bang Theory. He was a contemporary of Albert Einstein and based his work on Einstein's theory of general relativity. Fr. Lemaître also spent time serving as the Director of the Pontifical Academy of Sciences. Gregor Mendel was an Augustinian friar and was the founder of the modern science of genetics. These scientists and many others help Catholics today to repute the popular misconception that the Catholic Church is anti-science.

Examination of Conscience

A reflection on one's moral state, scrutinized by an honest reflection of actions, thoughts, and choices, sometimes involving a broad series of questions. It is often used to prepare for the sacrament of Confession.

Such an examination should be performed regularly but especially before the sacrament of Reconciliation to ensure no sin and detail is forgotten and that one is prepared to confess. Examinations should not only illuminate what one has done but also what one has failed to do in conformity with the will of God.

An examination of conscience can include recollecting moments of the recent past or, in some cases, of one's whole life, such as when one is preparing for a general confession. This examination should include one's circumstances and intentions aligned with good moral catechesis. Thorough examinations are often presented as a series of questions one may ask him or herself to be sure nothing is missed.

The point of an examination of conscience is not to scrutinize everything we've done wrong for the sake of guilt but to give Christ all our worries and even all our wrongdoing and to receive His mercy. Then we can live in peace and sanctity after receiving absolution. If a sin is forgotten in this examination or in the sacrament of Confession, it is still covered by the absolution given by the priest, but if it is later remembered, it is best to include it in the next confession. For those who pray—or want to pray—the Divine Office (see "**Divine Office**"), the night prayer (or "compline") contains a short examination of conscience to make each night.

Excommunication

A legal censure administered by the Church that deprives a person of communion with the Church.

There are two types of excommunication: *latae sententiae* ("sentence already passed") and *ferendae sententiae* ("sentence to be passed"). A *latae sententiae* excommunication is a direct and automatic result of a person's action. A *ferendae sententiae* excommunication occurs when a person is found and pronounced to be excommunicated.

Excommunications are ordinarily the result of heresy, apostasy, or creating a schismatic church. The 1983 *Code of Canon Law* details a number of specific actions that would result in an excommunication, which include abortion, scandal, perjury to an ecclesial authority, or attempts to give a sacramental absolution that is not authorized.

Excommunication is a serious penalty, but it is a medicinal one, and it is not intended to last indefinitely. Reconciliation with the Church occurs through an act of absolution, which is not to be confused with the sacramental act. Absolution from excommunication is purely jurisdictional, reinstating the individual(s) to communion with the Church and allowing them to receive the sacraments. Such an absolution would, then, occur before a full sacramental Confession and absolution.

Exorcism

A sacramental of the Church whereby a demon is expelled from a person, place, or object.

In an exorcism, the Church asks publicly and authoritatively in the name of Jesus Christ that a person or object be protected against the power of the Evil One and withdrawn from his dominion (CCC 1673).

The Old Testament contains no references to men performing exorcisms. This is because it is Christ who gave the apostles the power—His power—to cast out demons as a sign of their faith (Mark 16:17). Tobias, though, used the intercession of the Archangel Raphael to expel a demon with the burnt ashes of the heart and liver of a fish, as the angel had instructed two chapters prior (Tob. 6:16–17; 8:3). The New Testament contains a new fervor for this holy enterprise. In these accounts, we read that the Church was given the authority to exorcise demons. Acts 19:11–12 recounts that when handkerchiefs and aprons that had touched Paul's hands were applied to the sick, diseases were cured and evil spirits exorcised.

A simple exorcism is given with Baptism (three in the Extraordinary Form), and a major exorcism may be administered by a trained priest in strict compliance with the rules of the Church and with the approval of the bishop. The introduction of catechumens to the Church also involves a series of exorcisms.

Fr. Gabriele Amorth (1925–2016), an exorcist in Rome

Further reading: For an eye-opening look into exorcisms and the problem of evil in today's world, we recommend all of the books from and about Fr. Gabriele Amorth, the late Chief Exorcist for the Vatican who performed thousands of exorcisms. However, the study of demons and the demonic is incredibly dangerous territory. It is permissible for a faithful person to read one or two books in order to understand the realities of spiritual warfare, but one must guard oneself against a growing fascination or interest in evil.

Faith

A supernatural, infused gift from God by which a person accepts and believes in the truth.

Faith is equally an internal attitude and an act, driving a believer to seek understanding, to exercise freedom, and to obtain certainty. Christians do not have or gain faith through persuasive arguments and clever facts. Rather, we believe "because of the authority of God himself who reveals them, who can neither deceive nor be deceived" (CCC 156).

The author of the letter to the Hebrews describes faith as "the assurance of things hoped for, the conviction of things not seen" (Heb. 11:1). The early Church struggled against the dualistic belief that the material and spiritual were at odds with one another. This dualism challenged the idea that knowledge and faith could work together. St. Augustine's handling of the subject articulated the concept of faith with precision, preserving the double meaning of believing in the unseeable but to such an extent that it moves our hearts and dictates our actions—something we can actually savor and depend upon. The next breakthrough was with St. Thomas Aquinas, who famously wrote that faith was nothing more than the assent of the human mind to God's self-revelations as truth. These definitions do not disagree with one another; rather, each helps capture the characteristics of faith.[33]

"To make this act of faith, the grace of God and the interior help of the Holy Spirit must precede and assist, moving the heart and turning it to God, opening the eyes of the mind and giving 'joy and ease to everyone in assenting to the truth and believing it,'" says the Dogmatic Constitution on Divine Revelation, *Dei Verbum*.[34] Therefore, obtaining and increasing faith is a two-way relationship in which the person cooperates with God's free gifts of grace. Practically speaking, this comes through study, charity, exercising hope, and living in obedience to the Holy Spirit.

CATHOLIC TIP

A long-standing tradition among Catholics is the recitation of the Act of Faith. It is a prayer that acknowledges the truth of God and our personal assent to the teachings of the Catholic Church. This Act may be prayed daily, when faith seems to dwindle, or when we wish to rededicate ourselves to the Lord:

> *O my God, I firmly believe that You are one God in three divine Persons, Father, Son, and Holy Spirit. I believe that Your divine Son became man and died for our sins and that He will come to judge the living and the dead. I believe these and all the truths which the Holy Catholic Church teaches because You have revealed them who are eternal truth and wisdom, who can neither deceive nor be deceived. In this faith I intend to live and die. Amen.*

When we talk of faith, we are speaking about the individual beliefs of a person. But when we discuss the Catholic Faith, or more simply, the Faith, we refer to the complete system of beliefs revealed by God in Sacred Scripture and Sacred Tradition, which the Church presents to the world.

Family

The first unit of all societies, made by God in the beginning and blessed by Jesus in the sacrament of Holy Matrimony.

The family has the Church as its guide, reflecting in a special way the intimate love and life-giving nature of Christ and the Church as His Bride. The family is, therefore, a "domestic church" (see "**Domestic Church**" for more).

The chief mission and right of the family, as recognized by the Church, is to educate and catechize children to accept the Faith and follow God as Christians. *Gravissimum Educationis* boldly states:

> Since parents have given children their life, they are bound by the most serious obligation to educate their offspring and therefore must be recognized as the primary and principal educators.... Parents are the ones who must create a family atmosphere animated by love and respect for God and man, in which the well-rounded personal and social education of children is fostered. Hence the family is the first school of the social virtues that every society needs.[35]

Many ideas and social norms of modern society threaten the integrity of the family: birth control, abortion, increasing rates of divorce, careerism, premarital sex, materialism, inadequate wages, extravagant taste, immodest behavior, unemployment, social grooming through liberal higher education, sexual ideologies, and too many more to name here. In light of these threats, it is incumbent upon the consciences of every Catholic to be prepared to explain Catholic teaching and defend the family to better preserve its place and rights within society.

The family of St. Thérèse of Lisieux

The family can be an image of Heaven on earth, a true "domestic church," or it can be a Purgatory, even a Hell, depending on how committed parents are to their duties. The Church fittingly teaches that the family will determine how well children retain life lessons such as endurance, the joy of work, fraternal love, forgiveness, and above all their personal faith and divine worship in prayer (CCC 1657).

CATHOLIC TIP

A good priest always spoke firmly during his homilies: "The family that prays together stays together. But that prayer is more than the twenty seconds before meals."

It can seem daunting to busy parents, but time for prayer and devotion as a family needs to be part of the family schedule. My personal recommendation is to start with bedtime or mornings: a time when little else is going on and a short assortment of prayers can be fit in together. Start with a set of Hail Marys, the Our Father, and a Glory Be, and then proceed from there. A spiritual reading from the Bible or the work of a saint should eventually be added. Novenas are short and simple (and highly efficacious) prayers too. Consider a family Rosary after Mass on Sundays to further consecrate the Lord's Day as special in a way that is clearly visible to any child.

However you choose to add more prayer to your family life, remember that the best way to start praying together is to *start*. Catholic family prayer as a norm comes from building a habit, and all habits have to start with intentionality. Parents should also have the resolution to encourage some sense of accountability with each other: Even if one is tired or sick, the prayer should not be skipped—and even when hunger is strong after Mass on Sunday or the game is on TV, a pause must be applied to do what is right. "The family that prays together stays together."

Fasting

Intentionally refraining from the consumption of food or drink.

Fasting is an extraordinary aid to prayer and growth in spiritual perfection. It helps us to grow in self-control and is a devout act of penance and mortification. Jesus says, "*When* you fast" not "*if* you fast" (see Matt. 6:16), confirming that at various times, all Christians should take up this act.

Fasting should be accompanied by prayer in order to be efficacious. When coaching the disciples on performing the miraculous works He intended for them, Jesus reminded them, "This kind [of demon] cannot be driven out by anything but prayer and fasting" (Mark 9:29). Because Catholic fasting coexists with prayer, it is vastly different from fasting as part of a diet regimen whose main purpose is to lose weight.

Fasting is also a private act of penance. Jesus offers some important instruction: "When you fast, do not look dismal, like the hypocrites, for they disfigure their faces that their fasting may be seen by men.... But when you fast, anoint your head and wash your face, that your fasting may not be seen by men but by your Father who is in secret" (Matt. 6:16–18). In other words, don't boast about your fasting and don't show it off—hide it if possible. The best practice is to not mention it at all.

The Church requires that Catholics ages eighteen to fifty-nine fast on Ash Wednesday and Good Friday each year. This fast restricts food to a maximum of one full meal and two smaller meals that together do not equal the full meal. Excluded from the obligation to fast on these days are the chronically ill (such as diabetics) and pregnant and nursing women.[36] The Church also requires that Catholics fast from food and drink (except water and medicine) for one hour before receiving the Eucharist (CIC 919). The Eucharistic fast is a wonderful way to show our love and devotion to Christ, who is truly present in the Paschal meal.

Fathers of the Church

Early Christian theologians and writers who had a strong connection with the apostles and maintained the apostolic teachings.

The earliest of the Church Fathers are known as the Apostolic Fathers. The Fathers of the Church include recognizable writers such as Ignatius of Antioch, Polycarp, Irenaeus, Clement, and Cyril. An early Christian writer does not need to be a saint to be considered a Church Father, although there are a few unofficial characteristics recognized today that allow one to be considered a Church Father: antiquity, personal holiness, approval by the Catholic Church, and orthodoxy in teaching (their teachings should contain no deviation from the apostolic tradition). Lack of such characteristics explains why some commonly cited early Christian writers such as Tertullian (A.D. 155–200) and Origen (A.D. 184–253) are excluded from the title of Father, though their writings illuminate much for apologists and historians of the early Church.

All the Fathers of the Church witness to the clarification of Church doctrine in their time. Church Fathers are recognized from just after the time of the apostles all the way to St. Gregory the Great (d. 604) in the West, and St. John Damascene (d. 749) in the East, and so they occupy and demonstrate eight centuries of Christian thought, tradition, and life.

Further reading: Excellent reading on the Fathers of the Church is Pope Benedict XVI's Church Fathers: From Clement of Rome to Augustine. *Another highly regarded source is Mike Aquilina's* Fathers of the Church.

Feast Days

Days within the liturgical calendar to celebrate a specific saint, event, or aspect of Church teaching.

Also known as Holy Days and Ecclesiastical Feasts, there are three general types of feast days in the Church: solemnities, feasts, and memorials. A solemnity is the highest type of feast and indicates

Eucharistic procession for the feast of Corpus Christi, Bielsko-Biała, 2023

immensely joyful observance. Solemnities celebrate the most important events in the lives of Jesus and Mary or are dedicated to certain saints, especially Sts. Joseph, John the Baptist, Peter, and Paul. Sunday is also always a solemnity, as it is the day on which we celebrate Jesus' Resurrection from the dead. Some solemnities always land on Sunday (such as Easter), while others are celebrated on specific calendar dates or may be moved (these last are therefore known as "movable feasts"). A feast honors a mystery or title of the Lord or recognizes saints of particular importance. A memorial is usually an optional celebration of a saint, but we also celebrate memorials of Our Lord and of Mary. Two examples of memorials are the Holy Name of Jesus on January 3 and Our Lady of Loreto on December 10.

On any given day there are dozens of saints to be celebrated, but the Church usually highlights just one in her Mass of the day. Some feasts also may celebrate groups or multiple saints, such as the North American Martyrs (October 19) or Sts. Cosmas and Damian (September 26). Other times, the feast celebrates an event, such as the Dedication of the Basilica of St. Mary Major in Rome (August 5) or the Solemnity of the Immaculate Conception (December 8).

Understanding the treatment of feast days on the liturgical calendar can be frustrating without in-depth study and education, since there are a number of rules that are not always obvious. For example, the Gloria is sung on all solemnities no matter what day they land on. And often times, local dioceses and regional sees (such as the United States Council of Catholic Bishops) will alter their practices of transferring and observing certain feasts from year to year. Sometimes noticing these peculiarities just requires time and observation, and also asking questions. The best practice is to refer to an accurate calendar and to take each day, season, and year one at a time.

Final Perseverance

Continuing in a state of grace until the end of life.

The notion of final perseverance comes from Matthew 10:22: "He who endures to the end will be saved." The reward for final perseverance is Heaven and eternal life. While we hope to remain in a state of grace throughout our lives, most of us will fall short at some point (see Rom. 3:23). Through faith, man recovers from sin to be brought back into friendship with God, and lost grace and forgiveness for sin can be recovered through sorrow for sins, penance, and the sacrament of Reconciliation.

Catholic teaching on final perseverance does not limit it to the final hours of one's life or the

Stained-glass window of Christ revealing His Sacred Heart to St. Margaret Mary, St. Margaret Mary Alacoque Church, Woodbridge, Ontario

moments before death. Rather, final perseverance entails maintaining a continual life in a state of grace *up to* our final hours and moment of death. Because we require grace to sustain faith, final perseverance is a gift from God, and Catholics must pray for the specific grace of final perseverance throughout their whole lives. One way in which we may beg for this grace is through the Devotion to the Sacred Heart of Jesus (see "**Sacred Heart of Jesus**"). As Jesus Himself said to St. Margaret Mary Alacoque:

> I promise you in the excessive Mercy of My Heart that My all-powerful Love will grant to all those who communicate on the First Friday in nine consecutive months the Grace of Final Penitence; they shall not die in My disgrace nor without receiving the sacraments; My Divine Heart shall be their safe refuge in this last moment.

Theologian and spiritual master Fr. Reginald Garrigou-Lagrange offers the following recommendation for souls who wish to achieve final perseverance: "[To obtain this grace of final perseverance], we should frequently unite ourselves with the Eucharistic consecration, the essence of the sacrifice of the Mass, pondering on the four ends of sacrifice: adoration, supplication, reparation, and thanksgiving."[37]

Forgiveness

The free act of pardoning or releasing one who has caused injury in some way.

Only God can forgive sins, since sin is an offense against an infinite being and we are not able to restore our friendship with God after we have broken it through sin. But the Church teaches that at the moment a person has sorrow for his sins, he has obtained forgiveness (CCC 1452). This forgiveness

The parable of the prodigal son illustrates God's forgiveness.

even includes mortal sin if the sorrow for sin includes the intention to go to Confession as soon as possible.

The sacrament of Reconciliation is the ordinary means of forgiveness. It restores our relationship with God, offers peace of mind that one's sin is truly forgiven, and is the instrument by which sanctifying grace is received (see "**Reconciliation**").

As Christians, we also believe that forgiving the transgressions of others against us is one of the supreme acts of imitating Christ. Jesus makes it clear that forgiveness is a requirement of the divine law: "If you do not forgive men their trespasses, neither will your Father forgive your trespasses" (Matt. 6:15). When we are hurt by others, we should be quick to forgive even when an apology is not offered, since Christ has forgiven us (Eph. 4:32) and died for us while we were still unrepentant sinners (see Rom. 5:8).

Four Last Things

Death, judgment, Heaven, and Hell.

Death is the natural end of a human life on earth. It marks the separation of man's mortal body and

The Last Judgment, by Fra Angelico

immortal soul. All persons are subjected to death as a result of Original Sin.

At the moment of death, each person will undergo judgment for his conduct during his life and will then receive his reward or punishment. This judgment immediately after death is called the particular judgment. There will be another judgment at the end of time, when Jesus Christ will "come again in glory to judge the living and the dead," and it is in this final judgment (also called the general judgment) that God's whole plan for the world is to be revealed.

Heaven is the eternal state of perfect happiness, the state of union with God. Hell is the eternal state of torment and despair for those who have freely rejected God. The Church teaches that there is an intermediate state called Purgatory for those who are bound for Heaven but whose love for God is still blemished by some imperfection. These souls undergo a temporary period of being purged of the effects of sin (see "**Purgatory**"), after which they enter Heaven and eternal joy.

The branch of theological study that deals with the four last things and the destiny of man is eschatology.

Four Marks of the Church

Essential characteristics of the true Church founded by Christ: one, holy, catholic, and apostolic.

The four marks of the Church are contained in the Apostle's Creed. Only the Catholic Church bears these four marks. That the Church is *one* represents unity: the profession of one faith, one form of worship, and the authority of the pope. The *holiness* of the Church is found in its faith, discipline, worship, laws, and doctrine, all of which sanctify its members. The *catholicity* of the Church refers to its universal nature, which is inclusive of all peoples of the earth regardless of their race, language, or economic status, solely due to their identity in Christ's Body. The *apostolicity* of the Church means that the Church was founded on the authority given to the apostles and continues their teachings.

Free Will

A power within man's soul to choose the good and seek God, rooted in being created as a rational being with a spiritual soul.

Man was created in the image of God, with a rational soul. This means that human beings can freely choose how they will act, given their judgment and ability to reason. God created man this way so that, of his own volition, he might choose to seek God and love Him (CCC 1730).

According to the *Catechism*, "Freedom is the power, rooted in reason and will, to act or not to act, to do this or that, and so to perform deliberate actions on one's own responsibility" (CCC 1731). God has given man the freedom to forge his own life. Our freedom in life should cause us to be happy, and this is only achieved when our will is aligned with God's will. "By free will, he is capable of directing himself toward his true good. He finds his perfection 'in seeking and loving what is true and good'" (CCC 1704).

This freedom is like a liberation from the forces of temptation and evil, which seek to detract us from seeking God. It is different from the freedom the world portrays: an independent, self-seeking entitlement to do anything pleasing to oneself. Free will instead is that power within the soul to seek the *truly good* things in life that avoid sin and accomplish God's will. Indeed, running away from God's love and refusing His plan for our life completely removes our true freedom and makes us slaves to sin (CCC 1739).

God could never forces man's will because doing so would not be in keeping with man's dignity. Man's will is truly free. Because we have free will, however, we are responsible for our actions; we reap the benefits of our good choices as well as the consequences of our bad ones. The conclusion is not that we are in constant conflict with God, since we are susceptible to the consequences of Original Sin, but that we are liberated and absolutely unrestricted in our role as "collaborators in his work in the Church and in the world" (CCC 1742).

The freedom of will is not in conflict with God's providence or His knowledge of what will happen in the future. God is outside space and time, and He knows all things that will happen to all people—even the results of our free will. While He knows how we will choose, though, He does not control our choices, and He governs all things according to His will.

Freemasonry

An international secret fraternal society whose norms include conspiracy and that professes problematic teachings that are incompatible with the Catholic Faith.

Freemasonry is a secret fraternal society with deep anti-Catholic roots and motives. Because of the seriousness of the teachings of freemasonry, many of which are opposed to the Catholic Church (such as

Freemasons' Hall, London

their views on Jesus and the papacy), Catholics are forbidden to join the Freemasons.

The Freemasons appear to be an ordinary fraternal society, and many within the lower ranks do not realize that their philosophies and morals are inconsistent with Christianity. But in reality, their teachings include things like rites, sun cults, altars, and sacred books that sharply conflict with Catholic teaching.

Fruits of the Holy Spirit

Acts and characteristics of Christians who allow the Holy Spirit to work through them.

St. Paul names nine fruits of the Spirit in his letter to the Galatians: love, joy, peace, patience, kindness, goodness, faithfulness, gentleness, and self-control (Gal. 5:22–23). According to the *Catechism*, "The tradition of the Church lists twelve of them," adding generosity, modesty, and chastity to Paul's list (CCC 1832).

These fruits are not "proofs" of Christian behavior, since they are possible with any person, but are assured through grace when a Christian responds to God's inspiration. Their purpose is to sanctify the Christian. The fruits of the Spirit respond to and correct the fruits of evil, or "works of the flesh," which are also named by Paul in his letter to the Galatians: fornication, impurity, licentiousness, idolatry, sorcery, enmity, strife, jealousy, anger, selfishness, dissension, party spirit, envy, drunkenness, and carousing (Gal. 5:19–21). As we strive to live a truly Christian life, the fruits of the Spirit become in us "the first fruits of eternal glory" (CCC 1832).

Gifts of the Holy Spirit

Permanent dispositions of one in the state of grace that complete and perfect all other virtues and make one open to the promptings of the Holy Spirit.

Each person receives the gifts of the Holy Spirit at Baptism and is strengthened and confirmed in them through Confirmation (CCC 1830). The list of seven gifts traditionally comes from Isaiah (11:2–3): wisdom, understanding, counsel, fortitude, knowledge, fear of the Lord, and piety. That these, in the words of the prophet, would "shoot from the stump of Jesse" is a reference to Jesus, who gifted the Spirit to His Church (Isa. 11:1).

These gifts were not often discussed in the theological writings of early Christians, but Justin Martyr (d. A.D. 165) confirmed that all of the seven gifts are given at Baptism. Later, St. Thomas Aquinas developed the most complete theology regarding the seven gifts, distinguishing them from all other virtues and explaining that they are qualitatively different and superior to the moral and theological virtues. Moreover, he regarded the Holy Spirit, not the human person, as the actuator of these gifts in each individual. What is important about Aquinas's teaching is the reality that Christians shouldn't think that more effort and exertion will produce these gifts or produce them in more vivifying abundance—the gifts of the Spirit are freely given, and our goal is to remain in a state of grace and cooperate with them so that we may listen to the Holy Spirit, who will aid us in the practice of virtue.

Because of the way Paul presents these gifts as emanating from the Holy Spirit (1 Cor. 12), it is very easy to confuse these seven gifts with the charisms (see "**Charisms**"). The key distinguishing feature of the gifts of the Holy Spirit is that they are given to all the faithful through Baptism, first for one's own sanctification and then for that of others.

Gnosticism

An early heresy developed from pre-Christian dualist philosophies.

Gnosticism, from the Greek *gnosis* ("knowledge"), stems from dualism, a philosophy that pits the material world against the spiritual. Gnosticism arose from the idea that through knowledge a person could free himself from the evils of the flesh, and it quickly infected Christian doctrine as early as the first century A.D.

In early Christian times, gnostic heretics would disassociate Christ's divine personhood from His

Stained-glass window depicting the Holy Spirit in the form of a dove, Church of St. Pothin, Lyon, France

human, bodily nature. In essence, they rejected the Incarnation and Hypostatic Union (see "**Incarnation**" and "**Hypostatic Union**"): that Jesus was both God and man with a fully human nature and a fully divine nature fused in the one Person of Christ.

Gnosticism caused much division in the early Church and was the catalyst for some of the early synods. The apostle John wrote against Gnosticism in his epistles, warning the followers of Christ about "those who would deceive you" (1 John 2:26) and teaching them to discern the truth: "By this you know the Spirit of God: every spirit which confesses that Jesus Christ has come in the flesh is of God, and every spirit which does not confess Jesus is not of God" (1 John 4:2–3).

In some ways, dualist gnostic errors are still present today. Such is the case of the modern notion of idealism, a system of philosophy that relates knowledge as a reality that solely exists in the mind, rather than the physical world. Gnostic-esque dualism is also more manifestly present in world religions such as Mormonism, which profess that Jesus is not God but the firstborn "spirit-child" of God.

The Nativity with God the Father and the Holy Ghost, by Giambattista Pittoni

God

The one, supreme, eternal, infinite, and personal Being who created and rules the universe.

Christianity teaches that God is triune, meaning that He is three persons in one divine nature. This teaching is known as the doctrine of the Trinity (see "**Trinity**" for a more complete discussion)—"the central mystery of Christian faith and life" (CCC 234). God the Father is the first Person of the Trinity, God the Son is the second Person, and God the Holy Spirit is the third Person of the Trinity.

St. Thomas Aquinas goes to great lengths to describe the attributes of God: simple (lacks composition), good, perfect, omnipresent, infinite, immutable (cannot change), eternal, omniscient (all-knowing), and omnipotent (all-powerful). St. Thomas focuses on the idea that God doesn't merely *have* these attributes, but that He *is* these in perfection. Whatever God has, God was, is, and will be perfectly.

Theologians have also articulated that God *is His own existence*. All things exist because of an act of another, resulting in what is known as an "actual existence," but because God was existing, is existing, and always will exist, He is the only self-existent being: *He is His own existence, and He is Himself.* This notion of God simply "being Himself" is understood best in the traditional name of God as Yahweh, presented to Moses as "I AM" (Exod. 3:14–15). (See "**Yahweh**" for more on this important Old Testament name of God.)

Further reading: The first twenty-one questions of the Summa Theologiae *of St. Thomas Aquinas; and* The One God *by Fr. Reginald Garrigou-Lagrange.*

Godparents

The sponsors of a person who is baptized in the Catholic Church.

The Church requires the presence of at least one godparent at Baptism, but someone may stand in as a proxy for the godparent(s) if he or she cannot physically be present. This requirement also pertains to adult Baptisms that coincide with the Order of Christian Initiation of Adults (see "**OCIA**").

The conditions for this sponsor, pursuant to the Code of Canon Law (CIC 873–874), are that the person:

+ be designated by the one to be baptized, by the parents or the person who takes their place, or, in their absence, by the pastor or minister;
+ has the aptitude and intention of fulfilling the function of godparent;
+ has completed the sixteenth year of age, unless the diocesan bishop has established another age or the pastor or minister has granted an exception for a just cause;
+ be a Catholic who has been confirmed and has already received the most holy sacrament of the Eucharist and who leads a life of faith in keeping with the function to be a sponsor;
+ not be bound by any canonical penalty legitimately imposed or declared;
+ not be the father or mother of the one to be baptized.

A non-Catholic Christian cannot be a godparent but can be a witness of the Baptism together with a Catholic sponsor. The qualifications for a proxy (a stand-in) are the same: they must be a Catholic or a Christian of another denomination.

The duties of the godparent are to make a profession of faith for the child or adult to be baptized and to assume responsibility for the Christian upbringing or Christian education of the baptized, to ensure that the baptized lives a life in communion with the Church and its teachings (CIC 872). While the parents are meant to be the first and principal educators of children in catechesis, when they cannot or do not fulfill this obligation, it is the duty of the godparent to care for the spiritual development of their godchild. Even when parents do fulfill their obligation, godparents should remain involved in the development of the person's faith as a visible and sure example of Christian living.

Gospel

The good news that God loves mankind so much that He sent His only Son to be a perfect and final sacrifice for the sins of the world, and that God has called all people to share in eternal life with Him.

The word "gospel" comes from the old English *godspel*, or "good spell." Preaching the Gospel is the duty of all Christians (see "**Evangelization**" and "**Kerygma**").

The word "Gospel" may also refer to one of the four New Testament books written by the evangelists Matthew, Mark, Luke, and John that tell of the earthly life, teachings, and works of Jesus Christ. These four books are the only canonical Gospels in the Bible. Other ancient books referred to as "gospels," such as the gnostic "Gospel" of Thomas, are not accepted in the Canon of Scripture (see "**Canon of Scripture**").

The gospel is not just a book or a collection of stories and sayings but is also something to be lived out. Christians are called to "live the gospel," meaning we are to be converted, to be sanctified, and to be changed by the message of the gospel in order to be conformed to Christ. As St. Paul wrote to the Ephesians, "Put off your old nature which belongs to your former manner of life and is corrupt through deceitful lusts, and be renewed in the spirit of your minds, and put on the new nature, created after the likeness of God in true righteousness and holiness" (Eph. 4:22–24). This message is the gospel in action.

Grace

Supernatural aid bestowed on the will as a free gift of God in order that we might participate in the divine life by choosing and accomplishing good.

The *Catechism* defines grace as "*favor*, the *free and undeserved help* that God gives us to respond to his call to become children of God, adoptive sons, partakers of the divine nature and of eternal life" (CCC 1996) and "a participation in the life of God" that "introduces us into the intimacy of Trinitarian life" (CCC 1997). Although we refer to many "types" of grace, all grace comes from God and helps us and others achieve sanctification and reach Heaven.

Grace is a participation in God's own life that prepares man to perform good works and enables him to reach Heaven. The word "grace" comes from the Latin *gratia*, which indicates "favor, esteem, and regard." The grace we understand as Christians is a biblical and theological concept, but it is not too different from this secular use. In the Bible, we find that grace is God's divinely favorable disposition to a person or people. To live in a "state of grace" means to be in favor, in friendship, with God.

Graces are named by their relation to their effect or their origin. While all grace is really one, we speak of it in different ways depending on how God is acting in our lives. Sanctifying or habitual grace is the grace that places a person in permanent friendship with God; this is the grace that was lost by Original Sin and is restored in Baptism. Sanctifying grace can also be lost through mortal sin and regained in the sacrament of Reconciliation (or, if sacramental Confession is not possible, through perfect contrition; see "**Contrition**"). Actual grace allows us to act in a way that is pleasing to God.

Guardian Angel

The angel assigned to each person to watch over and protect him throughout his natural life and to act as an intermediary between God and the person.

Tradition and many of the saints teach that each person is given an angel as protector and aid (CCC 336). Pope Paul V authorized the feast of the Guardian Angels for the general calendar in 1609, and it was later elevated to a mandatory feast for the whole Church to observe on October 2 by Pope Clement X.

CATHOLIC TIP

Pray the traditional prayer to your Guardian Angel:

> *Angel of God, my guardian dear,*
> *to whom God's love commits me*
> *here, ever this day [or night] be*
> *at my side, to light and guard, to*
> *rule and guide. Amen.*

Angel statue, Castelo Sant'Angelo, Rome, Italy

Perhaps the clearest indication of the guardian angels in the Gospels occurs in Matthew 18:10, in which Jesus warns His followers: "See that you do not despise one of these little ones; for I tell you that in Heaven their angels always behold the face of my Father who is in Heaven." The Church encourages the faithful to ask their guardian angels for intercession, safety, and wisdom.

Further reading: For one saint's teachings on the guardian angels, see the Summa Theologiae *of St. Thomas Aquinas—the "angelic doctor"—part 1, question 113.*

Happiness

Possession of the good, satisfying man's soul.

Happiness is the ultimate goal of all persons. "We all want to live happily; in the whole human race there is no one who does not assent to this proposition, even before it is fully articulated" (CCC 1718, quoting St. Augustine). The desire for everlasting and satisfying happiness is written on our very hearts.

The things of the world—possessions, physical pleasures, monetary gain, or power—may make us feel happy for a time, but eventually that happiness diminishes and we want more, or something else. Human beings have an inherent longing for happiness that lasts, and ultimately we can only find this happiness in God. The eternal happiness in God that we were created for is called beatitude, and "God calls us to his own beatitude" explains the *Catechism* (1719).

Experience demonstrates that Christians are not always happy in the sense of *feeling* happy. Life provides enough struggles to give us seasons of an elevated outward happiness, but there are also moments of interior displeasure and *un*happiness. *Feeling* happiness and *having* happiness are different concepts for the Christian, because we are called to seek happiness as a thing to be achieved and to wait for—sometimes until the end (for example, the meek will inherit the earth; see Matthew 5:5). Christian wisdom informs our conscience of this important distinction: sometimes in this life we will not *feel* happy, even if we know we are in possession of the Good that satisfies our soul.

Heaven

Where God dwells and where the faithful hope to live with Him eternally.

Heaven is the state of perfect happiness obtained by those who die in God's grace. In this state of perfect happiness, all suffering is ended, and the elect will behold God's glory and live with Him forever.

In the Old Testament, "the heavens" referred to domed layers above the earth's sky, not unlike the layers of atmosphere we know of through science today. When Elijah was carried to Heaven (2 Kings 2:11), the writers were literally describing his ascent into the clouds. In the New Testament, Jesus described Heaven in parables to give it substance and depth. He even taught that we should strive to bring Heaven to earth when we pray: "Thy kingdom come. Thy will be done, on earth as it is in Heaven" (Matt. 6:10). Heaven, then, is not just something to be gained but something to build and something to share.

Eschatologically, we find a vast amount of imagery of Heaven in the Book of Revelation. A city with high gates and walls (21:10–27), white-robed

CATHOLIC TIP

Catholics do not spend a lot of time, energy, and resources trying to nail down what Heaven is or isn't, or when and how it will come. What Catholics are preoccupied with is the divine mission of bringing Heaven to earth: sharing Jesus and happiness with others as a taste of the heavenly promises yet to come.

martyrs (7:13), saints bringing prayers to God (5:8), and angels endlessly praising Him (4:8) are vivid descriptions the writer provides in his translation of his visions. Revelation also says that, in the end, there will be a new Heaven and a new earth, with a new Jerusalem (21:1–2). The *Catechism* tells us that "The universe itself will be renewed" and that in this new universe, "the heavenly Jerusalem, God will have his dwelling among men" (1042–1044).

Hell

The state of eternal punishment for the damned (those who have freely rejected God).

Hell is the dominion of Satan and his demons who have rejected God. Human beings who die without grace (in a state of mortal sin) will spend eternity in Hell by their own free choice (CCC 1035). This teaching implies an enormous responsibility and desire to shepherd all souls to Heaven; it should call all Christians to immediate work. In a General Audience, Pope St. John Paul II offered a very encouraging response to this reality:

> Damnation remains a real possibility, but it is not granted to us, without special divine revelation, to know which human beings are effectively involved in it. The thought of Hell—and even less the improper use of biblical images—must not create anxiety or despair but is a necessary and healthy reminder of freedom within the proclamation that the risen Jesus has conquered Satan, giving us the Spirit of God who makes us cry "Abba, Father!"[39]

The Old Testament does not provide a lot of details about Hell. The *sheol* described in the Old Testament was more of a place of waiting, a consignment location for the dead, though this idea later evolved in ancient Jewish thought into a place for the wicked, which was contrasted with Paradise as the place for the good. When the Hebrew Scriptures were later translated into Greek in the third century B.C., *sheol* was rendered as *Hades*, which implied an invisible, hidden, dark place. In the New Testament, Jesus assures His followers of the great suffering in Hell. It is a place of inextinguishable fire (Matt. 25:41), vast darkness (Matt. 8:12), and weeping and gnashing of teeth (Luke 13:28).

Before Jesus opened Heaven to the blessed through His death and Resurrection, "Hell" referred generally to the state of all the dead, both righteous and unrighteous. When we say that Jesus "descended into Hell" as we recite in the Apostles' Creed, we refer to the belief that Jesus, as His Body lay in the tomb for three days, was liberating the souls of the righteous who had died before His coming. This belief is known as Jesus' "Harrowing of Hell." There is an allusion to this event in 1 Peter 4:6, "For this is why the gospel was preached even to

CATHOLIC TIP

What about Dante's Hell? Dante Alighieri, one of the most respected and celebrated poets of all time, wrote extensively on the punishments of Hell in the *Inferno* of his *Divine Comedy*, relating each sin to a particular punishment. Of course, Dante drew from biblical imagery, historical poets, and his own imaginings, but he also drew from some substantial moral wisdom and an acute application of divine justice. We will, hopefully, never know if Dante was right, but we should pay attention to his link between our acts and their consequences: we are in a very real way tormented by our sins even in this life.

The "Harrowing of Hell":
Christ in Limbo, by Fra Angelico

the dead, that though judged in the flesh like men, they might live in the spirit like God." Now that Jesus has died and risen again, opening Heaven to all the just who lived before His coming, Hell refers only to the eternal and final place of punishment for those who have definitively rejected God's mercy even up to the last moment of their lives.

When Hell is discussed in academic Catholic circles, the idea of a "limbo" is also sometimes brought up. "Limbo" is a historical theological hypothesis within the Church that has not found as much popularity or further academic development in recent years. Historically, academics have contemplated two ideas: the limbo of infants (*limbus parvulorum*), the destination of souls who die in Original Sin (that is, without Baptism) but without personal mortal sin; and the limbo of the Fathers (*limbus patrum*), which includes the souls of the just who died before Christ and awaited their admission to Heaven (these were liberated in the Harrowing of Hell). The theory of limbo for infants, however, is not Church doctrine; instead, the *Catechism* wisely preaches on the reality of Christian hope in God's infinite mercy for children who are not baptized:

> The Church can only entrust them to the mercy of God, as she does in her funeral rites for them. Indeed, the great mercy of God who desires that all men should be saved, and Jesus' tenderness toward children which caused him to say: "Let the children come to me, do not hinder them," allow us to hope that there is a way of salvation for children who have died without Baptism. (CCC 1261)

Heresy

The formal rejection of a tenet of Christian doctrine.

Derived from the Greek word *haíresis*, meaning "sect," in early Christian times "heresy" was used to describe a particular erroneous teaching (or a division of teaching) among Christians. Heresy is a grave sin.

"Heresy" is a word often misused even in Catholic circles. Heresy is not simply an inaccurate statement. The sin of heresy can only be committed when we consciously and deliberately deviate from Christian teaching. In his epistles, St. John refers to those Gnostics who rejected Christ's Incarnation as "deceivers" (see 2 John 7), equating them with the enemy such a label.

Heresy is to be distinguished from heterodoxy (see "**Heterodoxy**").

Heresies are a grave evil. They corrode Christian doctrine and confuse truth and morals, causing the rejection of good and often leading people to sin. For example, the Albigensians of the twelfth century, much like the early Gnostics (see "**Gnosticism**"), taught a dualistic theology that rejected

Luther Burns the Papal Bull in the Square of Wittenberg, by Karl Aspelin

the material world as evil. As a result of this false teaching, this heretical group banned marriage and procreation, removing the sacrament of Holy Matrimony and denouncing the first command given to mankind: "Be fruitful and multiply" (Gen. 1:28).

Although there is no reason to be grateful for a heresy, "we know that in everything God works for good with those who love him" (Rom. 8:28). Throughout the Church's history, the investigation of heresy has led to better clarity in orthodox Catholic doctrine. Through the challenges of dealing with heresies over the centuries, the Church has been forced to articulate and elucidate her teachings, helping to reconcile souls and eliminate confusion for future generations.

Heterodoxy

Disagreement with or misunderstanding of some aspect of Church teaching.

A biblical example of heterodoxy exists in the book of Acts, in which there was a group known as Judaizers who continued to adhere to Jewish customs and even elements of the Mosaic Law that were problematic with the Christian revelation. They were requiring Gentile believers to be circumcised—a deeply problematic position that opposed divine revelation about the Old Law and showed there was a tacit misunderstanding about the reality of circumcision as a forerunner to the sacrament of Baptism. An admonishment was given, as was formal corrective guidance, but since the Church was still in a general state of development, and these types of ideas had not been fully articulated, the Judaizers were not treated as heretics but were given a fraternal correction.

Heterodoxy is less serious than heresy, though it is still problematic. Ideas are infectious, and when a heterodox person or group holds a simple disagreement with what is widely taught by the Church, great division often results. Even if these individuals or groups are not formally schismatic, there is legitimate concern that heresy may eventually result.

Avoiding heterodoxy is important, and it begins with being careful to not only accept what the Church teaches but to *understand why*. Secondly, we should be diligent to check any and all new ideas—or even the ones we are unsure of—with a solid reference or a person of orthodox repute. With astounding wisdom, Thomas á Kempis writes, "It is truth that must be sought in Holy Scripture, not beauty of expression.... Do not be critical of the sayings of the ancient Fathers, for they were not written without reason."

Hierarchy

The order of the body of rulers in the Catholic Church.

The hierarchy of the Church is made up of clergy, ranked based on expertise, function, and need. The term "hierarchy" refers to a system of both governance and ministry in the Church. In ministry, we refer to the hierarchy of holy orders: deacons, priests, and bishops. In jurisdiction, the hierarchy starts at the top with the pope and then extends to the bishops under his authority. The ministerial group and the governing group can be mixed with delegated roles, such as Curial staff (mostly cardinals) who help in specific affairs and offices, rectors in seminaries, and pastors in parishes.

A hierarchy is visible in the Bible: Jesus handselected His apostles, who then selected replacements, and we also find a system of presbyters and deacons. St. Paul mentions a set of angels to which Thomas Aquinas assigns a hierarchy. Observing hierarchy in the Bible is important to discovering that the Church we know and see today is not much different from the Church we find in Sacred Scripture. A hierarchy is necessary for the authoritative administration of the sacraments, and it also is requisite for the good administration of the Church as a whole.

Holiness

The state of perfection and nearness to God that we obtain through grace and separation from sin.

God is holiness itself, as Sacred Scripture testifies: "For thou alone art holy" (Rev. 15:4). We also believe that the Church is holy, as we recite in the Nicene Creed: "I believe in one *holy*, catholic, and apostolic church." This holiness is a mark of the Church that makes her distinguishable from any other Christian sect (see "**Four Marks of the Church**"). Her pure worship, discipline, firm and wholesome teaching, and saints are our surety. Catholics also refer to the supreme pontiff, the pope, as "His Holiness." For individuals, holiness means separation from sin and union with God.

In the Bible, "holy" means "set aside," and it refers to those things belonging to God either through His endowment or through consecration. In the first centuries of the Church, the eremitical life (where we get the term "hermit") became the prevailing form of growing in and witnessing holiness (and later monasticism). People chose to live their lives set aside for God, away from the lures of the world and physical appetites. But while monasticism presents something of an ideal in the quest for holiness, the Church recognizes that holiness can be achieved in all circumstances and with all vocations. To be holy, then, we must seek to grow closer to God according to our state in life, participating in the sacraments, making time for prayer, obeying God and the Church, and showing charity to our neighbor.

Holy Days of Obligation

Liturgical feast days on which the faithful are obliged to attend Mass.

Part of the precepts of the Church (see "**Precepts of the Church**"), holy days of obligation are feast days in the liturgical calendar that are observed through attendance at Mass and, when possible, rest from servile work (as on a Sunday). Attendance at Mass is obligatory on these feasts, thus the name.

Around the world, especially in countries that have a rich Catholic history, such feast days are recognized as national holidays (on which businesses shut down), offering populaces the opportunity to observe the feast properly and thoroughly. Secularization of countries has seen the removal of observing such feasts as national holidays.

Canon 1246, no. 2 of the Code of Canon Law, provides that a conference of bishops can abolish certain holy days of obligation or transfer them to a Sunday with prior approval of the Apostolic See. Since 1991, the United States Conference of Catholic Bishops (USCCB) has maintained their general decree that six holy days of obligation are required. They are: the Solemnity of Mary, Mother of God

(January 1); the Ascension of Christ (forty days after Easter; although some dioceses have abrogated this day to the following Sunday); the Assumption of the Blessed Mother (August 15); All Saints Day (November 1); the Immaculate Conception (December 8); and Christmas (December 25).

Holy Family

The family consisting of Joseph, Mary, and the Child Jesus.

By His divine will, God chose Mary and Joseph out of all people out of all times to raise and love His Son, Jesus. The Holy Family doesn't appear often in Scripture, but the few times they are mentioned provide an instructive example for all families. Despite often having to endure difficult circumstances, Mary and Joseph sought understanding in moments of confusion, helped each other when under threat, and supported each other when they lost Jesus in the Temple for three days when He was twelve years old. This family is an example to all mankind and the archetypal domestic church (see "**Domestic Church**"). The Feast of the Holy Family is celebrated on the Sunday after Christmas.

Mary and Joseph with the Infant Jesus, by Julius Frank

Holy Orders

A sacrament of the New Law instituted by Jesus Christ by which a man joins the order of bishops, priests, or deacons.

Jesus instituted the sacrament of Holy Orders. In this sacrament, men receive spiritual power and special graces to minister and lead the Church in accord with the degree to which they are ordained. The degrees of Holy Orders as a whole consist of the diaconate, the priesthood, and the episcopacy.

The first degree in Holy Orders is the order of deacons, who are called to witness in a special way to service in the Church. All priests are first ordained as deacons. This ordination happens, usually, a year before a man becomes a priest, and this period is known as the "transitional diaconate." Transitional deacons possess the full faculties of the diaconate. Among many other duties, deacons may baptize, witness and bless marriages, and preside at funeral liturgies. Deacons also may read the Gospel at Mass and are able to preach the homily. Some men, however, are ordained as permanent deacons, meaning they do not plan to be ordained priests. To become a permanent deacon, a man must be over thirty-five years old (depending on the rules of his episcopal see), a baptized and practicing Catholic for at least five years, and, if he is married, his wife must approve his ordination. (A married man can become a permanent deacon, but he cannot remarry after ordination.) Deacons often belong to a particular parish, but the diocese may move them based on needs and circumstances.

The second order of Holy Orders is the priesthood or presbyterate. A priest in the Catholic Church is a man who has received the sacrament of Holy Orders and has accepted the duties of celebrating the Sacrifice of the Mass, hearing confessions, giving absolution, and celebrating other sacraments *in persona Christi* ("in the person of Christ"). Priests also perform many other duties of pastoral ministry and, sometimes, administration.

The third and highest order is bishop, or the episcopacy. Bishops, then, represent the fullness of Holy Orders. A bishop is directly appointed by the pope—often at the suggestion of a Curial team—to oversee a diocese. A bishop is a priest, and he is entrusted with the responsibility to ordain new priests. Some bishops are of higher rank than other bishops; these are known as "archbishops."

Before the Second Vatican Council, there were lower orders, called "minor orders," bestowed upon those who were seeking the priesthood or other religious life. These included doorkeepers, lectors, acolytes, and exorcists. Today, their duties are assumed in the hierarchy of Holy Orders as a whole. However, there are still some priestly orders who have retained the minor orders, such as the Priestly Fraternity of St. Peter (FSSP); these orders often exclusively celebrate the Latin extraordinary form of the Mass (see **"Extraordinary and Ordinary Form of the Mass"**).

For more on each of these orders, see the topics for **"Deacons," "Bishops,"** and **"Priesthood."**

Holy Spirit

The third Person of the Holy Trinity, also known as the Advocate and the Paraclete.

The Holy Spirit is fully God, equal to the Father and the Son. He is not begotten, as the Son is begotten of the Father, but proceeds from the love between the Father and the Son. The Holy Spirit proceeds from the Father and the Son as from one principle and as by one spiration. This term "spiration" designates the loving activity between the Father and the Son that results in the term of their love, namely, the Holy Spirit. This Spirit sanctifies us by infused grace. He is often symbolized by a dove, and we receive Him through Baptism and more fully in the sacrament of Confirmation. The study of the Holy Spirit is known as pneumatology.

As "paraclete," the Spirit is a wise counselor, and as "advocate," He helps us when needed, as Christ promises: "the Holy Spirit will teach you in that very hour what you ought to say" (Luke 12:12), and "I will pray the Father, and he will give you another Counselor, to be with you for ever" (John 14:16).

Jesus' Incarnation (see **"Incarnation"**) was made possible by the power of the Holy Spirit, as the Nicene Creed professes: "Jesus Christ, his only Son our Lord, *who was conceived by the Holy Spirit.*"

As the only one who "comprehends the thoughts of God" (1 Cor. 2:11), the Holy Spirit inspired the writings of Sacred Scripture and is the reason Catholics can be absolutely sure that the Church teaches promptly, accurately, and correctly: "But the Counselor, the Holy Spirit, whom the Father will send in my name, he will teach you all things, and bring to your remembrance all that I have said to you" (John 14:26). The primary work of the Spirit is to testify to Christ.

We are encouraged to pray to the Holy Spirit, asking Him for of all of His fruits and gifts, so that we can go to Heaven and help others to journey well through the pilgrimage of life on Earth.

Homosexuality

The experience of same-sex attraction.

The Catholic Church offers a message of love toward homosexual men and women while nevertheless affirming that homosexual activity is intrinsically disordered (see CCC 2357). Sacred Scripture affirms the disordered nature of homosexuality (see Gen. 19:1–29; Rom. 1:24–27; 1 Cor. 6:9–10; 1 Tim. 1:10), and *Persona Humana* (Declaration on Certain Questions Concerning Sexual Ethics) states the Catholic Church's teaching that homosexual acts are intrinsically disordered[40] and are thus contrary to the natural law. The genesis of homosexuality—that is, whether the inclination to same-sex attraction is innate or acquired—is still largely unexplained.

Cultural acceptance or rejection of homosexuality has shifted and will continue to shift over time, but the Church's pastoral approach toward the people involved is clear:

> [People who experience same-sex attraction] must be accepted with respect, compassion, and sensitivity. Every sign of unjust discrimination in their regard should be avoided. These persons are called to fulfill God's will in their lives and, if they are Christians, to unite to the sacrifice of the Lord's Cross the difficulties they may encounter from their condition. (CCC 2358)

Men and women who struggle with homosexuality are called to remain chaste and to seek self-mastery in order to gain true freedom through prayer and sacramental grace.

Statue depicting the virtue of hope, Cathedral of the Assumption of Mary, Guadalajara, Mexico

Hope

The theological virtue by which we are given the desire to please and possess God and that gives us confidence that we will receive every necessary grace to accomplish this end.

Hope, along with faith and love, is a theological virtue, meaning it finds its meaning and end in the desire for God—it is a response to our aspiration for eternal happiness in Heaven. As a theological virtue, it is infused into the soul with the sacrament of Baptism. This hope means that we are not confident in our own strengths and merit but in the grace of the Holy Spirit (CCC 1817). The *Catechism* reminds us that "Christian hope takes up and fulfills the hope of the chosen people which has its origin and model in the *hope of Abraham* … 'Hoping against hope, he believed, and thus became the father of many nations'" (CCC 1819, quoting Rom. 4:18).

According to our own circumstances, all Christians share a hope for a better future, but we are reminded that our ultimate hope or ultimate happiness is in our ultimate destination of Heaven. Hope takes shape in the believer as he follows God and seeks to accomplish His will, remaining in communion with Christ's Church and prevailing against the sins of despair and presumption.

CATHOLIC TIP

The Act of Hope is a powerful and encouraging prayer and intention to say on a regular basis:

O Lord God, I hope by Your grace for the pardon of all my sins and after life here to gain eternal happiness because You have promised it who are infinitely powerful, faithful, kind, and merciful. In this hope I intend to live and die. Amen.

Hypostatic Union

The theological teaching that Jesus Christ is one divine Person with two natures, one divine and one human.

Cyril of Alexandria (d. A.D. 444) and the Council of Chalcedon (A.D. 451) clarified, defined, and formalized the doctrine of the Hypostatic Union as we articulate it today. The term "hypostasis" means subsistence, which is the underlying reality of a thing. Catholic theologians use these philosophical terms to better define the nature of Christ. The Catholic Church teaches that Christ is fully God and fully man; *He is a divine person with a human nature*. The substance of God (what God is) cannot be changed, as God is immutable, and so even in the person of Christ, God's substance is unchangeable. In the Creed, we supremely acknowledge and emphasize the reality of Jesus' divinity when we say He is "consubstantial with the Father."

Because Christ has two distinct natures, He therefore has two distinct wills—one divine, one human. These wills do not compete, but the human will must submit to the divine. Hence, Jesus in the Garden of Gethsemane knowingly surrenders to the imminent agonies of the Passion, as His human will submits to His divine will.

One question that often arises as people consider the divine personhood of Jesus is whether God died on the Cross. Jesus is God, and Jesus did die on the Cross, but that does mean that God died on the Cross. In order to understand this idea, let us consider the Incarnation. Mary is truly the mother of God (see "**Theotokos**"), but we do not say that when Mary gave birth to Jesus, God's existence as a divine person started that day. In the same way, we also do not believe or profess that God's existence as a divine person ended on the Cross, especially since the Cross was not the end of Jesus' life, as was manifested in the Resurrection.

CATHOLIC TIP

The teaching of the Hypostatic Union is highly philosophical, since we are using words with strict definitions such as *nature*, *person*, and *substance*. In the end, believing that Jesus—a man who walked the earth in flesh and blood—is God is most certainly a matter of faith. It is a mystery, and mysteries are to be appreciated, not understood.

Immaculate Conception

The dogma that Mary, by the merits of her Son, was preserved from Original Sin from the moment of her conception.

This teaching was defined in 1854 by Pope Pius IX, who wrote in *Ineffabilis Deus* that Mary, "in the first instance of her conception, by a singular grace and privilege granted by Almighty God, in view of the merits of Jesus Christ, the Savior of the human race, was preserved free from all stain of Original Sin." The pope specified further that this "is a doctrine revealed by God and therefore to be believed firmly and constantly by all the faithful."

The document's title, *Ineffabilis Deus*, is translated "Ineffable God," which is fitting because this teaching is truly indescribable. That God chose Mary from all women and preserved her from Original Sin is an indescribable favor, and the entire teaching centers on Christ. Mary's Immaculate Conception was not by random chance or by the wonderful virtues of Mary but through the merits of Christ as her savior. Mary herself confirms this: "My soul magnifies the Lord, and my spirit rejoices in God my Savior" (Luke 1:46–47). Therefore, the dogma of the Immaculate Conception centers on the victory of the Cross over sin and the unearned gift of God's freely given grace.

Statue of the Immaculate Conception, Malalos City, Bulacan

Further reading: Although there are more than a dozen excellent books to choose from that illuminate the Church's teachings on Mary, to learn more about the Immaculate Conception, there is no better place to start than with Pius IX's Ineffabilis Deus. *This Apostolic Constitution covers the subjects of Mary in commanding and convincing detail.*

Immigration

The migration of individuals, families, refugees, and the oppressed from their country of origin to another country, often in search of safety or opportunity.

Immigration remains a top concern for the Catholic Church, which is itself spread throughout the world. While today's political and social climate may push some to consider immigration as a sensitive topic that forces us out of our comfort zones regarding security, economics, culture, and welfare, the Church's position is clear:

> The more prosperous nations are obliged, to the extent they are able, to welcome the *foreigner* in search of the security and the means of livelihood which he cannot find in his country of origin. Public authorities

Immigrants on a ferry boat near Ellis Island

> should see to it that the natural right is respected that places a guest under the protection of those who receive him. (CCC 2241)

Host nations are not the only ones under certain moral obligations, however: "Immigrants are obliged to respect with gratitude the material and spiritual heritage of the country that receives them, to obey its laws and to assist in carrying civic burdens" (CCC 2241).

There must be a just cause for each act of migration, and each immigrant has the responsibility to respect the culture and religion of his new home, while the state has the responsibility, when able, to safely protect this migratory right and those who do so. "Today there is an inescapable duty to make ourselves the neighbor of every man, no matter who he is, and if we meet him, to come to his aid in a positive way."[41]

For further reading on the topic of immigration, I recommend Archbishop José Gomez's Immigration and the Next America.

Incarnation

The divinely revealed teaching that Jesus Christ, the second Person of the Holy Trinity, was made flesh, conceived in the womb of a woman by the work of the Holy Spirit.

The Incarnation of Christ is the central and defining mystery of the Christian Faith, since it means that God the Son became man in order to save mankind from sin. Christians profess belief in the Incarnation both in the Apostles' Creed—Jesus was "conceived by the Holy Spirit and born of the virgin Mary"—as well as more explicitly and with more thorough theological language in the Nicene Creed—"He came down from Heaven, and by the Holy Spirit was incarnate of the Virgin Mary, and became man."

The word "incarnate" comes from the Latin *incarno*, whose root word means "flesh." This use of "flesh," though, involves more than God taking on human form or appearances; such a teaching would imply that Christ is divine but only human as far as looks are concerned. Orthodox teaching on the Incarnation professes that Jesus was fully human, with a human nature, and also fully God, with a divine nature. These two natures are united in the one divine person of Christ, who has one singular substance—this doctrine is formally known as the Hypostatic Union (see "**Hypostatic Union**").

The Incarnation reveals much to us about the personhood and life of Christ. It means that God Himself took on human nature, that He became a helpless newborn, learned to walk as a toddler, was obedient to human parents, worked, sweated, ate, drank, and walked the earth that He created. It means that His human will had to prayerfully submit to His divine will in moments such as His agony in the Garden of Gethsemane. It means that He suffered the temptation to sin, just as we do, but that He overcame the temptation and rejected sin. The doctrine of the Incarnation also concerns more than merely a formula for Jesus' conception or birth. Rather, it impacts the entire redemptive

Baby Jesus with St. John the Baptist, by Felicián Moczik

history of the Word made flesh. Through this lens, we set a constant doctrinal rule for all questions pertaining to Jesus' personhood, nature, life, mission, and all other associated consequences.

Indulgence

"The remission before God of the temporal punishment due for sins already forgiven as far as their guilt is concerned."[42]

The Church's teaching on indulgences is closely related to its teaching on the sacrament of Reconciliation (CCC 1471). As the *Catechism* instructs, this teaching hinges on the understanding of the "double consequence" of sin: each sin entails an eternal punishment—separation from communion with God—in addition to a temporal punishment—the means through which man makes his adjustment to God. The eternal effect of sin is forgiven in the sacrament of Reconciliation. Indulgences have an effect on the latter consequence: since no sin or imperfection may enter Heaven, indulgences help remove the temporal consequences of sin, just as a penance does.

Because of their unique and abiding effect, the Church commends and encourages the seeking of indulgences by all the faithful (CCC 1032). There are two types of indulgences that we can seek: partial and plenary. A plenary indulgence remits all temporal punishment required to cleanse the soul from attachment to anything but God, and a partial indulgence remits part of the temporal punishment due to sin. We can seek either type of indulgence on behalf of ourselves or on behalf of the souls in Purgatory.

There are a number of ways to obtain an indulgence, and these are found for the most part in the *Enchiridion of Indulgences.* Other indulgenced acts may be attached to a specific event, such as solemn prayers during a conclave. To obtain a plenary indulgence, aside from doing the indulgenced work, there are three consistent actions that must be performed, and one must be in the state of grace with no attachment to sin (even venial sin). The three actions required to receive a plenary indulgence are making a sacramental Confession, receiving Holy Communion, and praying for the intentions of the Holy Father. All of these are to be performed ideally on the same day but at least "within several days (about twenty) before or after the indulgenced act." One can only receive one plenary indulgence per day.

The *Enchiridion of Indulgences* further clarifies that indulgences may not be obtained by happenstance but must be intentionally sought:

> In order that one who is capable may actually gain indulgences, one must have at least a general intention to gain them and must in accordance with the tenor of the grant perform the enjoined works at the time and in the manner prescribed.[43]

Further reading: Any Catholic can and should have a copy of the Handbook of Indulgences, *which describes the norms and acts that are given to the many indulgences approved by the Church.*

CATHOLIC TIP

Indulgences are one of the most controversial teachings of the Church and are frequently associated with the Protestant Reformation. Like most controversies regarding the Catholic Faith, indulgences are often misunderstood. They are not a ticket to Heaven nor some cosmic scoreboard for merit. Here's something I always tell people when explaining indulgences after clearing up the misconceptions: If the sacrament of Confession is that tremendously gracious gift that frees us from the guilt of sin, and an indulgence is the gift that frees us from the punishments of our sin, why not free yourself of guilt and punishment?

The legitimacy of indulgences, though, rests in the power and authority of the Church to "bind and loose." Not by our own merit, but by the intervention of the Church will Christians access the treasury of merits gained by Christ. "Thus the Church does not want simply to come to the aid of these Christians, but also to spur them to works of devotion, penance, and charity" (CCC 1478).

Infallibility

The dogma that the pope's official teaching on matters of faith and morals is incapable of error.

Papal infallibility does not mean that the ordinary teachings of the pope are free from error nor that the pope is morally perfect or somehow prevented from sin. Instead, the teaching on papal infallibility provides the Church with the assurance that the Holy Spirit will not permit her visible head to lead her into error. The *Catechism* explains, "Christ endowed the Church's shepherds with the charism of infallibility in matters of faith and morals" (890).

This infallibility pertains to the pope in virtue of his office when he teaches *ex cathedra* (Latin for "from the chair") and "proclaims by a definitive act a doctrine pertaining to faith and morals" (CCC 891). The First Vatican Council established four conditions for papal infallibility: 1) The pope must be acting as supreme pastor and teacher of all Christians; 2) he must use his supreme apostolic authority; 3) the substance of his teaching must concern faith and morals; 4) he must expressly indicate that the doctrine is to be held universally.[44] The whole college of bishops, acting as teachers and judges for the universal Church in harmony with the pope, is also infallible when teaching on matters of faith and morals.

Some confusion emerges as a result of this teaching: *How can a man be free from any error?* But the doctrine of infallibility actually indicates more about the power of the Holy Spirit and the Church as the Bride of Christ than it does about any pontiff. Christ promises that we will be protected from error and continue to be led in truth: "But the Counselor, the Holy Spirit, whom the Father will send in my name, he will teach you all things, and bring to your remembrance all that I have said to you" (John 14:26).

Islam

An Abrahamic monotheistic religion centered on the teachings of the Quran, its holy book, as revealed to their prophet Muhammed.

Islam is the world's second largest religion, and it began in the seventh century on the Arabian Peninsula near Mecca. The religion spread through caliphates—a governing office of Islam—in later centuries. The word *Islam* means "submission," and it implies submission to their God, whom they address by the Arabic word *Allah*. Most of the world's Islamic followers belong to the two major groups, Sunni and Shia, which split over disagreements regarding the successor of Muhammed. Followers of Islam are known as Muslims.

Islam teaches that God, Allah, is one, all-powerful being unassociated with other partners or persons. This teaching conflicts with Christianity's doctrine of the Trinity (see "**Trinity**"), and so Muslims consider Christians to be idolaters. The name of Allah is genderless and has no plurality. Islam further instructs that Allah is a personal God with no intermediaries like clergy or priests. Adherents to Islam value a moral life and worship God with prayer, almsgiving, and fasting.

Muhammed, who is known as the "Seal of the prophets," is the central and final prophet in the Islamic Faith. Islamic tradition states that Muhammed ascended to Heaven in A.D. 620 in a night's journey to tour Heaven and Hell and to speak with older prophets such as Abraham and Moses. He fought a handful of battles and is believed to have died in A.D. 632. None of the prophets sent by God with a specific message are considered to be divine, including Muhammed.

Islam, together with Judaism and Christianity, is an Abrahamic Faith, since they worship the God of Abraham. *Nostra Aetate*, the Second Vatican Council's Declaration on the Relation of the Church to Non-Christian Religions, states that

A mosque

Muslims "adore the one God, living and subsisting in Himself; merciful and all-powerful, the Creator of Heaven and earth."[45] Muslims believe Jesus was a just prophet, and they honor Mary as His virgin mother; but they do not regard Jesus as divine, and they reject the Incarnation, Crucifixion, and Resurrection of Christ.

Other practices of Islam include a number of restrictions on diet and behavior, and Muslims must pray five times per day. Traditionally, Islam also allows for polygamy and slavery.

Further reading: An excellent and important read on Islam for Catholics is Not Peace, But a Sword *by Robert Spencer. Other useful readings about Islam are the* 20 Answers: Islam *booklet from Catholic Answers and* The Crucifix on Mecca's Front Porch *by David Pinault.*

Jansenism

A seventeenth-century theological movement founded by Bishop Cornelius Jansen (1585–1638).

Bishop Jansen propagated a heretical message of determinism and rigid predestination that taught that man's nature is completely flawed by Original Sin and is only recoverable through a special and selective grace determined by God that affords salvation only to some. Jansen's teachings are mostly found in the *Augustinus*, a publication of his works after his death.

Jansenism was condemned over the course of the next century by Popes Innocent X in 1653, Alexander VII in 1656, and Clement XI in 1713, as it was a determined foe of true Catholic teaching on Original Sin and grace (see "**Original Sin**" and "**Grace**"). Jansenism opposes Catholic teaching in several ways, primarily in regard to man's free will: God cannot force any person to accept His grace, nor can any man be compelled against his will to accept God's free gift of grace. Every man has freedom and personal responsibility for his actions, including his acceptance or rejection of the divine law (see "**Divine Law**"). Every human person is created to love God and to share in the gifts of salvation.

The Jansenist movement within Catholicism was a scourge on France and other parts of Europe, but it eventually died out. However, Jansen's teachings are still strongly remnant in Calvinist Protestant denominations that believe in all or part of the following ideas that they see as consequences of Original Sin: Total depravity, Unconditional election, Limited atonement, Irresistible grace, and Perseverance of the saints (these ideas within Calvinism are often represented by the acronym "TULIP").

Cornelius Jansen

Jehovah's Witnesses

A religious sect formed in 1872 by Charles Taze Russell that emphasizes doomsday preaching and door-to-door evangelization.

When Russell formed the society it was initially known as "Bible Students" and after founding a printing company in 1881 the group became known as The Watchtower and Bible Tract Society. The assembly believed that they had uncovered the true teachings of Christianity after all was evidently lost with the death of the apostles. Charles Taze Russell heavily preached that the end of the world would come in 1914, and later when this date passed he stated that he made a miscalculation and edited the date to sometime in 1915. Charles died in 1916. His successor, Joseph Franklin Rutherford, continued this doomsday prediction and calculated 1925 as the year all would end and the earth world be transformed.

Charles Taze Russell

Prior to his death in 1942, Rutherford changed the name of the religious group to the Jehovah's Witnesses. His successor Nathan Knorr advanced the propagation of Watchtower teachings and evangelization through a door-to-door missionary scheme. He also directed a translation of the Bible exclusively for the use of the growing sect. This translation, known as the *New World Translation*, has received criticism from its initial publication continuing to the present for its unique translation and handling of key verses which aid the Jehovah's Witnesses' theological teachings.

Members of the Jehovah's Witnesses believe in one Almighty God. They call this God Jehovah after the medieval practice of spelling of Yahweh (see "**Yahweh**") not as the traditional tetragrammaton YHWH, but as JHWH and pronouncing this name as *Jah-hov-ai*. And according to the Watchtower's own literature, the name is so important because the Bible says, "For everyone who calls upon the name of the Lord," translated as Yahweh or Jehovah, "will be saved" (Joel 2:23; Rom. 10:13).

This Jehovah is the only true and supreme God. Jesus Christ is recognized as a lesser God, created by Jehovah. Additionally, the Jehovah's Witnesses believe that, as the highest of all of God's created beings, Jesus Christ is the Archangel Michael prior to becoming man and after his return to Heaven. The *New World Translation* Bible contains several mistranslations to verses which would otherwise directly challenge this teaching. John 1:1, as the best example, is ordinarily rendered as "In the beginning was the Word, and the Word was with God, and the Word was God," but the New World Translation reads, "and the Word was a God." This subtle alteration completely changes the meaning of the text to the defense of their theological teachings.

Jehovah's Witnesses also do not believe in the Holy Spirit as a divine person or even as a God or lesser God, but rather as the active force for God's work in man and in the world. To posit this belief, they contend that God cannot "fill" a person (as in Acts 2:4) but rather that such a spirit is a nuanced thing God uses. Additionally, they do not include the article "the" for any use of "holy spirit." Thus, Acts 2:4 is written in the New World Translation as "and they all became filled with holy spirit."

Jehovah's Witnesses do not believe in the Trinity – one God in three persons – which is the Christian God, and are completely separated from Catholic and Evangelical Christian denominations – their beliefs are not Christian.

The religious life of the members of Jehovah's Witnesses includes a Sunday service where readings are given and preaching is heard, but they have no firm structure of clergy or pastoral leadership – a concept they detest – and only know one another as brother, sister, and elder. Their facilities are known as Kingdom Halls and are established in strategic places they identify as "mission territory." Members continue to believe in the imminent doomsday spoken of by their founders. They strive to generate converts through door-to-door preaching, a practice required of every member of their sect. Should one of these members fall away from this missionary activity and "break the Bible's moral code" without repentance they will be shunned (a practice they call "disfellowship"),[46] meaning they are cut off from

CATHOLIC TIP

The day is certainly approaching when the knock at your door is not your neighbor's asking to borrow a cup of sugar, but is a group (often a family) of Jehovah's Witnesses who have come to convert you. What should you do? *Remain calm!* Experience shows that these door-to-door groups pose no threat to those expecting a tense conversation. Secondly, these missionaries are well-trained, but they *do* listen. I have had them knock at my door at 20-below zero in Alaska, and at my residence in Northern Italy, and what I usually find is a set of people who engage in a scripted conversation and as soon as I show I have a firm understanding of their teachings, they are generally more amiable to other discussions. Chances are, they have never been presented with the clear teachings of Christianity and rarely encounter a person who can point out their inconsistencies. When conversing, show the love of Christ and your intense passion for your own faith—a superior witness to Christ over any argument. In the meantime, prepare with the short reading suggestion below, which will fill in many of the "blanks" you will need when the doorbell eventually rings.

their fellow Jehovah's Witnesses regardless of their relation–a harsh social consequence that prevents many from converting away from the sect.

Further reading: 20 Answers: Jehovah's Witnesses, *by Trent Horn provides a fast and knowledgeable set of details regarding the beliefs and practices of the Jehovah's Witnesses and counter-arguments to use when the timing is right.*

Jesus Christ as the Good Shepherd, by Philippe de Champaigne

Jesus Christ

The Second Person of the Holy Trinity, the Christ, God's Word made flesh and born of the Virgin Mary.

The entire story and method of God's salvation of mankind is constructed through, with, and in Jesus. Thus, the Old Testament contains forty-four distinct prophecies (and hundreds in general) about Him so that we would know His identity and believe in His message. Jesus is also known as the "second Adam" because He fulfilled God's plan for mankind after Adam fell into sin.

"Jesus" is the anglicization of the Hebrew name *Yeshua* or *Yehoshua*, which literally means "God saves." Salvation through the person of Christ, the Son of the Living God, is the core of our Christian Faith: "But when the time had fully come, God sent forth his Son, born of woman, born under the law, to redeem those who were under the law, so that we might receive adoption as sons" (Gal. 4:4–5). As the central figure of our Faith, Jesus is the entire purpose and aim of catechesis: we must instruct others to be in communion with Christ (CCC 426–429).

The name of Jesus is much more than an item of identification. His is the name above all names precisely because it manifests the supreme saving power of God. Therefore, His name is to be invoked in prayer and to be used with exceptional reverence.

Joseph

The earthly and legal father of Jesus whose lineage traces back to King David, lawfully giving Jesus the title Son of David (Matt. 1:6–16).

The Bible contains no words spoken by Joseph, and very little can be gleaned about his life from reading the New Testament. However, we do know that he was a just man (Matt. 1:19), that he was a carpenter or artisan from Nazareth, that he likely taught Jesus his craft, and that he received divine dreams directing his actions. It is also possible that the "brothers of Jesus" referred to in the New Testament narrative are the children of Joseph from a previous marriage, but scholars are uncertain, since the word translated as "brother" was often used for cousins as well. What is certain is that these were not children born from Mary, who was a virgin before the birth of Jesus and maintained this state for the remainder of her life.

The *Protoevangelium of James* (A.D. 150) contains many details about Joseph's life leading up to the scenes in the Bible. Though this source is apocryphal and not included in the Canon of Scripture, it is often valued as a source of strong tradition and understanding of the Holy Family and the events leading up to the Gospel narratives. The narrative says that when Mary was twelve years old, leaders in the Temple wanted to find her a suitable arrangement to continue her consecration to God. A crowd of widowers were summoned, Joseph among them, and their rods were drawn. A dove landed on Joseph, which the priest acknowledged as a sign that Joseph was to be the caretaker of Mary. Joseph was afraid of the decision, but he submitted with godly encouragement from the priest.

St. Joseph Carrying the Child Jesus on the Left Arm, by Pieter van Lint

We know little about Joseph, but what is certain is that he is a superior patron and model for fathers and workers of the world. The Church celebrates three feast days specifically in his honor: the Solemnity of St. Joseph on March 19, the Feast of St. Joseph the Worker on May 1, and the Feast of the Holy Family, which is celebrated on the Sunday after Christmas.

Further reading: Patris Corde: With a Father's Heart *by Pope Francis.*

Judaism

The Abrahamic religion revealed to the ancient Israelites.

Judaism is a monotheistic religion that comprises the collective beliefs and customs of the Jewish people rooted in the revelations of the one true God to Abraham and the prophets of the Old Testament. It includes the system of theology, life, laws, and various traditions that have developed through many generations and important events. It takes its name from the tribe of Judah, who returned to the land of Israel after the Babylonian Exile (538 B.C.).

Judaism today is significantly different from the religion of the Hebraic people of the Bible's Old Testament. Since A.D. 70, when the temple of Jerusalem was destroyed by the Romans, Jews have not practiced proper sacrificial worship according to the old laws. Since that time and up to today, the Jewish religion conducts worship in synagogues that consists of readings, teaching, and prayer. The holy book of Judaism is the Tanakh (the Hebrew Bible), which consists of the Torah (the Pentateuch or Mosaic books) as well as the Prophets and Writings. Jewish people also consider the Mishnah and the Talmud, books of ancient and rabbinical teachings, to be sacred.

The Second Vatican Council document *Nostra Aetate*, the Declaration on the Relation of the Church to Non-Christian Religions, speaks positively of the Jewish people, acknowledging our common patrimony and that Christianity's proclamation of Christ as the Messiah sprang forth from the Jews, although they reject Christ as the Savior.

Further reading: Salvation Is from the Jews *by Roy Schoeman.*

Central panel of the triptych *The Last Judgment* by Hans Memling

Judgment

Eternal reward or retribution given to the immortal soul of man and the revealing of the merits of every person who ever lived.

After death, man will be judged according to his works, deeds, and overall acceptance of the grace manifested by Christ. The Bible refers to two distinct judgments: the particular judgment and the Last Judgment. These judgments proclaim "the 'blessed hope' of the Lord's return, when he will come 'to be glorified in his saints, and to be marveled at in all who have believed' " (CCC 1041).

Jesus' parables and descriptions of life after death make it clear that each person will enjoy different rewards or punishments based on his actions (see, for example, Luke 16:22–23). This is the particular judgment: "Each man receives his eternal retribution in his immortal soul at the very moment of his death, in a particular judgment that refers his life to Christ: either entrance into the blessedness of Heaven—either through a purification or immediately—or immediate and everlasting damnation" (CCC 1022). Jesus gives us the same imagery: "For the Son of man is to come with his angels in the glory of his Father, and then he will repay every man for what he has done" (Matt. 16:27). St. Paul writes, "For we must all appear before the judgment seat of Christ, so that each one may receive good or evil, according to what he has done in the body" (2 Cor. 5:10).

The Last Judgment is a bit different. It is focused on two events: the Second Coming of Christ and the revealing of all truth to all those who have died. This "truth" will include all actions, good and evil, public and secret, of every person who ever lived. The purpose of the Last Judgment, however, is to demonstrate God's justice and love: "In the presence of Christ, who is Truth itself, the truth of each man's relationship with God will be laid bare. The Last Judgment will reveal even to its furthest consequences the good each person has done or failed to do during his earthly life" (CCC 1039). This moment of Christ's coming is only known to the Father (Matt. 24:36) and is the final act of history.

It is natural to feel some fear and anxiety about God's plans for mankind. Knowing that we will face judgment forces every man to look at his life and wonder in which direction the Son of Man will separate him. But wonder and holy fear of God should spark man to reform himself, to weigh the retribution of eternity against a few moments of rebellious amusement on earth. These judgments "[proclaim] the 'blessed hope' of the Lord's return, when he will come 'to be glorified in his saints, and to be marveled at in all who have believed'" (CCC 1041).

Justification

The event and state of being justified before God through grace.

The Old Testament presents justification as a perceived legal state before God's judgment, but through the revelation of Jesus Christ, we understand that justification is friendship with God, contrary to a state of bondage to sin. To be justified is to remain in a state of righteousness. The only way we can be justified is through cooperation with the free gift of grace through Christ.

Justification points more to the works of Christ on our behalf than it does our own works, however meritorious. In his letter to the Romans, Paul puts it this way:

> They are justified by his grace as a gift, through the redemption which is in Christ Jesus, whom God put forward as an expiation by his blood, to be received by faith. This was to show God's righteousness, because in his divine forbearance he had passed over former sins; it was to prove at the present time that he himself is righteous and that he justifies him who has faith in Jesus. (Rom. 3:24–26)

Protestant reformers emphasized Paul's teaching on justification by faith, but they largely rejected or ignored the teaching of St. James, which is also in the Bible: "You see that a man is justified by works and not by faith alone.... For as the body apart from the spirit is dead, so faith apart from works is dead" (James 2:24, 26). The Catholic Church sees both our works and faith as graces resulting from the works of Christ, and they are not contradictory or combatant with one another. The *Catechism of the Catholic Church* articulates it this way:

> Like conversion, justification has two aspects. Moved by grace, man turns toward God and away from sin, and so accepts forgiveness and righteousness from on high.
>
> Justification includes the remission of sins, sanctification, and the renewal of the inner man.
>
> Justification has been merited for us by the Passion of Christ. It is granted us through Baptism. It conforms us to the righteousness of God, who justifies us. It has for its goal the glory of God and of Christ, and the gift of eternal life. It is the most excellent work of God's mercy. (CCC 2018–2020)

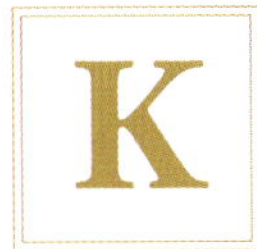

Kerygma

The proclamation of the gospel of Christ.

Kerygma involves both the act of proclaiming and the content of the proclamation itself. The content of the gospel proclamation is the good news that Jesus Christ was crucified for our sins and was resurrected in glory from the dead as the final act of salvation in history, opening the gates to Heaven for all mankind.

Each of the Gospels are the literary form of the kerygma, and each Gospel writer offers a perceptive angle of the divine message. Mark presents Jesus' words against the backdrop of the approaching Crucifixion. Matthew leans on the preaching of Christ and His relation to Moses. Luke persists in unfurling the meaning of the life of Christ. John presents the glory of Christ, the supernatural gifts instituted by Him, and the personal response required by all believers. We also find Paul's restatement of the kerygma in his first letter to the Corinthians: "For I delivered to you as of first importance what I also received, that Christ died for our sins in accordance with the scriptures, that he was buried, that he was

The Sermon on the Mount, detail of altarpiece by Henrik Olrik in St. Matthew Church, Copenhagen, Denmark

raised on the third day in accordance with the scriptures" (1 Cor. 15:3–4).

It may seem that this kerygma has already been announced, especially in the western world so heavily influenced by Christianity and Judeo-Christian principles. Oftentimes, this idea leads Christians to take evangelization for granted. But the fact is, the message of Christ is lost on the majority of people, and Christians still have an opportunity and responsibility to announce the gospel, as we always acknowledge at the end of Mass.

How can Christians preach the kerygma today? First of all, Christians can announce the gospel with their lives, by living according to Christian moral principles, being compassionate toward others, and serving God. Yet we should not be intimidated by speaking the kerygma, and opportunities in daily life abound. Some have never *really* heard the good news, others entertain incompatible activities and notions that deserve correction, and still others require guidance, friendship, and encouragement. Praying for the wisdom to select the right moments to bring others closer to Christ is key.

Further reading: Everyone should read Evengelii Nuntiandi *by Pope St. Paul VI. For intuitive and practical instruction on evangelization and the proclamation of Christ, pick up* Filling Our Father's House *by Shaun McAfee,* Forming Intentional Disciples *by Sherry Weddell, or* The Contagious Catholic *by Marcel LeJeune.*

Kingdom of God

A central piece of Christ's teaching that states that the reign of God in Heaven shall gradually and imminently be brought also to earth.

In Jesus, "the kingdom of God is at hand," as announced by John the Baptist (Mark 1:15). "The Kingdom of God has been coming since the Last Supper and, in the Eucharist, it is in our midst. The kingdom will come in glory when Christ hands it over to his Father," says the *Catechism* (2816).

The idea of the Kingdom of God is not limited to the New Testament. God ruled the people of Israel in justice and judgment (Deut. 33:5), and His reign was not limited to any earthly tenure but was eternal (Exod. 15:18). In the Lord's Prayer, Christ teaches us to pray that this perfection of living under God's rule be brought to earth "as it is in Heaven." By this, Christ is also foretelling His return as our supreme ruler.

Working toward the establishment of the Kingdom of God on earth is exemplified in the rejection of the common culture that tends to reject God. "Man's vocation to eternal life does not suppress but actually reinforces his duty to put into action in this world the energies and means received from the Creator to serve justice and peace" (CCC 2820).

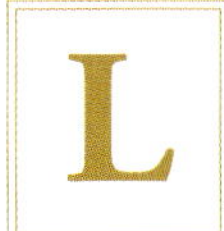

Laity

Members of the Church who are neither clerics nor religious.

Established by God in and through divine action, the laity are the community of Christian believers of the Church, God's people, who are not part of but are subject to the leadership of the hierarchy. According to *Lumen Gentium* (The Dogmatic Constitution on the Church): "The term 'laity' is here understood to mean all the faithful except those in Holy Orders and those who belong to a religious state approved by the Church."[47]

The laity play a pivotal role in the life of the Church. Because of their unique role in secular affairs, the laity can penetrate culture, influence social orders, and evangelize nations, thereby participating in the priestly, prophetic, and regal office of Christ and the work of the salvation of the world. This mission is the "apostolate" of the laity.

Popes and ecumenical councils are not short on words that detail the enormous role of the laity in the Church. The Second Vatican Council insisted,

> Our own times require of the laity no less zeal: in fact, modern conditions demand that their apostolate be broadened and intensified. With a constantly increasing population, continual progress in science and technology, and closer interpersonal relationships, the areas for the lay apostolate have been immensely widened particularly in fields that have been for the most part open to the laity alone. These factors have also occasioned new problems which demand their expert attention and study. This apostolate becomes more imperative in view of the fact that many areas of human life have become increasingly autonomous. This is as it should be, but it sometimes involves a degree of departure from the ethical and religious order and a serious danger to Christian life. Besides, in many places where priests are very few or, in some instances, deprived of due freedom for priestly work, the Church could scarcely exist and function without the activity of the laity.[48]

Lectio Divina

A method of reading the Bible that enables us to focus on meaning, discernment, and applying God's Word to our lives.

Lectio divina is Latin for "divine reading" and was popularized by monks beginning with St. Benedict of Nursia in the sixth century. It is still a strong form of prayer in the Church and is used by religious, lay people, and priests.

Lectio divina is composed of four parts: *lectio*, *meditatio*, *oratio*, and *contemplatio*. In the first part, *lectio*, the Scripture passage is read, ideally aloud, slowly and attentively. Some groups choose to read the passage multiple times. If in a group, each person may read the passage once aloud. In the second part, *meditatio*, one ruminates thoroughly on the reading, grabbing and considering each detail as a child is told to chew each bite in order to digest all nutrients properly.

In the third step, it's the reader's turn to reply. The *oratio* is a prayerful response to the reading. Following this, *contemplatio* is the quiet, still contemplation that allows our hearts and minds to consider the meaning and effect of what God wants to say to us.

Lectio divina may be done in private or in a group setting, where it can prove fruitful to listen to various reactions to Scripture. It is important to beware of disorganized and unorthodox interpretations of the Scripture reading through additional study and reference to traditional Catholic commentaries. Staying within these rubrics, *lectio divina* is a powerful form of reading Sacred Scripture and growing closer to God.

Lent

A liturgical season of penance that starts on Ash Wednesday and ends on Holy Thursday.

The season of Lent lasts forty days (excluding Sundays, on which we still commemorate the Lord's Resurrection). The liturgical color of this season is violet, and we omit the Alleluia and the Gloria from the liturgy.

In the Roman Catholic Church, during Lent, the faithful are called to *increase* their acts of prayer, almsgiving, and fasting (since they should be present throughout the life of every Christian). The faithful who are between the ages of eighteen and fifty-nine are obliged to fast on Ash Wednesday and Good Friday (exceptions to this rule are made for the chronically sick and for pregnant and nursing women). Those who are fourteen and older must abstain from meat on Ash Wednesday and all the Fridays of Lent. A penitential fast from some activity or intake is also traditionally observed by the faithful.

Historically, the required fasts and penances of Lent were more severe, and they still are in some respects in the Eastern Catholic Churches. Roman Catholics, too, are welcome to increase their personal mortifications in this season. The laws and norms of the present day allow for a more universal application of the Lenten penance, yet they still offer pastoral flexibility for those who desire more and for those who must observe less by virtue of their state of life.

The final week of Lent is known as Holy Week. Holy Thursday (also known as Maundy Thursday) through Holy Saturday is known as the Triduum, and these three days are set aside to remember the Lord's Passion and death. On Holy Thursday, the Church celebrates the Last Supper, the institution of the priesthood, and the agony in the Garden. On Good Friday, we commemorate when Christ was crucified. And on Holy Saturday, we remember the time Christ spent in the tomb and prepare to celebrate the Resurrection on Easter.

A priest administers ashes on Ash Wednesday.

Liturgical Year

The cycle of seasons and feast days in the Catholic liturgical calendar.

The first Sunday of Advent marks the beginning of the new liturgical year. The seasons in the liturgical year are Advent, Christmas, Ordinary Time, Lent, Easter, and Ordinary Time following Pentecost. The USCCB also counts the Triduum as a season of the liturgical year.

The liturgical calendar has evolved over time. It underwent significant changes after the Second

Vatican Council and has been amended since. The aim of the liturgical calendar is to enable Christians to live the cycle of the year around the events of Christ's saving work. To live liturgically is to live in closer union with Christ in and through His Church.

The liturgical year is highly organized. It includes both fixed and movable feasts, readings, and prayers. Events throughout the year (particularly Easter) are calculated and systematized well before they are observed and celebrated.

Liturgy

The official, public worship of the Church.

"Liturgy" comes from the Greek term *leitourgia*, meaning a service completed, and applies to a variety of things. The scope of liturgy in the Roman Catholic Church can refer to the order of the Mass, the rite of Baptism, ceremonies of Christian initiation, and other rituals and published prayers. The Eucharistic Sacrifice, the Divine Office, and the administration of the sacraments make up the primary liturgies for the Church.

Sacrosanctum Concilium describes the liturgy as "the outstanding means by which the faithful can express in their lives, and manifest to others, the mystery of Christ and the real nature of the true Church."[49]

Easter Vigil liturgy, collegiate church of Gdańsk-Wrzeszcz

Sometimes the term "liturgy" can cause confusion, especially among new Catholics who were not formally part of a liturgical church such as the Anglican or Lutheran denominations. To say that anything the Church or its members do, even in a formal setting, is liturgy, is incorrect. Stations of the Cross, the Rosary, and novenas, for example, are private devotional practices but are not the Church's liturgy because they are not part of the Church's official public worship.

Further reading: Every Catholic should read Sacrosanctum Concilium, *the Second Vatican Council Constitution on the Sacred Liturgy, to grasp the Church's vision of liturgy in the modern Church. St. Robert Bellarmine's* On the Sacrifice of the Mass *is also a classic treatise on everything about this powerful liturgy.*

Lord's Day

Sunday, the day we celebrate Jesus' Resurrection from the dead and observe a day of rest.

Biblically, the term "Lord's Day" comes from the book of Revelation: "I was in the Spirit on the Lord's day, and I heard behind me a loud voice like a trumpet" (Rev. 1:10). The Lord's Day stems from the Sabbath, which in the Old Law was the day commanded by God to be set aside for rest. For the Jewish people, the Sabbath was observed on the final day of the week (Saturday), commemorating God's rest on the final day of the creation account (Gen. 2:2). Christ was resurrected on a Sunday, and Christians thus preserved Sunday as the Lord's Day.

The *Catechism* reads: "The Church celebrates the day of Christ's Resurrection on the 'eighth day,' Sunday, which is rightly called the Lord's Day" (2191).

Sundays, then, are the days Christians keep holy, and they are set aside for rest. The Code of Canon Law stipulates that "Sunday … is to be observed as the foremost holy day of obligation in the universal Church" (CIC 1246, no. 1). On Sundays, Catholics are required to attend Mass unless it is impossible because of sickness or other restriction. This weekly celebration of the sacrifice of the Mass defines our communion as a Church and our testimony as believers. On Sunday, Catholics are also required to refrain from servile works—those that hinder worship, joy proper to the Lord's Day, and proper relaxation of mind and body (CCC 2185). Practically speaking, observing Sundays is the very best means of grounding us, allowing us to recharge and ensuring meaningful productivity throughout the week.

CATHOLIC TIP

"The Sabbath, which represented the completion of the first creation, has been replaced by Sunday which recalls the new creation inaugurated by the Resurrection of Christ" (CCC 2190). Many today will argue that the Catholic Church moved the Hebrew Sabbath, but this is clearly not what the Church teaches. The Sabbath of the Bible rightly belongs to the Old Law, a law fulfilled by Christ. His followers are called to celebrate and observe the New Law, the law of love. Paul proclaims that "the law of the Spirit of life in Christ Jesus has set me free from the law of sin and death" (Rom. 8:2). In this New Law, entrusted to be applied and regulated by the Church, which has been given rightful authority over such things, the Church teaches with continuity throughout the centuries that Sunday is not the new Sabbath, but that it is the Lord's Day.

Love

The theological virtue by which we love God above all things for His own sake, and our neighbor as ourselves for the love of God.

St. Paul informs us that love is the most important of all of the virtues: "So faith, hope, love abide, these three; but the greatest of these is love" (1 Cor. 13:13). Love is also known as charity and is considered the whole of authentic communion with God and others. As characterized and lived out by Christians, love is discernibly different from the love the world knows as mere elevated attraction and care. Love is selfless.

A handful of types of love are recognized by scholars using their classical Greek names: *storge, philia, eros, and agape*. *Storge* is familial love, a general bond that exists between persons, animals, and other things. *Philia* is love of friendship, which grows out of compatibility and common values. *Eros* is passion of a sexual nature, though it also has a spiritual component when one loves what is perceived as beautiful and desirable. *Agape* love, the strongest and most desirable for Christians, is love that is generous and selflessly manifested without concern for reward or return.

Love, we are told in Paul's beautiful litany, "is patient and kind; love is not jealous or boastful; it is not arrogant or rude. Love does not insist on its own way; it is not irritable or resentful; it does not rejoice at wrong, but rejoices in the right. Love bears all things, believes all things, hopes all things, endures all things" (1 Cor 13:4–7).

This charity ought to be the center of private life and relationships, but it is the supreme essence of redemption, which the Church, as the community of believers and imitators of Christ, is called to bring into the world. When asked which is the greatest commandment,

> Jesus answered, "The first is, 'Hear, O Israel: The Lord our God, the Lord is one; and you shall love the Lord your God with all your heart, and with all your soul, and with all your mind, and with all your strength.' The second is this, 'You shall love your neighbor as yourself.' There is no other commandment greater than these." (Mark 12:29–31)

CATHOLIC TIP

Increasing in charity is a daily process that comes from listening to the promptings of the Holy Spirit and recognizing moments in which charity would prevail. To assist in this active listening to the Holy Spirit, a beautiful prayer, known as the Act of Love, is recommended for those hoping to increase in charity:

> *O Lord God, I love You above all things and I love my neighbor for Your sake because You are the highest, infinite and perfect good, worthy of all my love. In this love I intend to live and die. Amen.*

Magisterium

The living teaching office of the Church, given authoritatively to the apostles and to their successors to interpret divine revelation.

The bishops in communion with the pope have the authority to interpret the Word of God (both written Scripture and Sacred Tradition) not as its superior but as its servant (see CCC 85–86). The Church exercises this teaching authority in the name of Jesus Christ.

The Magisterium guides the Church through doctrinal continuity and hierarchical stability. There are two distinct functions of the Magisterium exercised by the Church: universal (also called extraordinary or solemn) and ordinary.

The Church exercises her universal Magisterium in promulgating doctrinal definitions and explaining moral judgments. Examples include the declaration of the dogma of the Assumption of Mary by Pope Pius XII in *Munificentissimus Deus*; the definition of indulgences by the Council of Trent; or the discussion of the Church's position on abortion and contraception in Pope St. Paul VI's *Humanae Vitae*.

The Church exercises her ordinary Magisterium in the regular teaching duties of bishops. This faculty may consist of preaching, apostolic letters, contributions to books, circulars, or joint faith statements.

An important thing to remember is that the Magisterium is not always *de facto* infallible, but it is authoritative: bishops have the authority to teach doctrine, and the faithful ought to listen carefully to the Church's Magisterium. The *Catechism* urges the faithful to "receive with docility the teachings and directives that their pastors give them in different forms" (87). We must therefore read and be aware of new papal documents in continuity with received tradition and ensure that we do not merely rely on internet sources and social media to understand Church teachings.

Marriage

A mutual covenant between a qualified man and woman to enter into wedlock, giving themselves to each other freely for the purpose of having children and sanctifying each other through a common life.

Marriage between baptized persons is a sacramental union. When two Catholics are married in the Latin Church, the sacrament normally takes place within a nuptial Mass. The essential characteristics of marriage are indissolubility and unity. Indissolubility means that the covenant cannot be broken. Jesus Himself said of marriage, "So they are no longer two but one flesh. What therefore God has joined together, let not man put asunder" (Matt. 19:6). The unity of marriage requires that it be solely between the man and woman, "undivided and exclusive" (CCC 1645).

Through the sacrament of Holy Matrimony, grace is conferred upon the couple to meet and maintain the responsibilities of the married state. The Latin church teaches that together, they—not the priest, deacon, or bishop—are the ministers of this great sacrament. "The priest (or deacon) … gives the blessing of the Church. The presence of the Church's minister (and also of the witnesses) visibly expresses the fact that marriage is an ecclesial reality" (CCC 1630).

In the Catholic Church, the following norms are required for a valid marriage: capacity, consent, and canonical form. Capacity refers to the

The Wedding at Cana, by Bernardino Poccetti

personal competence of the people exchanging vows, including psychological and physical capacity. This concept of capacity also means that the marriage partners are free from impediments, such as prior marriages or religious vows. Free consent to a lifelong, exclusive marriage that is open to childbearing is the second requirement. Consent initiates a marriage, later intercourse completes and consummates a marriage. Finally, the marriage must take on a canonical form, meaning the marriage must be performed in the presence of clergy with proper faculties, with at least two witnesses present.

If someone enters the Catholic Church already married, his marriage is presumed sacramental if both spouses were baptized. The process to confirm this is known as convalidation, or regularization.

Martyr

One who gives his life in witness to the Faith.

Since the earliest days of the Church, martyrdom has served as the ultimate witness of belief. The word "martyr" comes from the Greek *mártys*, meaning "witness."

Martyrdom for one's faith in God finds its roots in Scripture. St. Stephen, the first Christian martyr (Acts 6:8–7:60), is known as the "protomartyr." In the early Church, persecutions created numerous martyrs, especially since the religious practices of Christianity were outlawed in the Roman Empire. Throughout the course of the Church's history, many thousands of martyrs have been killed due to their doctrinal opinions, status as clergy, and especially missionary work.

The Stoning of St. Stephen, by Gabriel-Jules Thomas

The cult of martyrs is a strong tradition in the Church, since martyrdom is the ultimate means of conformity with the suffering Christ. Churches were built on the sites of martyrdoms, and altars were placed over the remains of the martyrs as a means of inspiration and intercession.

Many Catholics also recognize an unofficial classification of martyrs. Those who physically give their lives for the Faith are "red martyrs" who shed their blood. However, as Christianity became accepted and even popular in parts of the world, the call to give one's life for the Faith became less common, though many Christians still desired to give God this ultimate gift of their lives. Pious tradition speaks of two other types of martyrdom by which a Christian can witness to Christ even if he is not called to shed his blood: the first, "green martyrdom," emerged in Ireland and includes those who perfectly devote themselves to strict asceticism and extreme forms of penance; the second is "white martyrdom," which can mean suffering persecution for the Faith or living a life of penance.

Mary

The sinless, ever-virgin mother of Jesus Christ, known widely as the Blessed Virgin Mary or simply the Virgin Mary.

There are four dogmas concerning Mary: she is truly the mother of God; she was immaculately conceived; she was a perpetual virgin; and she was assumed body and soul into Heaven.

A native of Nazareth, Mary was from the tribe of Judah as a descendant of Nathan, the son of King David. Her parents were Sts. Anne and Joachim. The Bible tells us nothing about Mary's early life, but commonly sourced writings from early Christians suggest she was entrusted to the Temple at an early age. When she came of age to marry, Mary was betrothed to Joseph. Shortly after this ceremony, she was visited by the Archangel Gabriel, a story recounted in Luke chapter 1. Mary is mentioned in all four Gospels as well as the Book of Acts, but the Bible tells us nothing about Mary's life after Pentecost. However, the Catholic Church teaches dogmatically that she was assumed bodily into Heaven—scholars date this event to around

A.D. 48 (see "**Assumption**" for more about this teaching).

Theologically, Mary is known as *Theotokos*, meaning "God-bearer," as she is the mother of the second Person of the Trinity, Jesus Christ (see "**Theotokos**"). This theological title was used in Syriac Christian communities in the third century, and it was ecumenically introduced at the Council of Ephesus in A.D. 431. However, the theological title "Mother of God" does not imply that Mary is the source of the divine nature of Christ. Rather, this title is a magnification of her role in salvation history: she is the mother of the Incarnate Jesus, who is God (see also "**Incarnation**"). Mary also has many other titles and patronages, since she is the universal mother of Christians and Queen of Heaven.

The Blessed Virgin Mary and the Christ Child

It is also a dogmatic teaching of the Church that Mary was born without the stain and effects of Original Sin, and through this act of mercy through the work of Jesus Christ, she remained sinless throughout her entire life (see "**Immaculate Conception**").

The final dogmatic teaching about Mary concerns her virginity. The Church teaches that Mary remained a virgin before, during, and after the birth of Christ for the rest of her life. She did not bear any other children. This doctrine was established along with the title of *Theotokos* at the Council of Ephesus, but it is rejected by almost all Protestant denominations.

Catholic devotion to Mary begins with our understanding that when Jesus looked to John from the Cross and stated, "Behold, your mother" (John 19:27), He not only entrusted the care of Mary to the disciple but He also assigned Mary as mother to all believers. This idea is simple when we also consider that the faithful are, in reality, the spiritual Body of Christ—of which Mary is also mother. As she is our spiritual mother, we look to her for intercession and imitation of her complete trust in God.

CATHOLIC TIP

There is beauty and happiness in accepting the motherhood of Mary. Her status as our mother is not dependent on our feelings and reservations; she loves us as a mother regardless of our personal placement of her motherhood. But when we are ready to grow closer to her, we may consider an act of consecration. The Consecration to Jesus through Mary is a pledge process by which a person sets himself aside for the purpose of serving God under the patronage of Mary as the perfect disciple of Jesus. St. Louis de Montfort's method—which is a process by which one prepares for such a consecration—is by far the most popular and suggested. One can find many books with guidance and commentary for this consecration, or it is also available for free through a handful of online resources.

Mary was not an apostle, but she is the proto-follower of Christ and a perfect example of Christian virtue. Catholics do not worship Mary as a god, but we do venerate her, ask her for her prayers, and honor her above all other saints (see the final paragraph in the "**Adoration**" entry). Catholic devotion to Mary can be one of the most misunderstood aspects of Catholicism for non-Catholics, but the important thing to remember about Mary is that she always points us to her Son, not to herself, just as she did at the wedding feast in Cana: "Do whatever he tells you" (John 2:5).

Further reading: Those who wish to imitate and devote themselves to Jesus through Mary can consecrate themselves through the method provided by St. Louis de Montfort's popular Total Consecration to Jesus through Mary. *In addition, a personal favorite on Mary and her status as the Mother of Christians, as well as a solid defense of Marian dogmas, is* Behold Your Mother *by Tim Staples.*

Meditation

A form of mental prayer by which one seeks deeper knowledge of God's revelation with the intention of moving the will to resolution, action, or decision.

Two popular forms of meditation in Catholicism today are the Ignatian Method and the Sulpician Method. Ignatian contemplation often involves reading Scripture while using the imagination to enter the scene and experience Scripture in a personal way. In the Sulpician Method, one focuses on reflections of unworthiness and the desire for virtue. This method also involves adoration and active prayer.

There are other forms of meditation in the Church, and all methods aim to help one progress in the Christian life, whether in virtue or in making an important life decision. All meditation should begin with an invocation of the Holy Spirit and be rooted in an intention of advancing closer to Christ.

"Meditation" can be a buzzword in today's culture, and it is often used by those who consider themselves to be "spiritual but not religious." Popular culture tells us that meditation is a process by which we calm ourselves, reduce stress, and become "mindful." True meditation might indeed produce these fruitful results, but for the Catholic, meditation is about action: "The mind seeks to understand the why and how of the Christian life, in order to adhere and respond to what the Lord is asking" (CCC 2705).

Mercy

The attribute of God by which He forgives us our sins and welcomes us back into friendship with Him.

Mercy is correlated to God's will, as He chooses to be merciful or chooses to express His mercy in various ways. God's infinite mercy in no way competes with or impedes His justice. Pope Francis calls justice and mercy "two dimensions of a single reality that unfolds progressively until it culminates in the fullness of love."[50]

God's mercy is such that He reaches out to those in need, not because of anything they have done to deserve it but out of His faithful love and kindness. "The Lord is gracious and merciful, slow to anger and abounding in steadfast love" (Ps. 145:8). St. Thomas Aquinas argues that God could have saved mankind in any way He chose, but that sending His Son to die for our sins was the most merciful—the most suitable—way.[51]

Out of love for God and desire for holiness, Christians also strive to be merciful. It is a moral virtue and Beatitude that returns what one provides: "Blessed are the merciful, for they shall obtain mercy" (Matt. 5:7). In a practical sense, Christians show mercy by lessening the severity of judgment and tempering punishments. The Catholic Church also encourages the faithful to practice works of mercy (see "**Works of Mercy**"), both corporal and spiritual.

Miracle

A supernatural event in which God intervenes in the world in a way that cannot be attributed to a natural cause.

Miracles are solely attributable to God, and although they cannot be explained by science, they are observable. God's power in a miracle is directed through His own immediate action, or through the mediate action of His creatures as His instruments.

Theologians agree that there are three general purposes for a miracle: to lead someone to belief, to verify the sanctity of a person or place, or to validate a truth or divine mission. Christ performed miracles for these very same purposes, demonstrating His divinity, His Church, and His salvific work on Calvary. "Thus the miracles of Christ and the saints, prophecies, the Church's growth and holiness, and her fruitfulness and stability 'are the most certain signs of divine revelation, adapted to the intelligence of all'; they are 'motives of credibility' (*motiva credibilitatis*), which show that the assent of faith is 'by no means a blind impulse of the mind' " (CCC 156). Miracles are therefore the servants of faith. Miracles such as those that result in a healing serve to help someone temporarily, but they also show us that that healing is important in this life; after all, Christ Himself healed many during His earthly ministry.

Jesus Healing the Sick, by Heinrich Hofmann

Miracles continue to this day, and we hear of many miracles big and small in the life of the Church. For example, a priest watched as the host bled in his hands at the words of consecration in Bolsena, Italy, in 1263. In 2008, in Sokolka, Poland, a Host that had fallen on the ground was placed in water to dissolve but instead began to bleed. Some Christians are also given a charism (a

CATHOLIC TIP

If we stop to contemplate God's infinite mercy, it's not hard to imagine, and we may even dare to expect, that God performs miracles every day. Think about it: the Eucharist truly is the Body, Blood, Soul, and Divinity of Jesus, and this happens at every Mass. This miracle occurs every day, all over the world. Indeed, we have all witnessed God's astonishing intervention in the natural world—and in perpetuity no less!

unique spiritual gift—see "**Charism**") to perform miracles by the power of God (CCC 2003).

Miracles, usually referred to as signs and wonders, are abundant in the Old Testament. These miracles range from the plagues in Egypt to the exploits of Elijah and Elisha. The New Testament indicates a wider and fuller outpouring of the Holy Spirit on believers, in which those followers of Christ are the instruments of numerous miracles as promised by Christ (Mark 16:17–18).

Miracles are a constant topic in the Catholic Church because they are required in the process of canonization (see "**Canonization**"). Although several miracles may be investigated at the same time, the current norms to canonize a saint require only one miracle to be approved for beatification and another miracle for canonization (with the exception of martyrs, who may be approved for both beatification and canonization without approved miracles).

Further reading: Compendium of the Miraculous, *by Deacon Albert E. Graham, is a vast encyclopedia of miracles and miraculous events in the history the Church.*

Mission

The special work of preaching the Gospel and ministering to Christ's people, whether local or abroad.

The word "mission" comes from the Latin verb *mittere*, meaning "to send," as Jesus Christ sent the apostles into the world (Matt. 28:19). The Decree on the Missionary Activity of the Church, *Ad Gentes*, describes missions as those "particular undertakings by which the heralds of the Gospel, sent out by the Church and going forth into the whole world, carry out the task of preaching the Gospel and planting the Church among peoples or groups who do not yet believe in Christ."[52] It also declares, "The pilgrim Church is missionary by her very nature, since it is from the mission of the Son and the mission of the Holy Spirit that she draws her origin, in accordance with the decree of God the Father."[53]

This sense of mission in the Church transcends every culture and institution, every government and every human order: "Faithful to her own tradition and at the same time conscious of her universal mission, she can enter into communion with the various civilizations, to their enrichment and the enrichment of the Church herself."[54] Indeed, whether we are lifelong Catholics or newly converted, and regardless of our state of life, God's command is for us to be missionaries—sent, itinerant, intentional. "This duty ... is one and the same everywhere and in every condition, even though it may be carried out differently according to circumstances."[55]

As Christians, we strive to carry out our mission to convert the world with the same mindset as the itinerant prophets and missionaries who delivered Christ's message to the ends of the earth from the Church's earliest days. As believers and disciples of Jesus Christ, our mission work in the world is our Christian witness: how we live our life, our collaboration with others in the social and economic life, and our treatment of others with true charity.[56]

Further reading: I wholeheartedly recommend, in addition to the sections in this book on "Evangelization" *and* "Kerygma," *that all read* Ad Gentes, *The Decree on the Mission Activity of the Church from the Second Vatican Council, for information on living out the missionary spirit of the Church.*

Missionary

One sent on mission to evangelize, teach, and preach the Faith.

Missionaries have held a special office of the Church's apostolic mission since its foundation. St. Paul was a well-traveled missionary, but other apostles, such as Thomas and James, took the Gospel to great distances too. The role of missionary continued as a selective vocation but exploded with the mendicant orders (Franciscans and Dominicans) in the twelfth century, whose members brought

St. Francis Xavier, patron of missionaries

CATHOLIC TIP

It could seem as if missionary activity in the world is a thing of the past, but this idea is far from accurate. Active missions continue throughout the world in places such as Africa, China, the Middle East, and many parts of the West. These missions are dedicated to ministering to the poor, comforting those in prison, and aiding those enduring persecution.

All Christians, however, are called to be missionaries. "Missionary activity is a matter for all Christians, for all dioceses and parishes, Church institutions and associations" (*Redemptoris Missio*, no. 2). The laity have a unique ability to be missionaries wherever they are in all states of life:

> To obtain all these things, the most important and therefore worthy of special attention are the Christian laity: namely, those who have been incorporated into Christ and live in the world. For it is up to them, imbued with the spirit of Christ, to be a leaven working on the temporal order from within, to dispose it always in accordance with Christ. (*Ad Gentes*, no. 15)

the mission field depth, organization, and regularization. This work was later furthered with orders such as the Jesuits in the sixteenth century. Today, religious orders continue to send out missionaries throughout the world, as they provide the stability, training, funding, and succession approach required for missionary success.

Missionaries work in two different types of mission fields: foreign and domestic. Foreign missions announce the gospel to the whole world. Domestic missions serve within one's own country. You might be surprised to learn that much of the United States is still considered mission territory, and missionaries are sent here to help preach the gospel. In areas where there are not enough priests to serve the needs of the local Church, missions might take over a parish church (becoming a "parish mission") for a weekend and set aside time for instruction, refresher catechesis, and reception of the sacraments. As the availability of priests increases, these missions typically diminish in frequency.

Modernism

A cultural movement that opposes true Christianity by proposing freedom from all religious authority and the emancipation of the individual's conscience.

Pope St. Pius X condemned Modernism as the "synthesis of all heresies" in his 1907 encyclical *Pascendi Dominici Gregis*. He taught that Modernism is the result of unchecked curiosity and pride: "It is pride which fills Modernists with that confidence in themselves and leads them to hold themselves up as the rule for all ... as the sole possessors of knowledge ... which rouses in them the spirit of disobedience and causes them to demand a compromise."[57]

The problem with Modernism is not solely that it rejects this or that article of faith but that it makes the individual the sole judge of religious truth. Modernism teaches people to challenge everything; no religious authority should be accepted. Under the pretense of Modernism, anything can be rejected. It is from Modernism that the more recent problem of moral relativism has emerged (see "**Relativism**").

At the turn of the twentieth century, the Church led important initiatives to combat, remedy, and address the rampant and rapid advancement of Modernism. As the world turned to the self to understand and define truth, the Church, especially under the leadership of Popes Pius X and Leo XIII, encouraged her members to return to our past, specifically, to classical philosophy and the scholasticism of St. Thomas Aquinas.

Present-day men and women—even those with great intentions—are not immune to the dangerous ideas of Modernism. Indeed, Modernism pervades social thinking in the twenty-first century, perhaps more than it ever has. The Church's defense against this creeping ideology begins in the home: wholesome, practical Catholic teaching on authority and the formation of conscience can help to abate the influence of Modernism on the future leaders and thinkers of the Church and will help to keep them *in* the Church!

Further reading: The Gods of Atheism *by Fr. Vincent Miceli, S.J., is an excellent look into the characters and philosophies that have shaped modernist thinking and have lead many into atheism.*

Monasticism

The state of life of those religious who, living in a community, operate under a systematic lifestyle according to an approved rule.

The origins of monasticism stem from the early eremitical Christians (from whom we derive the word "hermit") who, living solitary or in small communities, desired to live perfectly the evangelical counsels (see "**Evangelical Counsels**"). They followed the teaching of Christ, who told His followers, "If you would be perfect, go, sell what you possess and give to the poor, and you will have treasure in Heaven; and come, follow me" (Matt. 19:21), in imitation of the Master who had "nowhere to lay his head" (Matt. 8:20). These hermits, such as St. Anthony of Egypt or the acclaimed Desert Fathers, attracted diverse people, and their devout lifestyle spread across the East and West.

Over time, many famous monks gathered and organized communities, such as St. Martin of Tours and St. Honoratus. But it was St. Benedict of Nursia who wrote the first widely adopted rule that productively governed the existence and regimen of a community. Discretion and moderation within this rule not only gave its users flexibility but also preserved the discipline necessary to cultivate devotion and sanctification in them. St. Benedict is therefore considered to be the Father of Western Monasticism. Meanwhile, his sister St. Scholastica made an identical impact for the rule of female cloistral and conventual communities.

Members of monastic orders live a life of prayer and penance, and most of these orders focus on a

Benedictine Monastery of Subiaco

All members of monastic orders make vows of poverty, chastity, and obedience (see "**Evangelical Counsels**").

Male members of monastic orders are known as monks or friars and are generally referred to as "brother." Some religious brothers are also priests, and some are even bishops. Monks and friars vow obedience to their abbot (if living in an abbey) or prior (if in a priory).

Female members of monastic orders are either known as nuns (if they are cloistered) or as religious sisters. Note that "nun" is not interchangeable with "sister," yet because both nuns and sisters belong to religious life, they can also be called "women religious." Catholic nuns, known in Canon Law as *moniales*, are women who profess solemn vows and live in a religious community that is either cloistered or semi-cloistered. Their ministry and prayer life are centered around the monastery

specific labor of some sort, depending on the rule of life for their respective religious order. Some monastic orders are cloistered, while others are active in the world. To be cloistered is to be "enclosed," meaning the monks or nuns spend their daily life within the boundaries of their campus.

CATHOLIC TIP

There are two types of vows religious can take: solemn or simple. The *New Commentary on the Code of Canon Law* explains the distinction this way:

> The older religious orders (monastic, canon regulars, mendicants, Jesuits) make perpetual solemn vows, and the more recent apostolic congregations make perpetual simple vows. The chief difference between the two is that religious who profess a solemn vow of poverty renounce ownership of all their temporal goods, whereas religious who profess a simple vow of poverty have a right to retain ownership of their patrimony (an estate, endowment or anything inherited from one's parents or ancestors) but must give up its use and any revenue. (John Beal, *New Commentary on the Code of Canon Law* [Mahwah, NJ: Paulist Press, 2000], 1417.)

for the good of the world. Sisters, however, *sorores* in Canon Law, are women who belong to various religious orders and communities and yet live, minister, and pray in the world. We use the terms "active" or "apostolic" to explain a sister's life because she is engaged in the works of mercy and other ministries that take the gospel to others wherever they are. Sisters profess perpetual simple vows to live according to the evangelical counsels of poverty, chastity, and obedience.

Some common monastic orders include the Benedictines, Carmelites, Norbertines, and Trappists.

Montanism

An apocalyptic movement and heresy of the second century named after its chief preacher and leader, Montanus.

Around A.D. 160, Montanus, a convert to Christianity and possibly a priest, began to prophesy, claiming he was under the influence of the Holy Spirit. He was joined by Prisca (or Priscilla) and Maximilla. His most famous adherent was Tertullian, a famous and often reliable Christian apologist who joined the sect later in his life. Montanus claimed that the Spirit had granted him a new revelation, exclusively for him and his followers. Montanists also claimed that these revelations were final. Montanism was opposed as a heresy in the early third century, and Emperor Justinian I's legislation effectively destroyed it.

Montanism promoted strict moral rigors and prohibited marriage, but it was more problematic because of its insistence that the revelations its founder received were exclusive and final, which implies that something could be added to the teachings of Christ and therefore contradicts the teachings of the apostles. Montanists also believed that the Second Coming was to occur within months or years, and that they knew when it would take place.

The central problem with Montanism was not the inclusion of prophecy in the preaching of Montanus. The Church regards prophecy as a genuine charism, although she believes that it should be tested (1 Thess. 5:20–21). The Church teaches that divine revelation, however, ended with the death of the apostles. The *Catechism* says, "Christian faith cannot accept 'revelations' that claim to surpass or correct the Revelation of which Christ is the fulfillment, as is the case with certain non-Christian religions and also in certain recent sects which base themselves on such 'revelations' " (67). Although Catholics are welcome to believe in approved private revelations, such as the messages of the Virgin Mary at Fatima, Catholics are not bound by conscience to believe these things, and Catholics may not accept any revelations that contradict or change Church doctrine. The "deposit of faith" is transmitted through the successors of the apostles, who are the bishops, and is not subject to correction.

Montanism is best known today for its association with the Church Father Tertullian. Near the end of his life, Tertullian renounced the Catholic Church and embraced this sect. That is why, despite his substantial contributions to Christian theology, he has not been canonized.

Morality

Norms of human conduct that determine whether actions are right or wrong, and the amount of responsibility for these actions.

Morality is part of the natural law and is written on every human heart (see Rom. 2:15; also see "**Natural Law**"). Through centuries of careful study of human nature and Sacred Scripture, the Catholic Church teaches that the morality of human acts depends on: "the object chosen; the end in view or the intention; and the circumstances of the action" (CCC 1750).

The object is the act itself. It can be morally good or a violation of the natural law. The intention is the purpose of the action, willfully considered and

CATHOLIC TIP

St. Paul warned the Corinthians: "Bad company ruins good morals" (1 Cor. 15:33), quoting Greek playwright Menander's comedy *Thais*, with which the ancient Greeks he spoke to would no doubt have been familiar. Paul issued this stern warning against bad influences who steer us away from Christ and therefore lead us to become less moral and less aware of the truth.

My favorite image of a "good moral compass" is the image of the Barque of St. Peter. This pious tradition, which sets Peter as the captain of a vessel, represents the Church and the authority of the pope. The pope steers the Church through rough seas—we are ever under threat, but ever protected. Our best moral compass in life is the moral teaching of the Magisterium. "Do not be deceived," St. Paul says. The world is complex and new challenges (and influences) to living a moral and upright life meet every generation. But the Church transcends every generation's moral struggles; she is unwavering in her moral wisdom regardless of changes in political patterns or philosophical tides. Catholics enjoy superior confidence that the moral position of the Church is guided by tested principles and protected by the Holy Spirit. This ship, the Barque of Peter, will always be guided to safety. Let's stay in the boat!

executed by the subject (the person). The intention (focused on the end) never changes the substance of the act; rather, it determines the true purpose pursued by an act. For example, an act that is good but was not done with any intent to be good would be of less merit. However, a good act performed with no expectation of reward is highly meritorious.

The most important item to remember in the application of morality is that if the object (the act) is evil, it is always evil, regardless of one's intention. This fact is important to keep in mind when considering many modern issues such as abortion, homosexual acts, and birth control.

Circumstances can impact the subject's responsibility and, in a way, can measure one's involvement in an act, but circumstances do not change the substance of the act. For example, an act done out of fear of death has an increased circumstantial moral application, usually reducing responsibility, than the same act not performed with any threat or fear of death. Another example might be the measure of the act: the widow in the Gospel who gave a little in poverty gave more than those who donated much from their abundance (Mark 12:42–44).

Catholic teaching says that the natural law of morality is written on the human heart, since the rational soul of man is able to discern between good and evil (see CCC 1956–1960). The Bible, the Word of God, is the principal tool in the formation of a good conscience (2 Tim. 3:16), but we must also remember that we are not alone. The experience of the Catholic Church and the guidance of the Holy Spirit aids believers in living good, moral lives, and the Church's authoritative documents are essential in the formation (and examination) of our consciences.

Further reading: the Handbook of Moral Theology *by Fr. Dominic Prümmer, O.P., has been a stable and trustworthy authority on the expansive topics of moral theology. Pope St. John Paul II's* Evangelium Vitae *is a very useful encyclical to laypersons who want to know more about morality.*

Mormonism

Popular name for the Church of Jesus Christ of Latter-Day Saints.

Mormonism was founded by the Vermont-born farm laborer Joseph Smith in Fayette, New York, in 1830. He claimed that an angel named Moroni, who was once a mortal man and son of a prophet named Mormon, revealed to him a new gospel of Jesus Christ and told him to found a church, since all others in existence were unworthy. Smith claimed that the revelation he received was an ancient record of the teachings of Christ, who appeared shortly after His Resurrection to a civilization of Jews who were living in North America.

The principal text of the Church of Jesus Christ of Latter-Day Saints is the Book of Mormon. According to Joseph Smith, this book was given to him by Moroni as a set of ring-bound golden plates. The Book of Mormon purports to be an abridged account of God's dealings with ancient civilizations who embarked to North America around the time that the Tower of Babel was purported to have been built.

Mormonism combines spiritualism and materialism with elements of Protestantism, Freemasonry, and other heretical groups. Mormonism teaches that God is a material being; He did not create matter but organized it. They also believe that God procreated with the Virgin Mary in order to create Jesus, and therefore Mormonism rejects the divinity of Christ and instead treats Him as a "spirit-son," not as God. A number of other seriously problematic teachings persist. They believe in a plurality of heaven—degrees of blessedness, not all of which include being with God; continued divine revelation that is binding upon its adherents, which directly contradicts the Christian idea that Jesus is the fullness of divine revelation—that the apostles were given a complete deposit of faith (see "**Revelation**"); and that the Book of Mormon is authoritatively superior to the Bible. The salvific and eschatological doctrine of Mormonism concludes with the regathering of the tribes of Israel and the building of the New Jerusalem in North America prior to the Second Coming of Christ.

Joseph Smith, founder of the Mormons

Adherents of Mormonism refer to themselves as Christians, but they are not Christian, primarily because their baptism is not valid and also because their heretical teaching rejects the divine nature of Jesus Christ as God.

Although they are popularly known as Mormons, the participants of this religion prefer to be called Latter Day Saints in contradistinction to the saints of the former churches (and former times). Mormons are strongly encouraged to spend a period proselytizing as missionaries, and so all Catholics must be prepared to answer and refute their claims by becoming familiar with Mormon teachings in detail. One may choose to read the Book of Mormon in order to understand their beliefs, but if reading the Book of Mormon is too uncomfortable, one can find Catholic resources on Mormonism in order to survey and understand their true teachings as well as learn persuasive arguments to help Mormon people discover the true Jesus.

Further reading: The booklet 20 Answers: Mormonism *from Catholic Answers is a must-have for anyone looking for the core beliefs of Mormonism as well as persuasive discussions. Listening to the testimonies of Mormon converts in various books, online resources, and especially the Coming Home Network's* The Journey Home *series are also effective means of learning what helps a Mormon come to understand the weaknesses in their faith and theology.*

Mystery

Truths of our faith that God has revealed but that men cannot know in their fullness during our lives and journeys as Christian pilgrims on earth.

The word "mystery," in the scriptural use, comes from the Greek *mysterion*, meaning "secret" and "hidden," as God's revelation is knowable only to God. Thus, the mysteries of the Christian Faith are known to God alone. The First Vatican Council declared, "If anyone shall say that in divine revelation there are no mysteries, truly and properly so called, but that all the doctrines of faith can be understood and demonstrated from natural principles by properly cultivated reason; let him be anathema."[58] In the hope of the Beatific Vision (see "**Beatific Vision**"), Christians believe knowledge of the mysteries of our faith will be revealed in Heaven.

All four Gospels speak of the chief mystery of the Incarnation and the Paschal Mystery (see "**Incarnation**" and "**Paschal Mystery**"), but St. John wonderfully presents the central Christian mysteries of the Christian Faith in his Gospel: that Jesus is the Incarnate Word of God; that in order to have life in Christ we must be reborn and die to self; that we who desire to see God are also called to eat His Flesh and drink His Blood as true food; and that it was necessary for Christ to be sacrificed for our sins.

"Mystery" was also the theological word used throughout the New Testament (see Mark 4:11, Rom. 11:25, Eph. 5:32) and through the patristic age to apply to the sacraments and sacramental celebrations. Where the word *mysterion* was applied by the Greek Fathers, their Latin counterparts used either *mysterium* or *sacramentum*. Today, we also refer to the sacraments as mysteries of our Faith. It is God's plan that through sacraments, the faithful are brought into God's eternal plan of salvation that has been realized in history by Christ and receive sanctifying grace.

Mystical Body of Christ

The Church as a spiritual union of believers under Christ as its Head.

The Mystical Body of Christ consists of all members of the Church, the laity and the hierarchy. St. Paul tells us, "For just as the body is one and has many members, and all the members of the body, though many, are one body, so it is with Christ.... Now you are the body of Christ and individually members of it" (1 Cor. 12:12, 27). St. Paul explains also that Christ is the head of this Mystical Body: "He is the head of the body, the Church" (Col. 1:18). Therefore, in a spiritual but also very physical sense, the Church exists and operates as Christ's presence on earth. Members are incorporated into this Body upon the reception of the sacrament of Baptism.[59]

As the Mystical Body, the Church shares in the life of Christ in multiple ways. The Church observes the life of Christ through the liturgy, shares in Christ's sufferings through exposure to torments and persecution, and has the responsibility of caring for this Body. The Mystical Body is sustained through the sacraments instituted by Christ, especially the Holy Eucharist.

Further reading: Learn more about the Church as Christ's Mystical Body in Pope Pius XII's encyclical Mystici Corporis Christi.

Mysticism

A deep spiritual knowledge and sense of the presence of God and of the things of God.

Mysticism results from the presence and movement of God in one's soul. The word "mysticism" is derived from the Greek verb *muō*, meaning to silence the mouth by closing it. Those who experience mysticism are also known as mystics.

Mysticism or contemplation is distinguished from meditation. St. Alphonsus Liguori writes definitively on this subject. The difference is that in meditation one encounters God through one's own efforts and mental faculties, whereas in contemplation God is present and active without the person's effort. Mystics in the Church's history have sometimes received extraordinary graces, such as the stigmata, locutions, ecstasies, bilocation, and levitation. Again, these are extraordinary accompaniments, and a person can be a mystic without experiencing any of these things. Famous mystics include saints such as Teresa of Ávila, Catherine of Siena, and Padre Pio.

Further reading: Prayers of the Women Mystics *and* Holding Hands with God *by author and professor Ronda Chervin, a modern authority on mysticism, are wonderful. Much of Chervin's prolific career has benefitted Catholic readers' understanding of mysticism and the mystic saints.*

St. Teresa in Ecstasy,
by Giovanni Battista Piazzetta

Natural Family Planning (NFP)

Methods of fertility care that follow the woman's natural cycle of fertility and infertility to help a couple achieve or avoid pregnancy.

While the Church teaches the objective immorality of birth control (see "**Contraception**"), she encourages the practice of Natural Family Planning methods: "Periodic continence, that is, the methods of birth regulation based on self-observation and the use of infertile periods, is in conformity with the objective criteria of morality" (CCC 2370). Because NFP does not ever close the couple off to the possibility of conceiving life and can always be adapted to try to achieve a pregnancy, it preserves the unitive and procreative aspects of moral sexual activity within marriage (see "**Marriage**" for more on these aspects).

Through self-sampling and observation of "biomarkers," couples can understand the characteristics and timing of the woman's cycle—and indeed her biochemistry and behavior patterns—to a near-precise degree. This knowledge allows couples to appreciate God's gift of fertility more fully and to space out pregnancies when necessary. It also provides health benefits to women beyond the interests of conception.

To try to achieve a pregnancy, a couple would monitor the fertile period and engage in sexual activity together when the woman is fertile. To avoid pregnancy, the couple would use the natural infertile periods for conjugal activity. The couple must always have just reasons for exclusively avoiding pregnancy (CCC 2368).

There are several methods of NFP, and couples are free to choose the method that best suits their needs and lifestyle. Some methods include: the

CATHOLIC TIP

A frequent objection to NFP is that it is just another method of birth control when the couple intends to avoid pregnancy, or that the couple who utilizes NFP has a "contraceptive mentality." However, the *Catechism of the Catholic Church* tells us that a couple has the responsibility to maintain a just cause for avoiding pregnancy (CCC 2368). These valid reasons may include health, child spacing, age, or other personal circumstances, as discussed by Pope Paul VI in *Humanae Vitae*; but couples should never avoid pregnancy simply for selfish reasons and must always involve God in their family decisions, through frequent family and spousal prayer.

NFP is not the same as birth control. Birth control is an artificial (unnatural) means to avoid the natural consequences of sexual intercourse. Meanwhile, NFP does not intervene in the natural process of fertility but simply gives the couple the knowledge to observe it and to choose to abstain from intercourse when the woman is fertile. The bottom line on the objective morality of NFP is that a couple is not "preventing" a pregnancy by not having sex, they are simply not having sex.

Creighton Fertility Method, the Billings Method, the Marquette Method, and the Sympto-Thermal Method; information about each as well as training programs are widely available online. These programs are all supported by scientific research and are much more accurate than the antiquated "rhythm method" or free apps and programs.

Further reading: For more on the Church's teaching regarding birth control, read Humanae Vitae, *the masterwork of Pope St. Paul VI. For more on NFP, read Simcha Fisher's* The Sinner's Guide to Natural Family Planning *for reflective and practical insights.*

Natural Law

The order of man's natural inclination to reason between good and evil; natural law is present in the conscience of each person by virtue of being created with a rational soul.

The natural law is what St. Paul refers to when he teaches, "They show that what the law requires is written on their hearts, while their conscience also bears witness and their conflicting thoughts accuse or perhaps excuse them" (Rom. 2:15).

Much of the Christian articulation of the natural law is derived from or influenced by ancient philosophers such as Plato and Aristotle, and it was developed with the understanding of divine revelation by philosopher-theologians such as Augustine and Thomas Aquinas. The notion of the natural law was accepted by most in Western society until recent centuries, when it has been gradually superseded by modernism, relativism, and other dominant philosophies that reject a moral law applicable to all persons. As a result of this shying away from definitive morality, modern society as a whole struggles to find a suitable basis for civil laws.

Roman Catholic theology affirms that the natural law of human conduct is based on mankind's creation in the image of God. Using his reason, man is able to reflect on his own human nature and natural experiences and thus determine the moral substance of an act. Paul refers to this idea when he testifies that the Gentiles do by nature what the Law (given to God's people) requires (Rom. 2:14).

Further reading: All Catholics should read The Catechism of the Catholic Church *paragraphs 1954–1960 carefully, in which the natural law is articulated as it applies to morality. Charles Rice's book* 50 Questions on the Natural Law *also offers imperative learning and insights.*

New Age

A range of philosophical thought and spiritual practices emerging in the West in the 1970s which holds that a person's reality is constructed through a connection with one's own mind, body, and spirit.

The New Age movement is not a religion per se, but it contains elements that can be mixed with religion. A common and strong thread in most adaptations of New Age spirituality includes an acceptance of astrology, reading one's fortune or deriving spiritual wisdom from interpretations of cosmological cycles. In this case, horoscope readings are considered a personal forecast and guide. Another common belief and practice of New Age movements is the rejection of modern conventional medicine in favor of a total reliance upon alternative medicine; New Agers follow "self-healing" practices that aim to "balance" the mind, body, and spirit.

New Age spirituality has no strict definition and could include a myriad of beliefs and practices, but many common ones are in conflict with orthodox Christian teaching. These often include ideas that replace man's need for God with himself as the center of his efforts. There is no clear authority in any New Age practice, and this lack of any solid doctrine or leadership results in an ultra-modernism that often replaces established sources of truth for religion and living with "hidden knowledge."

New Age spirituality is a sharp deterrent to wholesome, orthodox Christian thinking. It orients the individual to place confidence in things other than God;

According to some New Age beliefs, some crystals have healing properties.

to look to cosmological "signs" to tell us who we are rather than understanding who *God says we are*; and to accept a "law of attraction" that exalts the power of the person over dependence on divine grace. The ever-evolving nature of this spirituality forces many partakers to fall into indifferentism, and they soon become indifferent to the differences between actual religion and problematic New Age spiritualities.

Because many New Age adherents purport to be Christian but really aren't, faithful believers must recognize the confusion of New Age thinking by first of all taking time to study orthodox Christian teaching on critical topics, such as: the working and receiving of grace; Christ as the Son of God, the savior of mankind and the one mediator between God and man; and acceptance of human suffering and God's redemptive plan of salvation. Understanding these teachings will help one successfully identify and combat New Age ideas in conversation, media, and other societal influences.

Further reading is extremely encouraged, since the New Age movement is so deceptively active in modern society. Brian Mercier's book Counterfeit Spirituality: Exposing the False Gods *and Matt Nelson's* Just Whatever: How to Help the Spiritually Indifferent Find Beliefs that Really Matter *are excellent reads on the problems of New Ageism.*

New Evangelization

Evangelization in response to changes in the modern world, with a focus on those Catholics who have fallen out of the practice of their faith.

Pope St. John Paul II, Pope Benedict XVI, and Pope Francis have all preached on the need for continued emphasis on the New Evangelization in response to the millions of Catholics who, although catechized (to a varying degree), have not been evangelized.

In a "post-Christian" world devastated by secularization—as well as grave scandal within the Church, given by clergy and laity alike—many take the message of the gospel for granted. Many people have heard of Jesus and may even have been raised in a church, but they are indifferent to religion and moral absolutes and are suspicious and dismissive of the authority of the Church. The focus of the New Evangelization is to re-propose the message of Christ in a way that offers people a renewal or a rediscovery of the Faith.

The methods of the New Evangelization are not set in stone, but modern popes and saints have given us some important guidance. Evangelization in the modern world requires: a thorough catechesis that is capable of combating anti-Catholic messages; a greater knowledge of and closeness to our separated brethren (Christians who do not accept the Catholic Faith); and, more than anything else, a wholesome call to conversion to Christ in how we live, work, and worship.

"Nones"

Those in the United States who claim no religious or spiritual affiliation.

With no strict origin for the term, "nones" apparently derived in popular culture to refer to those who marked "none" on a survey used to draw data on religious affiliation. "Nones" may include atheists and agnostics. However, those who are called "nones" are fundamentally different from atheists, who actively don't believe in God, and from agnostic persons, who are uncertain about the existence of a higher power or the need to follow religious ideals. "Nones," rather, do not identify with any religious belief system or category—they represent an elevated form of ideological ambivalence and religious indifference. The "nones" are a growing affiliation in the modern secular world.

What draws "nones" away from Christianity is often a deep immersion in secular culture and the devaluation of Christ. With innumerable and ever-growing means of being distracted or entertained, and the increased treatment of Jesus as nothing more than a character from an ancient Christmas story, modern culture encourages the rapid rise of the "nones" as it fosters an environment of disinterest and meaninglessness.

How do we combat this cultural phenomenon? The New Evangelization points to the need for the testimony of Christians (see "**New Evangelization**"). In short, Christians should be dynamic witnesses of Christ. We should carry ourselves and even talk differently than other people as we live with joy, selfless love, and a brightness of life that can only point to a supernatural influence. An argument we often hear today is that "you don't need religion if you're a good person." But what does this statement really mean? The statement actually makes a tacit argument *for* religion: the absolutism of this statement firstly (and incorrectly) implies that "you need religion if you're a bad person." What's more is that the statement presumes that religion is simply a device used for moral enhancement. In reality, religion often brings forth concepts beyond morality—right and wrong—and serves man by giving him meaning, virtue, freedom, and many other intangible benefits. Catholics must be capable of pointing out the duplicity of this claim in order to get to the heart of the matter: religion has value, and morality has objective truth.

Awaiting the coming of the Holy Spirit for nine days

Novena

A nine-day prayer made for a petition or occasion.

The term "novena" comes from the Latin *novenus*, which indicates a set of nine. A novena is a popular form of prayer that may be accomplished in private or with a group. Most novenas follow a standardized form for nine consecutive days, but others are prayed once per week for nine weeks.

Historically, Christian novenas were mostly nine days of prayer for the dead, but other novenas, such as those in preparation for special feasts such as Christmas and the Annunciation, were used throughout the middle ages. Although novenas did not become widely popular until the seventeenth century, the formula is rooted in the pages of Sacred Scripture, as the nine-day period is symbolic of the nine days between Christ's Ascension and Pentecost in which Mary and the apostles waited prayerfully for the Holy Spirit. Therefore, the novena to the Holy Spirit is always promoted as a powerful plea for the light and strength and love so sorely needed by every Christian. It may begin on the day after the Solemnity of the Ascension.

Occult

A belief and practice in supernatural knowledge other than divine revelation and forces other than God.

People who dabble in the occult, or occultism, are attempting to manipulate spiritual forces in order to effect some outcome in the natural world. Occultism is deeply deceiving, as it plays on man's concupiscence and his fallen desire to be the master of his world and his destiny. It includes divination, magic, astrology, voodoo, alchemy, reiki, and witchcraft among many other practices.

Occultism is a moral evil. The *Catechism* makes it clear: "All practices of *magic* or *sorcery*, by which one attempts to tame occult powers so as to place them at one's service and have a supernatural power over others—even if this were for the sake of restoring their health—are gravely contrary to the virtue of religion" (2117). Occult practices done with the intent of harming a person or group are even more evil, but the *Catechism* makes an important point: participation in the occult even for a good intention is still a moral evil; the ends cannot justify the means.

Occult practices have been widespread throughout history. As modern science developed, there was an increased temptation to participate in the occult for one's own benefit. Examples of such practices include alchemy of souls—to awaken a person from the grave and obtain prolonged life—and the collection of charms for good fortune. Today, occult practices are growing in popularity.

Expert exorcists maintain that the occult is often overlooked, yet it is the easiest means by which demons can control a person. Even in the Catholic Church, well-intentioned believers sometimes fall prey to an occultist line of superstitious thinking: if I do *x*, the outcome will be *y* (for example, burying a statue of St. Joseph to sell a home). Occult practices break the First Commandment, putting other powers before God and His providence, in which we are called to trust.

Further reading: The works of Fr. Gabriel Amorth, Chief Exorcist of the Vatican, are highly recommended. Fr. Gabriel's extensive experience is marvelously presented to readers as informative and cautionary of the subtle ways evil pervades the everyday world. See especially his many books, including An Exorcist Explains the Demonic. *However, it is always wise to approach any study of the occult or demons with caution: it is commendable to learn in order to understand how to combat the forces of evil, but one must take care that such knowledge does not become an obsession, a distraction away from the holy, or an opportunity to despair; God has already won the battle of salvation!*

OCIA

The process for adults who wish to enter the Catholic Church in the United States.

OCIA stands for Order of Christian Initiation of Adults. Those who participate in OCIA (formerly known as RCIA, or Rite of Christian Initiation of Adults) are either catechumens (non-baptized people) or candidates (those already baptized but seeking full communion with the Catholic Church).

Most parishes offer an OCIA program that lasts a number of months and ends on the Easter Vigil, but the process may last longer. The program can take as much time as necessary to bring a person to a level of knowledge and comfort in his decision to enter the Catholic Church. Depending on people's unique situations, a priest may also help someone complete OCIA and the Sacraments of Initiation at other times in the year.

OCIA is a lengthy process, but it may be broken down into four periods with four steps. The first period is the evangelization and precatechumenate. In this early stage, the goal is to promote conversion through evangelization. When the person moves forward with conversion, he is accepted into the first step, the Order of Catechumens, and may undergo a series of optional rites that includes an exorcism, the renunciation of false worship, the presentation of a cross, and being given (choosing) a new name.

The second period is the catechumenate. Here, the Christian way of life through catechesis is the focus (see "**Catechesis**"). Catechesis involves study of Church doctrine and participation in the Sunday liturgy. Once the catechumen has been meaningfully evangelized to belief and action, he is admitted to the Rite of Election and the Enrollment of Names, the second step of OCIA.

The third period is known as purification and enlightenment. During this phase, "scrutinies" are administered as rites. The word "scrutiny" today often has a negative connotation, but these scrutinies are intercessions and exorcisms for the elect for healing and forgiveness. After the scrutinies comes the celebration of the Sacraments of Initiation: Baptism, Eucharist, and Confirmation (see "**Baptism,**" "**Eucharist,**" and "**Confirmation**"). When possible, the Church prefers that the catechumen or candidate receives these sacraments within the context of the Easter Vigil liturgy.

Finally, the fourth period is the post-baptismal catechesis, which is known as mystagogy. This period usually spans the fifty days of Easter and is meant to be a time of growth with the Christian community in order to achieve a deeper appreciation for the Paschal Mystery, sharing in the Eucharist, and devoting one's life to the gospel message.

Those interested in joining OCIA must contact their parish priest or deacon for instruction. The parish's director of religious education might also play a significant role in leading OCIA.

Pope Francis wearing green vestments during Ordinary Time

Further reading: For those who have just entered the Catholic Church, I'm Catholic. Now What? *by Shaun McAfee is a helpful resource.*

Ordinary Time

The liturgical season split between the time after Christmas and before Lent, and between Pentecost and Advent when the new calendar year begins.

Depending on where the first Sunday of Advent falls (between November 27 and December 3), Ordinary Time may be either thirty-three or thirty-four weeks in duration, making it by far the longest liturgical season. Green is the liturgical color worn throughout Ordinary Time to represent eternal life, hope, and growth in the Holy Spirit.

Being the longest liturgical season in duration, Ordinary Time contains many important feasts and solemnities. These feasts all serve the main concern of Ordinary Time: to keep the believing community focused on the redemption of Christ as an experience of everyday living. The Mass readings during Ordinary Time commonly concentrate on our responsibilities, whereas the readings in other seasons emphasize Christ's work for us.

Original Sin

The universal loss of original perfections, mainly sanctifying grace and bodily immortality, as the direct consequence of the sin of Adam and Eve.

Original Sin was rooted in man's distrust of God. It was an abuse of the freedom God had given to man. As a result of Adam and Eve's sin, all human beings come into the world tainted by sin.

The Council of Trent (1545–1563) confirmed a definition of Original Sin, still referenced by theologians today, as a response to the growing heresies and schismatic preaching at the time that were rooted in a poor understanding or outright rejection of Original Sin. The anathema confirmed that Adam immediately lost holiness and justice when he transgressed and that such an injury was not to him alone but also to his descendants: the entire human race. "By one man sin entered into the world and by sin death; and so death passed upon all men, in whom all have sinned."[60]

The tragic fall of Adam and Eve caused all mankind, except for the Virgin Mary (see "**Immaculate Conception**"), to lose what is known as Original Justice: the state of grace and resulting perfections given to mankind by God when He created them. By their sin, Adam and Eve fell from grace, and the result is a "fallen" nature of all people. St. Paul's teaching on this is almost always cited first: "Therefore as sin came into the world through one man and death through sin, and so death spread to all men because all men sinned" (Rom. 5:12).

Although appropriately focused on the effects of sin and man's fallen nature—the condition of guilt shared by all human beings—this pivotal teaching underscores the universal need for a savior and thus the universal application of Christ's sacrifice on Calvary. Therefore, the Christian message is the joyful news of a free offer of salvation to all humanity.

As one sin affected all mankind, one act of sacrifice offers grace to save all mankind. "If, because of one man's trespass, death reigned through that one man, much more will those who receive the abundance of grace and the free gift of righteousness reign in life through the one man Jesus Christ" (Rom. 5:17). We receive a rich picture of the Church's doctrine on Original Sin from other words of St. Paul (see Rom. 6:4, Col. 2:12).

The Church teaches that in the sacrament of Baptism, we are participants in the redemption of mankind, risen with Christ, and we receive the life of His grace and are completely forgiven of our sins—including Original Sin—and all punishments (CCC 405, 1263). This is wonderful news, but there is still work as far as our *choices* are concerned. Although the stain of Original Sin is removed, the consequences remain. Because of Original Sin, man is still subject to ignorance, suffering, natural death, and the inclination to sin (known as *concupiscence*—see "**Concupiscence**"). Therefore, we must ask for the gifts and graces of the Holy Spirit, make frequent Confession and Communion, and entrust ourselves to God so that we may live good lives and free ourselves from the bondage of sin.

Orthodox Churches

The Eastern European and Asian Christian churches that are not in communion with the Holy See.

In the Great Schism of 1054, the Eastern churches split from Rome. These churches operate with autocephalous authority, meaning the local bishop does not report to any other higher-ranking authority, although the bishops often view the Patriarch of Constantinople as a *primus inter pares* or "first among equals"—a spiritual leader but not a jurisdictional one. Today, the Orthodox churches form the second largest Christian church in the world. The theological teachings of the Orthodox churches are largely the same as Catholic beliefs, but they do reject the doctrine of papal supremacy, and they have not formally accepted any of the clarifications or dogmatized teachings pronounced by the pope since the eleventh century.

At the time of the Great Schism, a few Eastern churches remained in communion with the Bishop of Rome, and they have maintained an authentic liturgy and theological tradition that testifies to their Eastern roots. Others have since returned to communion with the Bishop of Rome. Both of these types of churches are what we call Eastern Catholic Churches.

Despite the differences between Eastern and Western Christianity, ecumenical advancements continue to produce hope in the reunification of Orthodox and Catholic churches. Concluding the Second Vatican Council, Pope St. Paul VI and Patriarch Athenagoras mutually lifted their excommunications in a highly symbolic act of hope for future unity.[61] Pope St. John Paul II detailed his efforts to advance reunification with Orthodox Churches in *Ut Unum Sint*, stating that "the Church must breathe with her two lungs!"[62] Activities between popes, bishops, and Orthodox leaders continue today, with the prayerful hope of full communion in the same spirit of Christ's prayer: "that they may all be one; even as thou, Father, art in me, and I in thee" (John 17:21).

The term "orthodox" may cause some confusion, as it simply indicates traditional, mainstream, or accepted practices. It does not solely relate to the Eastern churches not in full communion with Rome (see "**Orthodoxy**" below).

Orthodoxy

Holding beliefs consistent with Church doctrine.

The word "orthodoxy" comes from the combination of two Greek words: *orthos*, meaning "straight and correct," and *doxa*, meaning "view" or "belief." A teaching that is not in line with Catholic teaching is called heterodox (see "**Heterodoxy**"), *hetero* indicating "another" in the Greek. A critical note is that heterodoxy is not tantamount to heresy, which is the formal, obstinate rejection of a Christian doctrine.

Orthodoxy became an imperative rule and subject of Christian writers after the second century. Earlier than that, the instruction we find in the Bible (and in early Christianity) was more concerned with living and acting correctly, known as *orthopraxis*. But as the Church grew, confusion about the apostolic tradition spread, which led to a greater focus on orthodox teaching.

As practical help to today's theologians and thinkers, we have many writings that dispute history's heretical and heterodox teachers, along with an extensive archive of ecumenical councils and other documents that address and refute heterodox ideas. But it is

An iconostasis (a screen that separates the sanctuary from the nave) in a Russian Orthodox church

the Magisterium as a whole that acts as the benchmark, the teaching body of the Church that instructs the faithful on Christian doctrine and guides bishops when new challenges arise (see "**Magisterium**").

Further reading: Maintaining an orthodox faith and worldview is best achieved through an attentive reading of the Catechism of the Catholic Church. *Additionally, G. K. Chesterton's masterpiece,* Orthodoxy, *is one of the most beloved examinations of the ontology of belief and the application to one's personal faith.*

Benediction of God the Father, by Luca Cambiaso

Our Father

The prayer Jesus taught His disciples when they asked Him, "Lord, teach us to pray" (Luke 11:1).

The Our Father is also known as the Lord's Prayer. This prayer is an integral part of Christian liturgy and ritual and is among the most recognized in the entire world. St. Thomas Aquinas called it "the most perfect of prayers."[63] Throughout most of the Church's history, the prayer was said in Latin (*Pater noster* ...). Early Christians prayed this prayer three times per day, and today it is included in the Mass, the Divine Office, multiple sacramental rites, and other prayers such as the Rosary.

The Our Father is unique and profound among all Christian prayers, since it is the only prayer given to us by Christ and it therefore allows us to pray to God with the words Christ Himself gave us. The invitation is for believers to pray to God as their Father too. Thus, it is the master prayer of the entire Christian Body: Jesus instructs us to pray "Our" Father, not "My" Father.

Although the prayer appears in both Matthew's and Luke's Gospels, Christians traditionally use the one from Matthew:

> Our Father, who art in Heaven, hallowed be Thy name; Thy kingdom come, Thy will be done on earth as it is in Heaven. Give us this day our daily bread, and forgive us our trespasses, as we forgive those who trespass against us; and lead us not into temptation, but deliver us from evil. Amen.

The prayer is composed of seven petitions, requests to God that cover man's physical and spiritual needs. The addition of "For Thine is the kingdom, the power, and the glory forever" was favored by Protestant Bible translators in the seventeenth century but is not found in the earliest manuscripts of the Gospel of Matthew. Catholics include a doxology when we pray the Lord's Prayer at each Mass: "For the kingdom, the power, and the glory are yours now and forever."

Further reading: Pope Francis's book Our Father: Reflections on the Lord's Prayer *is a great (and thorough) reflection on the meaning of this prayer.*

Paganism

All religion outside of the one revealed by God.

Etymology of the word "paganism" is curious, given how we treat the word today. In the Latin, *paganus* was used by Christian missionaries to describe those who lived away from civilized society, in the countryside, since it was often those who were untouched by the work of the missions. Thus, these "pagans" kept to their beliefs and practices of the religions of the Romans, Greeks, Egyptians, or others.

Today, we use the term "pagan" to include those non-Christian religions that involve mythology, pantheism, animism, divination, and magic. The central issue with paganism is that it is idolatrous and therefore directly violates the First Commandment.

It may seem as though paganism is a thing of the past and that few, if any, still accept the belief in many gods held by the ancient Greeks, Egyptians, or others. Yet paganism is still present in many parts of the world, especially the Far East, where Buddhism and Hinduism are prevalent. Subtle forms of paganism are also growing rapidly in modern culture, even in the West, such as: common belief in the occult (see "**Occult**"); dualism; astrology; adoption and evolution of pagan practices; idolatry of money, status, and consumerism; and pantheism that mingles the divine with the universe. The reality is that as modern people look for truth and meaning in things other than God, they steadily accept unorthodox traditions that soon regress into pagan beliefs.

Further reading: An excellent read on the issues of neo-paganism and how Christians can win this culture war is How Christianity Saved Civilization ... And Must Do So Again *by Mike Aquilina and James Papandrea.*

Papacy

The office of the pope, the Bishop of Rome, as the civil and spiritual ruler of the Church.

The term "papacy," along with "pope," comes from the Ecclesiastical Latin word *papa*, meaning "father." Most people simply refer to this office as the office of the pope, but it is also frequently called the office of the supreme pontiff. The term "papacy" also may refer to the period of a pope's reign (for example, "the papacy of John Paul II spanned twenty-six years").

The pope is the visible head of the Church founded by Christ, and he teaches infallibly on truth and morals when speaking *ex cathedra* (see "**Infallibility**" for a detailed discussion). Peter was the first Bishop of Rome and head of the Church. This idea derives from the commission Christ gave to Peter in Matthew 16:18, as Christ called Peter the "rock" on which He would build His church. Peter's exercising of his authority is evident in the account of the Council of Jerusalem in the book of Acts: after arguments on circumcision had been presented, Peter declared the pastoral approach to resolve the division among the others present, "and all the assembly kept silence" (Acts 15:12).

Power and authority given to the papacy is derived directly from the authority of Jesus, not from any pope. Because the pope rules over Christ's Church as a steward, the pope is given the title Vicar of Christ. Although the pope is the supreme ruler of the Church, for efficiency and smoothness he delegates many of his powers through the Curia, the highest of his staff, which is normally headed by an appointed cardinal.

Since 1274, the pope has been elected by the college of cardinals in a process known as a conclave,

St. Peter, on whom Christ founded His Church

which is highly protected to ensure the integrity of the vote. Two-thirds of the entire college must vote for the candidate, and cardinals over eighty years of age cannot vote. Pope St. John Paul II's *Universi Dominici Gregis* eliminated some traditional procedures, leaving "scrutiny," the election of the pope by secret, paper ballot, as the only valid means of electing a new pope.

Further reading: An outstanding defense of the papacy and the primacy of Peter is available in Joe Heschmeyer's book Pope Peter: Defending the Church's Most Distinctive Doctrine in a Time of Crisis.

Parousia

The Second Coming of Christ.

The Greek term *parousia* means "arrival" and is used to refer to the event of Christ's Second Coming twenty-four times in the Greek New Testament. Scholars point out that the term originated in the third century B.C. to indicate a king's presence among his people. Likewise, the Parousia does not refer to an instance but a span of time when Christ will revisit the earth. The prophecy of the Parousia tells that Christ will come gloriously at the end of time to culminate His work: "But of that day and hour no one knows, not even the angels of Heaven, nor the Son, but the Father only" (Matt. 24:36).

The Parousia is an end- time event, but the term is not used interchangeably with end times or end-times study (the study of the end times is known as eschatology). The idea of the Savior returning

CATHOLIC TIP

The office of the pope is one of the most divisive issues between Catholics and non-Catholics. Most arguments center on what theologians refer to as the "primacy of Peter" (or Petrine primacy). There are too many scriptural proofs of Petrine primacy to mention all here, but a few convincing instances include: Peter is almost always named first among the apostles; he is mentioned more than one hundred and fifty times when all the other apostles are mentioned one hundred and thirty times *combined*; he was the first to recognize Jesus as the Christ (Mark 8:29); he alone received the keys representing his authority (Matt. 16:19); he was the spokesperson for Jesus' tax (Matt. 17:24–27); he made judgment on interpretations of Paul's letters and other scriptures (2 Pet. 3:16); and he addressed other bishops as a superior (1 Pet. 5:1).

CATHOLIC TIP

Catholics treat the coming of Christ—certainly eschatology as a whole—with substantially more imperturbability than our separated Protestant brethren. Especially in the modern era, Protestant leaders have been quick to claim personal knowledge of the unfolding of events and sometimes include private knowledge of the day and the hour, leading flocks of Christians to unfulfilled promises of Christ coming in glory at a given day and time. After several false claims, which none should make in the first place (see Matt. 24:36), many would-be believers have dismissed Christianity as a whole. A more balanced take is to treat the Parousia in accord with the words of Christ and Paul: The Son of Man is coming like a thief in the night (see Matt. 24:43–44, 1 Thess. 5:2). That we know the Son of Man is coming but not the hour should cause us to be expectant but not assuming, living our daily lives reflective of our hope and faith: "But he who endures to the end will be saved" (Matt. 24:13).

for His people is found throughout the prophetic sayings in the Old Testament, and the event is known as the "day of the Lord": "The sun shall be turned to darkness, and the moon to blood, before the great and terrible day of the Lord comes" (Joel 2:31). The New Testament writers draw imagery consistent with their revelation of the last days and the Second Coming from the writings of the prophet Daniel (Dan. 7:13–22).

Some New Testament writings indicate that the early Christians had a sense that the Second Coming was not just imminent but immediate and that the writers believed it might even occur within their lifetime (see 1 Thess. 4:17). But Paul softens this belief with a more moderate tone that emphasizes the immediate needs of personal holiness and union with Christ despite His departure from earth (2 Thess. 1:10).

As centuries have passed, Christians have not lost their belief in the integrity of the message of Christ's return. In Holy Mass, the Parousia is acknowledged when the Eucharistic acclamation of the Mystery of Faith is repeated: "We proclaim Your death, O Lord, and profess Your Resurrection until You come again."

Paschal Mystery

The salvific work of Jesus Christ, including His Passion, death, and Resurrection.

"The Paschal Mystery has two aspects: by his death, Christ liberates us from sin; by his Resurrection, he opens for us the way to a new life" (CCC 654). *Pasch* is the name of the Jewish Passover feast, coming from the Hebrew word *pasha*. St. Paul draws from his Jewish roots to tie Christ to the Pasch: "For Christ, our paschal lamb, has been sacrificed" (1 Cor. 5:7). The first Christians would slowly come to appreciate the importance of Paul's comparison of Jesus to the Passover lamb: *Why does this new message matter? Why did this God-man have to die?*

The Paschal Mystery is an answer eagerly awaited by all mankind. For ages, mankind walked and scoured the earth for answers to the greatest question of all: *What is it all for?* It is precisely in Christ's culminating work on the Cross that we understand the great mystery of our existence as the climax of history: to be forgiven and redeemed, and to anticipate eternal life in complete communion with our creator. That is to say, *Christ is the mystery*. As the *Catechism* says, "Only in the Paschal Mystery can the believer give the title 'Son of God' its full meaning" (CCC 444).

In Christian practice, the Paschal Mystery is at the core of the Church's entire liturgy. The Mass is particularly focused on Christ, who becomes our Paschal Lamb to be consumed by true believers in the Eucharist. We see this mystery in the other sacraments as well: Marriage is a reflection of the union of Christ with His Church; in Holy Orders, a man receives the powers to act *in persona Christi* and forgive sins as well as consecrate the Eucharist as Christ did at the Last Supper; in Baptism, we die with Christ to sin and rise again with Him to new life. We also witness the Paschal Mystery in Catholic funeral rites, in which the Christian faithful look forward to the resurrection of the dead with a celebration of Mass.

Passion of Christ

The sufferings and torture of Jesus that preceded His Crucifixion and death.

The Passion narrative is included in all four Gospels, but only the Gospel of John begins the Passion in the Garden of Gethsemane.

Jesus endured His suffering voluntarily, as a necessary instrument of atonement for the sins of mankind (CCC 1992). Thus, the Passion is a specific account from the life of Christ, but it is also an object of devotion since the earliest days of Christianity. In the spirit of St. Paul, who treated his own personal suffering as participation in Christ's Passion, and also as necessary sufferings for those who hope for Heaven, Christians perceive the Passion of Christ as something to share in willingly. The *Catechism of the Catholic Church* wisely reminds us of this teaching: "Suffering, a consequence of Original Sin, acquires

The Crucifixion, attributed to Pietro Perugino

a new meaning; it becomes a participation in the saving work of Jesus" (CCC 1521).

Passions

Movements of man's sensitive appetites or emotions, tending to seek an apparent good and avoid evil.

Our passions are directed toward attaining perceived goods (whether or not they are objectively good) or avoiding evil. These passions are present in man at all times, and man is always making decisions that use the passions to seek good. However, when man better understands the presence or animation of the passions inside him, he is better equipped to seek good and avoid evil, so long as his moral judgment is also well-formed. Here, we realize that the passions don't necessarily help us live *better* (or more holy) lives, but that they aid man in *understanding himself*.

Eleven passions are usually observed by philosophers and are broken into two groupings: the pleasure (or concupiscible) passions and the aggressive (or irascible) passions. The pleasure passions are love, hatred, desire, aversion, joy, and sadness. The aggressive passions are courage, fear, hope, despair, and anger. Passions are not good or evil in and of themselves, even if they seem negative. For instance, one is called to hate sin and evil (Prov. 8:13), and having pity and sharing in another's suffering and sadness can be works of mercy. The passions become morally good or evil when they cause us to act either for good or for evil, respectively. The passions, then, must come under the regulation of reason and will. "Passions 'are evil if love is evil and good if it is good'" (CCC 1766).

Patron Saints

Saints chosen for intercession (and often imitation) by a person, group, cause, profession, or place.

The emergence of patron saints came through the celebration of the martyrs, for whom churches were named since they were constructed over the places of their martyrdom or remains. With the belief in the Communion of Saints, the faithful entrusted their prayers and devotions to the intercession of the saints. And as saints (martyrs and non-martyrs alike) performed certain miracles, or their lives were associated with various causes and professions, their following became likewise associated. For example, it is said that St. Anthony of Padua lost a book of psalms to a thief who later returned it. Popular devotion to St. Anthony then led him to becoming the patron saint of lost items.

Official patron saints are approved by the Holy See. There are patron saints of many things, including the various arts, specific professions, and even entire continents—for example, St. Benedict of Nursia is the patron of Europe. A saint might have something particular in common with an area or a parish—perhaps the first immigrants to an area brought with them a great devotion to this or that saint. Sometimes saints become patrons of something because of miracles they performed. Saints also become patrons of an activity or interest because they themselves participated in or advanced it. Bernard of Clairvaux is the patron of hikers because he trekked vast distances in his ministry and preaching, and St. Rita of Cascia is the patron of lost causes because of her own difficulty in converting her husband, entering into religious life, and keeping her two sons safe from corruption.

CATHOLIC TIP

As Catholics, we have a multitude of saints to turn to for intercession and inspiration, but each of us will naturally gravitate to a few over all the rest. Choosing a patron saint deserves careful consideration. That saint is meant to be a lifelong intercessor and inspiration. The study of a saint's life, whether through reading books or trusted online sources, can help in choosing the most appropriate saint.

St. Anthony of Padua, patron saint of lost items

Each individual Catholic has a patron saint (or more than one) as well. Many people are given the name of a saint (or saints) at Baptism, and Catholics choose a patron saint when they receive the sacrament of Confirmation. The bishop (or delegated minister of the sacrament) calls the individual by the name of the saint as he administers the sacrament.

Further reading: A plethora of books about the saints are available for states of life, interests, and so on. The most admired and thorough catalog of saints with detailed hagiographies is Alban Butler's Lives of the Saints, *popularly known as "Butler's Lives."*

Peace

The establishment of order within man.

One of the effects of Original Sin is lack of peace, which we see in the division, confusion, disorder, and general frustration we face each day. This is the result of the separation from God that mankind must suffer as a result of sin. St. Augustine brilliantly wrote that peace is only achieved through well-ordered concord.

When we sin, we at once realize our lack of peace and that we are all the more restless now that we are separated from God. As Christ makes all things new, our closeness to Him brings us peace in measure. Jesus said, "Peace I leave with you; my peace I give to you; not as the world gives do I give to you" (John 14:27). The "peace of Christ," as it is known, is not the superficial peace that the world claims it wants but an inner quieting of the soul and an assent to the order of things as God created them. It is accessible through a life lived in union with God, especially through the sacraments.

Peace is a fruit of the Holy Spirit (see "**Fruits of the Holy Spirit**"), and Jesus tells us that being a peacemaker is a Beatitude. Therefore, as Christians, we strive to operate under the order of peace and goodwill in our decisions and interactions with others. The priest says at Mass and in other liturgical rites, "Peace be with you," after the model of Christ, who after His death and Resurrection used this greeting several times when He met with His disciples (see John 20:19–29). Peace thus becomes a sign of recognizing Christ's presence, and when we exhibit peace and peacemaking, we show that Christ is alive within us.

Penance

The repentance from past sins with the intention of avoiding future sin.

The word "penance" comes from the Latin *poenitentia*, which implies an undoing of sin through repentance.

For Catholics, penance has many meanings. Sacramentally, it is the satisfaction of sins, which is why the sacrament of Reconciliation is also known as the sacrament of Penance. Penance "consecrates the Christian sinner's personal and ecclesial steps of conversion, penance, and satisfaction" (CCC 1423). In the sacrament of Reconciliation, the penitent receives a penance to perform after absolution is given as satisfaction for the sin, in accord with the quality and number of sins. Common penances include saying a prayer, fasting, denying oneself of some pleasure, or performing some good work.

CATHOLIC TIP

A common objection leveled against the Catholic Faith is that penances assigned in Confession are a penalty. However, rather than a penalty, such as a fine for speeding that is meant to motivate the opposite behavior, a penance given in the sacrament of Reconciliation is an act that makes right the disorder that a sin has caused. If a person steals a wallet, it is right for the one harmed to say, "I forgive you," but complete satisfaction demands that the wallet be returned. By the same token, when a person receives absolution, he is forgiven, but full satisfaction for the sin is not achieved until the situation is righted. Thus, a prayer or other act of penance is assigned and performed.

The faithful are always welcome to perform penances outside of sacramental Confession out of sorrow for their own sins and for the good of others. In addition, because the Church teaches that a person can meritoriously suffer on behalf of others (this idea is called redemptive suffering), Catholics can perform a penance for the benefit of another or for the souls in Purgatory (see "**Purgatory**").

Ordinarily, penance refers to the sacrament, but closely related to this understanding is its meaning to describe the *act* of repenting, of being regretful for past sins committed. We are called to repent with our lips and to perform acts that satisfy our temporal punishment, but as Sacred Scripture points out, what God values above all is a truly repentant heart: "The sacrifice acceptable to God is a broken spirit; a broken and contrite heart, O God, thou wilt not despise" (Ps. 51:17).

Penitential Seasons

Liturgical seasons during which the faithful focus on penance and renewal.

Traditionally, Advent and Lent are known as the penitential seasons of the liturgical calendar. At these times, Catholic life is focused on renewal, although each of these seasons aims at a different renewal.

Lent (see "**Lent**") is the foremost season of penance. "The penitential days and times in the universal Church are every Friday of the whole year *and the season of Lent*" (CIC 1250, emphasis added). During this time, fasts are instated, and many believers take up practices such as mortifying their flesh, repenting their sins, almsgiving, and living simply. The reason for the penitential theme of Lent is clear: we join in sorrow for the suffering of our savior, and we reflect on our personal unworthiness of this immense sacrifice. Catholics prepare for Easter through the discipline of Lent.

Advent (see "**Advent**") is also a season of penance, though this penitential purpose can be a

CATHOLIC TIP

During times when we wish to express our sorrow for our sins (or for the sins of others), especially during the penitential seasons of Advent and Lent, Catholics are encouraged to pray with the aid of the penitential Psalms. Praying these Psalms during the penitential seasons has been part of Church Tradition since the seventh century A.D. Their prayerful recitation enables us to recognize our own sinfulness and ask for God's forgiveness. There are seven of these Psalms: Psalms 6, 32, 38, 51, 102, 130, 143.

cause of confusion when there is so much "Christmas in the air" culturally in the weeks leading to Christmas. Prior to modern liturgical reforms, Advent also included days of fasting. Advent is not the season of joy—that belongs to Christmas—but a season of *anticipation*. The anticipation of Advent is twofold: we anticipate the coming of the newborn Christ Child, and we also anticipate the Parousia, the Second Coming of Christ (see "**Parousia**"). As we prepare for the Second Coming, believers are called to examine our lives and repent of our sin in order to be ready for Jesus when He comes again.

Pentecost

The solemnity on which we commemorate the coming of the Holy Spirit in the Church.

Pentecost is celebrated at the end of the Easter cycle, fifty days after Easter Sunday, and it marks the end of the Easter season. The name comes from the Greek *pentēkostē*, meaning fiftieth day. Pentecost originated as a Jewish holiday, as the Old Testament mentions a "festival of the first fruits," which later also celebrated the Covenant, that occurred seven weeks after Passover (see Lev. 23:9–16, Exod. 23:16). Seven weeks are about fifty days,

Stained-glass window depicting Pentecost

CATHOLIC TIP

Non-Catholics tend to believe that the New Testament confirms that Mary had other children. They cite verses like Mark 6:3 to defend this: " 'Is not this the carpenter, the son of Mary and brother of James and Joses and Judas and Simon, and are not his sisters here with us?' And they took offense at him." How does a Catholic defend Mary's virginity against this claim?

In fact, the virgin birth of Jesus and perpetual virginity of Mary were accepted by several of the Protestant reformers, including Martin Luther, Ulrich Zwingli, John Calvin, Thomas Cranmer, and John Wesley. This doctrine was without challenge until well into the Reformation. Martin Luther writes:

> Christ, our Savior, was the real and natural fruit of Mary's virginal womb.... This was without the cooperation of a man, and she remained a virgin after that ... [and Jesus Christ] was the only Son of Mary, and the Virgin Mary bore no children besides Him.... I am inclined to agree with those who declare that "brothers" really mean "cousins" here, for Holy Writ and the Jews always call cousins brothers (Martin Luther, Sermons on the Gospel of St. John, ed. Jaroslav Pelikan [St. Louis, MO: Concordia Publishing House, 1957]).

and hence the New Testament, which was written in Greek, called the festival Pentecost, and the name was then adapted by Christians for their own festival to celebrate the day that the Holy Spirit descended upon the apostles and Mary in the Upper Room, where Jesus had told them to wait in anticipation.

Pentecost is considered to mark the beginning of the Church, since the apostles had been given authority but were told by Christ to wait until the Paraclete—the Holy Spirit—came so that they would be completely equipped for the divine mission of evangelizing the entire world.

Among the ways Catholics celebrate Pentecost is with a novena leading up to the solemnity. A novena (see "**Novena**") is a nine-day prayer (literally meaning "nine") for a particular intention and is believed to come from the account in Acts 1:12–14 in which the apostles and Mary prayed for nine days until the Holy Spirit came. In the days leading up to Pentecost, many Catholics pray the Novena to the Holy Spirit, asking each year for a special outpouring of the Spirit.

Perpetual Virginity

The dogmatic teaching that Mary maintained her virginity her entire life.

The Dogmatic Constitution on the Church, *Lumen Gentium*, adds that the virgin birth of Christ "did not diminish his mother's virginal integrity but sanctified it."[64] As it is the constant teaching of the Church, Catholics call Mary "ever virgin" in the Confiteor at Mass.

St. Thomas Aquinas explains in his *Summa Theologiae* that the virtue of virginity exceeds all chastity, even in a marriage, since it renders a person's soul perpetually open to divine things.[65] Hence, it is fitting that the sinless Mary, Mother of God, would perpetually demonstrate her openness to God's work in her life, perseverance in complete virtue, and preservation from all unchastity.

This teaching was officially recognized at the Lateran Council in A.D. 649 but was a topic of much discussion—and unanimity—among the

Church Fathers. Jerome (d. 420) was the principal apologist when Helvidius, a writer who rejected the perpetual virginity of Mary, made the assertion in Rome that the Bible contained proof that Mary had other children. Helvidius's argument was based on several texts that refer to "brothers and sisters" of Jesus, such as Mark 6:3. Jerome, however, the translator of the Vulgate Bible and the master linguist of his time, responded that "brother" and "sister" in those instances are understood either as cousins or as stepbrothers and stepsisters through a previous marriage of Joseph. The latter argument is a possible reference to the apocryphal but often referenced Protoevangelium of James. References to another Mary, such as the one in John 19:25, are also often cited by Protestants who reject Mary's virginity, but they are more likely allusions to the wife of Clopas and not to any siblings of Jesus.

Catholics rightfully defend that Mary was a virgin before, during, and after the birth of Christ, and in this unique perfection, she is also the spiritual mother of all mankind.

Pilgrimage

A religious journey to a holy place for the purpose of worship, spiritual aid, or fulfilling a vow.

A pilgrimage is an act of faith, and making a pilgrimage is an ancient practice. In the Old Testament, people of Israel longed to return to their provincial city, even after the various deportations they endured that scattered them across the known world. That's why, in the Gospels, we see so many scores of Jews returning to Jerusalem for the Passover feast.

Historically, Rome and the Holy Land have been the capital sites of pilgrimage for Christians because these were the places where the Christian Faith was planted and from which it spread throughout the world. As the Faith has grown in the world, places of pilgrimage have sprung up almost everywhere. People make pilgrimages to the

Pilgrims in Fátima

locations where great miracles have occurred or where the Virgin Mary has appeared (see "**Apparitions**"). Lourdes, France; Guadalupe, near Mexico City; Turin, Italy; and even Champion, Wisconsin, are all places where Our Lady has appeared, and all are highly praised destinations for pilgrims.

CATHOLIC TIP

Pilgrimages are not vacations. They can invite and result in relaxation, but they are not opportunities to splurge, be pampered, or purchase frivolous things or entertainment. Pilgrimages require a mix of sacrifice, silence, humility, contemplation, and prayer. If you put your desires aside for just a few days and allow yourself to be more available to the wisdom of the Holy Spirit, you can make a pilgrimage out of nearly any adventure.

Population Control

The practice of artificially limiting the size of a population.

Population control comes in a variety of forms. In China, active population control is propagated by the government through laws that limit the number of children a couple can have, and the Chinese people often make decisions about bearing children based on their baby's sex. In the Western world, population control is achieved through birth control and the active support of abortion, although these might not be directly advanced by the government. However, the practice of eugenics to reduce a certain minority from the population might be deceivingly legislated into law.

Population control has become a topic of great interest in recent decades as concern for the environment has increased. Concern for global climate change or general population expansion and inequality or inequity has created large support for population control as a solution: if there are fewer people to consume resources, then there will be less poverty, a more balanced eco-system, and more benefits for the people who are born.

But population control is a great moral threat to society. The Catholic Church views population control as an abuse of human rights. Parents have the right to regulate their birth and family size. Pope St. Paul VI argued, "The family is the primary unit in the state; do not tolerate any legislation which would introduce into the family those practices which are opposed to the natural law of God."[66]

Many opponents of population control consider over-population to be a myth, or at least exaggerated. Others see legitimate population problems in parts of the world but offer solutions that do not abuse human rights. Acknowledging the general issue of population density disproportionate to the availability of resources in some areas, Paul VI again asserted that "there are other ways by which a government can and should solve the population problem—that is to say by enacting laws which will assist families and by educating the people wisely so that the moral law and the freedom of the citizens are both safeguarded."[67]

Prayer

"The raising of one's mind and heart to God or the requesting of good things from God."[68]

Prayer is an expression of communion with God through thanksgiving, petitions, intercession, blessings, adoration, and praise. Prayer is the quintessential act of a believer as he acknowledges the Creator's ubiquity, perfect knowledge, and total authority over all things. Christ's followers are told to "pray without ceasing" (1 Thess. 5:17, NRSVCE), remaining steadfast and expectant (Col. 4:2).

Prayer comes in many forms, ranging from silent meditation on God's Word to the sacrifice of the Mass. At its end, prayer always aims to thank God, ask for forgiveness, supplicate for our needs, and come to know His perfect will. Prayer unites us to God and detaches us from the world.

Humility is the foundation of true prayer. This virtue exposes our inner lack of understanding and control and unlocks our need for God, leading us to turn to Him with greater trust. Prayer is not a

We communicate with God through prayer.

CATHOLIC TIP

Prayer is the central focus of our life in Christ, and our primary mission is to share the gospel message and the virtues of Christian living with our family and our neighbors, to the ends of the earth. This work is impossible without prayer! Novices who are eager to begin a prayer regime ought to start small, with the recitation of standard prayers such as the Lord's Prayer, Hail Mary, and Glory Be and between five and ten minutes of self-guided prayer and listening. Anyone who feels they are ready should commit to regularly reciting longer chaplets such as the Holy Rosary, the Seven Sorrows, or the chaplet of Divine Mercy and should also set aside more time devoted to contemplation.

magic wand to get what we want or a spiritual pill to make us happy but an unveiling of God's plan for our lives. All men desire this relationship with God. The *Catechism* reminds us: "Even after losing through his sin his likeness to God, man remains an image of his Creator, and retains the desire for the one who calls him into existence. All religions bear witness to men's essential search for God" (2566).

Further reading: There exist a wide variety of books on the topic of prayer from saints and recent authors too. St. Francis de Sales's Introduction to the Devout Life *is a classic, and* Time for God *by Fr. Jacques Philippe is a modern treasure. I highly recommend finding a robust assembly of Catholic prayers – the* St. Joseph Prayerbook *is a much-loved collection for all Catholics.*

Preaching

Proclamation of the Word of God and communication of God's plan of salvation to all mankind.

Preaching is an activity but also an office belonging to the teaching function of the Church. The apostles, the stewards of Christ on earth, were given charge of the duty to teach all nations what the Master commanded (Matt. 28:20). Christ the Lord commissioned the apostles to preach to all men the gospel that had been promised in former times through the prophets and that Christ Himself fulfilled and promulgated with His lips. They preached orally, by their example, and by observing what they were taught from the lips of Christ or what they had learned through the prompting of the Holy Spirit.[69]

Preaching, which is a vital part of evangelization (see "**Evangelization**"), is understood in four ways, related to the stages of evangelization:

1. *Pre-evangelization*: This stage of evangelization focuses on nonbelievers. In this stage, our preaching is an attempt to show how the gospel message fulfills man's deepest needs and desires.
2. *Evangelization*: This stage of evangelization seeks to bring inner conversion to the disposed non-believer, which must be the focus of our preaching.
3. *Catechesis*: During this stage of evangelization, our preaching must focus on the doctrinal and moral education of a believer.
4. *Mystagogy*: At this stage, we are preaching to those who are formed in the Faith, bringing them into a deeper union with Christ and the assembly of God.

Throughout the Church's history, the office of preaching has been reserved to the bishop and his delegates. Some controversy arose, then, in the early thirteenth century, when approval was granted to the Franciscans for preaching on humility and to the Dominicans for preaching on doctrine and morals. The

St. Anthony Preaching before the Fishes, by Gerard David

efforts of local bishops were greatly supplemented when the pope allowed preaching by these groups, which was largely uncanonical in those times.

Today, Canon Law and episcopal sees continue to maintain certain laws and norms regarding preaching. The 1983 Code of Canon Law still states that "the function of proclaiming the gospel has been entrusted principally to the Roman Pontiff and the college of bishops" (756) and elsewhere that the homily preached at Mass "which is part of the liturgy itself and is reserved to a priest or deacon, is preeminent" (767, no. 1).

Laypeople, too, by virtue of their Baptism and Confirmation, are called in a special way to witness to the gospel message with their lives, through catechesis, and within the context of their profession (teachers, religious educators, directors of conferences, and others), and care should always be given to ensure this preaching never opposes the local bishop's efforts and is free from errors that would lead the faithful astray.

Precepts of the Church

Moral and ecclesiastical laws that govern the life of Catholics.

The precepts of the Catholic Church are instituted to help members of the faithful better carry out their duties as members of the community. These precepts are also known as the Commandments of the Church. They are given for the spiritual good of the faithful and are obligatory. They are found in the *Catechism of the Catholic Church* paragraphs 2041–2043, and are also found in Canon Law:

1. You shall attend Mass on all Sundays and on holy days of obligation (CIC 1247).
2. You shall confess your sins at least once a year (CIC 989).
3. You shall receive the sacrament of the Eucharist at least once during the liturgical season of Easter (CIC 920).
4. You shall observe the days of fasting and abstinence established by the Church (CIC 1249–1253).
5. You shall help to provide for the needs of the Church (CIC 222).

A sixth precept is included in Canon Law, which requires the laws of marriage to be observed (CIC 1055–1165).

These precepts are meant to support the faithful in living the Christian life and in acknowledging, serving, and worshipping God. They are also meant to keep our souls clean and preserved in a state of grace. Practicing Catholics are those who observe these precepts.

CATHOLIC TIP

The Church's precepts are "the very necessary minimum in the spirit of prayer and moral effort, in the growth in love of God and neighbor" (CCC 2041). Even this "very necessary minimum" is overlooked by too many Catholics today—a symptom of the sickness of acedia (see more about this vice in "**Capital Sins**") plaguing the Church today. The precepts are the baseline of Catholic living, but we shouldn't settle for the minimum! We should give as much as we can to God and neighbor. The precepts outline the Church's ecclesiastical obligation for living, but the Gospels are replete with commands to live in love and virtue (John 13:34) and to participate in the missionary work of evangelization given to all Christians (Matt. 28:19–20).

Preferential Option for the Poor

The Church's attentiveness and responsiveness to the plight of the poor and vulnerable, in keeping with the Gospel.

The Preferential Option for the Poor, known simply as the "option for the poor and vulnerable," is the Magisterium's teaching that the spirit of evangelism and love for neighbor seeks to minister first to those most in need. As a baseline, this principle is evident throughout the Bible and in Christ's teachings: from the Exodus, emancipating God's people from harsh slavery, to the Beatitudes, which begin with, "Blessed are you poor, for yours is the kingdom of God" (Luke 6:20). Christ's parable of the rich man and Lazarus is an extraordinary elucidation of God's preference for the poor, as well as the impending judgment of those who ignore them (Luke 16:19–31).

The Old and New Testaments express a continuity of this preference for the poor and vulnerable. In Pope St. John Paul II's tremendous encyclical *Laborem Exercens*, he writes, "The Church is firmly committed to this cause, for she considers it her mission, her service, a proof of her fidelity to Christ, so that she can truly be called the 'Church of the Poor.'"[70] He confirms that the "poor" come in many forms, including not only the materially poor but those literally destitute of resources and those whose human rights are violated.

We are not called to prefer the poor simply because they are poor, nor is there any class war inherent in this teaching. Rather, as the Bible exhorts us: "You shall do no injustice in judgment; you shall not be partial to the poor or defer to the great, but in righteousness shall you judge your neighbor" (Lev. 19:15), and "You shall not be partial in judgment; you shall hear the small and the great alike" (Deut. 1:17). What Christ teaches is that Christian preference for the poor comes from love of God. When we serve the "least of these," we serve Christ and affirm our love of Christ, who is mysteriously present in the underprivileged of the world (Matt. 25:34–40).

Priesthood

The second order of Holy Orders and the universal mission of every baptized person to share in offering Christ's perfect sacrifice.

First of all, the priesthood refers to the ordained ministerial priesthood, and secondly, to the universal priesthood shared by all believers in a real and efficacious way through Baptism. Risen with Christ, we share in Christ's life and identity, which includes His priesthood. As St. Peter reminds us, "But you are a chosen race, a royal priesthood, a holy nation, God's own people" (1 Pet. 2:9).

The ministerial priesthood is a fulfillment of the priesthood of the Old Law, which was an office held by the Levites, the tribe chosen by God to produce male priests who would offer sacrifices on behalf of the people of Israel. Jesus then established at the Last Supper the priesthood that would minister to the people of God. Today these priests are given the authority to administer the sacraments, except for Holy Orders and Confirmation; however, these latter two can be delegated by a bishop under special circumstances (for example, when the bishop is unavailable or at the Easter Vigil in each parish—see CIC 883-884).

Jesus Christ is the supreme priest and is the model for the ministerial priesthood. The Catholic Church even teaches that priests act in the person of Christ (*in persona Christi*): "The ordained minister is the sacramental bond that ties the liturgical action to what the apostles said and did and, through them, to the words and actions of Christ, the source and foundation of the sacraments" (CCC 1120). Upon this foundation is a unique calling particular to the priesthood, that of *ministry*. The word often translated as ministry actually means "service" in Greek (*diakonia*). Being an ordained priest, then, gives a man the duty of building up the Body of Christ primarily through the sacraments, but also in a practical and pastoral way as he attends to his parish or community flock.

Priestly ordinations of members of the Institute of the Incarnate Word

In the Roman Catholic Church, ordained priests normally remain celibate, though priests can marry in some of the Eastern Catholic churches. This celibacy is a matter of practice and discipline but not dogma, meaning that it has changed and can change again throughout the history of the Church. However, the ordained priesthood is always reserved to men and always will be solely male because Christ established this priesthood and the Church does not have the authority to change this important teaching.

Private Property

The natural right of each person to own and use goods.

Private property is a natural right that governments must preserve and private citizens must use for God's purposes.[71] This right is included in the Church's social teaching (see "**Catholic Social Teaching**"). The Catholic Church's teaching on private property stems from its understanding of creation: "In the beginning God entrusted the earth and its resources to the common stewardship of mankind to take care of them, master them by labor, and enjoy their fruits" (CCC 2402). The Church thus is outspoken in opposition to governments who seek to seize or sanction their citizens' private property (which includes ecclesiastical property).

God created the wealth of the world, and all wealth belongs to Him first, so our ownership and use of property must acknowledge this reality. Thus, wealthy people have a directly correlated responsibility regarding private property, as the *Catechism* teaches: "The ownership of any property makes its holder a steward of Providence, with the task of making it fruitful and communicating its benefits to others, first of all his family" (2404).

In the circumstance where a central government treats property as a shared concern, bringing property under the supervision of the state, the Church concurs that this is a good social policy. "[When] the State brings private ownership into harmony with the needs of the common good, it does not commit a hostile act against private owners but rather does them a friendly service ... it does not destroy private possessions, but safeguards them; and it does not weaken private property rights, but strengthens them."[72]

Further reading: Quadragesimo Anno *by Pope Pius XI, and* Mater et Magistra *by Pope St. John XXIII.*

Protestantism

The denomination of Christians who first separated from the Catholic Church during the Protestant Reformation and who continue to be out of communion with the Church.

Although there were precursors to the Protestant Reformation, it is recognized to have officially begun in 1517 in Germany, when Martin Luther, an Augustinian priest, questioned and accused the Catholic Church with his *95 Theses*, which primarily attacked the pope's authority and the treatment of indulgences. In the decades that followed, further Protestant divisions quickly arose throughout Europe. The original Protestant churches remain to this day: Lutheran, Anglican, and Calvinist. But if we consider each Protestant church with independent hierarchy and beliefs to be separate from the others, there are now thousands of Protestant denominations throughout the world.

All Protestants share two core beliefs: that the Bible is the only source of faith and that a believer is justified by faith alone. These are known, respectively, as the doctrines of *sola scriptura* and *sola fide*, and they are generally traced back to the founding Reformers, such as Martin Luther, Ulrich Zwingli, and John Knox. All Protestant denominations are

CATHOLIC TIP

Regarding the Protestant doctrine of *sola scriptura*, it's important to understand that this doctrine cannot be found anywhere in Scripture. In the Old Testament, the Scriptures are never referred to as the dominant authority over God's people. There was not even an accepted list of books belonging to the Old Testament mentioned in the Hebrew Scriptures! The same is true of the New Testament writings. In Acts 15, for example, we read about the Council of Jerusalem, in which the doctrine about circumcision was addressed and clarified not by reference to Scripture but by the authority of the apostles.

The official Canon of Scripture was decided by the Church in the fourth century: it is not listed and named within Scripture itself. If the Church has authority over the Canon of Scripture, it also shares authority over the interpretation of those scriptures, which means that Scripture itself cannot be the only source of our belief as Christians.

also united in their rejection of the authority of the pope as the head of the Church.

Most Protestant denominations today have minimized the importance of liturgy, rejected the ministerial priesthood and its disciplines, and rejected the substance and effects of most sacraments. Baptism is the remaining sacrament common to most Protestants, though some Protestant denominations do not attribute much theological significance to it and many disagree on the practice of adult versus infant Baptism. Most Protestants today also deny Mary's perpetual virginity and freedom from Original Sin.

The Council of Trent (1545–1563) was the Catholic Church's response to the Protestant Reformation. During this ecumenical council, the Catholic Church defended the Church's teaching against the theological attacks of Protestant reformers and also provided ample time and care to fortify the social reform that was needed within the Church itself to reverse years of abuses and controversy. In full, the Church took nearly four hundred years to execute all of the reforms of Trent.

Further reading: The Faith of Our Fathers *by James Cardinal Gibbons. This book remains a treasured collection of systematic arguments that defend the Catholic Faith against Protestantism.*

Providence

God's personal act of ordering all things to the purpose, intent, and end of His perfect will.

The term "providence" comes from the Latin word *providere*, which means "to look ahead, prepare, and supply," and it speaks to the constant provision and portioning God gives to His entire creation for His purposes. The *Catechism* eloquently teaches, "The universe was created 'in a state of journeying' (*in statu viae*) toward an ultimate perfection yet to be attained, to which God has destined it" (302).

Jesus confirms that God's will is oriented to providing for everyone's true needs: "Look at the birds of the air: they neither sow nor reap nor gather into barns, and yet your heavenly Father feeds them. Are you not of more value than they?" (Matt. 6:26). We understand God's providence to be judicious and precise, not random: "The lot is cast into the lap, but the decision is wholly from the Lord" (Prov. 16:33).

In carrying out His plan, God allows us a level of participation: Because of our free will, we can choose whether or not to be in step with God's plan. This concrete providence and man's ability to choose reveals both God's supreme authority and His goodness: Our Lord calls us friends, not slaves.

The topic of divine providence always raises the question of the problem of evil. If God is good and supreme, why does He allow evil? But Christianity, apart from every other religion in the world, has a unique take on evil. Our faith is founded on our perfectly good God becoming man for the sole purpose of accepting an unjust accusation, a brutal Passion, and a horrifying death on a Cross. The problem of evil is at the core of Christianity, and at that core is the solution. The greatest evil the world has ever seen is the murder of the Son of God, but through this death, enormous good was brought forth: our eternal salvation. Thus St. Paul could write with confidence, "We know that in everything God works for good with those who love him, who are called according to his purpose" (Rom. 8:28). The world is looking for an explanation to the problem of evil, but Christianity answers with a perfect Person.

Further reading: Jean-Pierre De Caussade's Abandonment to Divine Providence.

Purgatory

The state of souls who require final purification from sin after death before they can enter Heaven.

In Purgatory, souls undergo temporal punishment due to their venial sins and forgiven mortal sins.

Madonna and Child with Souls in Purgatory, by Luca Giordano

Purgatory is the necessary state for believers and friends of God who have not achieved perfect sanctification, though they are assured of heavenly glory. It is not, contrary to some assumptions in modern times, a lost teaching of the Church but is still a core Catholic belief regarding the afterlife. Purgatory is a topic that is always mentioned along with death, judgment, Heaven, and Hell—the Four Last Things (see "**Four Last Things**").

Catholic teaching on Purgatory importantly reminds us that the Church is inseparable, regardless of the state of the soul of the believer. The souls in Purgatory, then, as part of the Communion of Saints (see "**Communion of Saints**"), are also known as the "church penitent" or "church suffering," due to the state of penance and punishment they must endure.

While the Bible does not use the term "Purgatory," it does depict the state. St. Paul writes, "If any man's work is burned up, he will suffer loss, though he himself will be saved, but only as through fire" (1 Cor. 3:15). In the Old Testament account of Judas Maccabeus, "he made atonement for the dead, that they might be delivered from their sin" (2 Macc.

CATHOLIC TIP

The souls in Purgatory endure a period of God's merciful purging that is beyond our understanding. But the theological certainty of the unity of the Church remains firm: "Therefore the union of the wayfarers with the brethren who have gone to sleep in the peace of Christ is not in the least weakened or interrupted, but on the contrary, according to the perpetual faith of the Church, is strengthened by communication of spiritual goods" (*Lumen Gentium*, no. 49). Accordingly, we are taught to pray for the souls in Purgatory and to apply our works (and indulgences) to their assistance.

Two excellent ways to pray for these souls are with the Divine Mercy chaplet and the recitation of the Holy Rosary. Another very efficacious (and practical) means of aiding the souls in Purgatory is by visiting a cemetery and praying for the departed. Each of these is given an indulgence should the correct requirements be satisfied (see "**Indulgences**").

12:45). The *Catechism* tells us, "From the beginning the Church has honored the memory of the dead and offered prayers in suffrage for them … so that, thus purified, they may attain the beatific vision of God" (1032).

Closely related to the teaching on Purgatory is the doctrine of indulgences (see "**Indulgences**"). Indulgences, which are the remission before God of the temporal punishment due sins, can be merited by us for the souls in Purgatory. This means that those on earth may directly aid those who are still undergoing their final purging. St. John Chrysostom wrote, "If Job's sons were purified by their father's sacrifice, why would we doubt that our offerings for the dead bring them some consolation? Let us not hesitate to help those who have died and to offer our prayers for them."[73]

Further reading: Purgatory Is for Real *by Karlo Broussard is a great resource on the topic of Purgatory.*

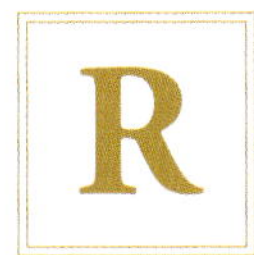

Racism

A prejudicial and discriminatory treatment of persons based on their race, color, beliefs, or culture.

Racism is condemned by the Church. Leaders in the Catholic Church, including various popes, have spoken out against racism and the systematic oppression of minorities, condemning not only the legalized racism of apartheid but also anti-Semitism, tribal conflicts, and other forms of racial prejudice. The Church has also strongly defended the rights of aboriginal people for centuries; one of the most famous defenders of native peoples, for example, is Bartolomé de las Casas, who called for the end of slavery in the Spanish Americas in the early 1500s. More recently, in 1989, the Pontifical Commission for Peace and Justice drew up *The Church and Racism* at the request of Pope St. John Paul II, which declares, "Harboring racist thoughts and entertaining racist attitudes is a sin."[74]

Racism is a societal disease that often creates generations of hate. The Church's treatment of racism stems from its teaching on the dignity of the human person. Each individual is created by God in His image and is equal to every other person in worth. Baptism further brings people of every nation together as brothers and sisters in the one Body of Christ. Racism, then, is a sin against the belief in God as Father to all mankind and is against the very nature of the Church, which is the promoter and vessel of unity among all peoples.

Further reading: Edward Feser's All One in Christ *contains a wealth of information on the Christian approach to modern racism.*

Reason

The cognitive capacity of a human being to query, investigate, discern, and resolve rational problems.

As a rational creature made in God's image, man is endowed with reason. St. Thomas Aquinas tells us that reason is an operation of the intellect of man. This classical view of reason is led by discursive thinking, wherein man applies what he knows about truths and principles and forms conclusions. Reason, then, is a faculty of the mind that enables man to consider his environment and his understanding of life, nature, and his awareness of himself, in order to better navigate the notions and problems set before him.

Catholic teaching also recognizes what is known as an "age of reason," a state of rational development at which a person has acquired the ability to distinguish between right and wrong and understands moral responsibility for his conduct. This age is traditionally observed to be seven years old, though depending on mental capacity, it may vary. This notion of the age of reason explains why children usually receive First Holy Communion around age seven.

The Church teaches that through reason, a person can know of God's existence. Particularly in our day, with the modern technology and science demanding "proofs," the Catholic Church preaches a consistent message: "God, the beginning and end of all things, can be known with certainty from created reality by the light of human reason" (*Dei Verbum*). The Bible, too, professes this truth: "Ever since the creation of the world [God's] invisible nature, namely, his eternal power and deity, has been clearly perceived in the things that have been made" (Rom. 1:20).

In an age of increasing relativism, it's essential for Catholics to know the truth and to be able to defend it reasonably, particularly through the study of good Catholic philosophy.

Further reading: Ralph McInerny's A First Glance at St. Thomas Aquinas.

CATHOLIC TIP

We want to be better thinkers, able to distinguish good philosophy from bad. The Church says that if we want the gospel to thrive, we must return to the study of philosophy, especially the Classics, such as Plato and Aristotle, and the writings of St. Thomas Aquinas. This was the position of Leo XIII in *Aeterni Patris* (1879) and, it was echoed by John Paul II in *Fides et Ratio*. "Faith is not opposed to reason" (CCC 35)—on the contrary, reason supports and bolsters our faith.

Reception of Holy Communion

The reception of the Eucharist, the sacrament of the Body and Blood of Christ.

Catholics believe that the celebration of the Eucharist is a sign of the oneness of our faith, life, and worship. The Church therefore provides pastoral guidance and law concerning worthy reception of the Eucharist.

Each person must examine his own conscience for worthiness and ensure he is in a state of grace before receiving Communion (1 Cor. 11:28). Catholics who are conscious of committing a mortal sin that has not been absolved through a sacramental Confession are obligated to abstain from receiving Communion unless there is a grave reason and there is no opportunity to confess (CIC 916). We must be in the state of grace to receive Communion, since it is the sacrament that most closely unites us to Christ. The *Didache*, an early Christian catechism, urges us: "But first make confession of your faults, so that your sacrifice may be a pure one."[75]

The Last Communion of St. Mary of Egypt, by Marcantonio Franceschini

CATHOLIC TIP

Receiving Communion is a sacred act. We should receive with humility, reverence, and respect at all times. In the United States, the established norm is to receive standing, preceded by a reverent bow. When the person distributing Communion says, "The Body of Christ" while holding up the host, the receiver should audibly say, "Amen" (demonstrating his assent of faith to the reality of the Eucharist), receive, and consume immediately. The same applies to receiving from the chalice.

The history of receiving Communion is generally clear to scholars. The apostles and Christians for the first centuries of the Church probably received in the hand, almost universally. Over time, a standard practice of receiving directly on the tongue was adopted in many places throughout Christendom. Today, in the Roman Rite in the Ordinary Form, Catholics may receive directly on the tongue or in the hand. No matter how one receives Holy Communion, the most important thing is to receive worthily, with love and reverence for the True Presence of Christ in the Eucharist. One should never look down on a fellow Catholic for their choice of reception. However, if one witnesses some abuse or alteration of the guidelines for reception, they should report it to the priest or offer a gentle and tactful correction.

In the Catholic Church, we "receive" Communion (rather than "take" Communion), since it is a gift and something to participate in: "The cup of blessing which we bless, is it not a participation in the blood of Christ? The bread which we break, is it not a participation in the body of Christ?" (1 Cor. 10:16).

In striving to maintain unity in the Church and the fundamental moral obligations of all Christians, the bishop plays a vital role in shepherding his flock in overseeing the distribution of Communion, and as such, he is fully authorized to refuse Holy Communion to public persons and lawmakers who refuse to abide by the moral guidance provided by the Church.

Non-Catholics are welcome to *celebrate* the Holy Eucharist, meaning that they attend and fully participate in the Mass but without receiving Holy Communion: "Because Catholics believe that the celebration of the Eucharist is a sign of the reality of the oneness of faith, life, and worship, members of those churches with whom we are not yet fully united are ordinarily not admitted to Holy Communion."[76] Canon Law and the United States bishops have provided clear guidance that unless extraordinary circumstances prevail and a diocesan bishop provides permission in accordance with Canon Law, non-Catholics are not permitted to receive Holy Communion (CCC 1401).

The Church also tells us to fast prior to receiving Holy Communion: "A person who is to receive the Most Holy Eucharist is to abstain for at least one hour before Holy Communion from any food and drink, except for only water and medicine" (CIC 919, no. 1).

Access to the Code of Canon Law is free on the Vatican.va website. All should make themselves familiar with the paragraphs that concern reception of the Eucharist, canons 912–923.

Reconciliation

The sacrament by which God renews our friendship with Him.

The sacrament of Reconciliation is known by several names, including Confession, penance, the sacrament of forgiveness, and the sacrament of conversion (CCC 1423–1424). All of these titles point to a special and distinct aspect of the sacrament. It is called "reconciliation" after the great act of reconciling in the redemptive work of Christ. Since sin separates man from God, Christ instituted a means of reintegrating Christians into His life through absolution (see "**Absolution**") and penance (see "**Penance**"). Thus, Jesus is at the center of each act of personal confession, but He is especially present in the context of the sacrament, where His presence is more fully demonstrated in the ministerial work of the priest giving absolution.

In the sacrament, the Church teaches that those who repent of their sins "obtain pardon from God's mercy for the offense committed against him, and are, at the same time, reconciled with the Church which they have wounded by their sins and which by charity, by example, and by prayer labors for their conversion" (CCC 1422). Christ bestowed this wonderful gift on the Church in the power He gave to His apostles: "Receive the Holy Spirit. If you forgive the sins of any, they are forgiven; if you retain the sins of any, they are retained" (John 20:22–23).

Before Confession, one must make a thorough examination of conscience (see "**Examination of Conscience**") in order to recall the type, number, and impact of our sins. We must confess any mortal sins we remember, and it is good also to confess any venial sins (CIC 988). We increase in virtue at an astonishing rate when we visit the sacrament regularly. If one suffers from some habitual sin, a consistent confession *and consistent confessor* is recommended. Honestly confessing our sins, obtaining the sacramental graces that are so powerful for our souls, and receiving absolution is the best way to overcome sin.

CATHOLIC TIP

Catholics often wonder how often they should go to Confession. According to Church Law, we are required to make a Confession at least once a year (CIC 989). Yet one must be free of mortal sin before receiving Communion, so adequate consideration must be applied, especially if we want to receive Communion regularly—a good practice that further intensifies God's grace and enables us to do good and avoid sin. So it is a good idea to make time for Confession more often than once a year—once per month or perhaps more frequently, depending on your state of life and obligations.

Redemption

The saving work of Jesus Christ in His life, death, and Resurrection, by which He restored man to friendship with God.

By Jesus' life-giving death and Resurrection, all men have the opportunity to be restored to the life of grace and a relationship with God. Man was created to live in perfect happiness with God, but sin caused a severe disruption: "By our first parents' sin, the devil has acquired a certain domination over man" (CCC 407). Despite this separation, God, in His perfect love and goodness, would not abandon man, and so God established a means of redeeming us.

Too often today, the word "redemption" describes an economic exchange, such as "Redeem this bottle for five cents." Or we think of it as a matter of satisfying the law: he was condemned, but later redeemed by his good behavior. But the redemption of Christ should not be treated as an economic or judicial transaction. Rather, His redemption is a justification, an undeserved restoration. Christ has bought us back at a high price, as St. Paul effectively pronounces (1 Cor. 6:20), but it is important to affirm that our redemption is not merely transactional but a *bringing back to our former state*.

The New Testament also contains an awareness of redemption as a *rescuing*: by His redemptive work, Jesus saves us from a life of emptiness and sin and restores us to life in God, in whose life we are capable of true happiness: "You know that you were ransomed from the futile ways inherited from your fathers, not with perishable things such as silver or gold, but with the precious blood of Christ" (1 Pet. 1:18–19).

The redemption of Christ instituted a *means* of salvation. Hence, man is redeemed, but we also must "work out" our salvation (Phil. 2:12), which comes through a participation in the ministry of the Church and a sacramental life that brings sanctifying grace required to regain the kingdom of Heaven. "Or do you presume upon the riches of his kindness and forbearance and patience? Do you not know that God's kindness is meant to lead you to repentance?" (Rom. 2:4).

Relativism

A philosophical worldview according to which knowledge, truth, and morality pertain to an individual person and culture and are not absolute.

Relativism may be a sort of heresy, perhaps the most menacing of our time. It is a heresy because it removes and replaces truth with self-identified realities that vary from person to person. For one person, for example, abortion may be a moral right, and for another, it may be a grave violence against the innocent. But under the ideas of relativism, anything goes, and all are free to decide for themselves.

Relativism has become increasingly popular in modern society because it is *easy* and it frees individuals from personal responsibility, but the consequences of relativism damage people and society. First, if we take relativism to its logical conclusions, we arrive at a society in which nobody is right. True justice and scientific inquiry are impossible to achieve because everyone is entitled to his own version of the truth. Second, relativism leads to indifference. If everyone's "truth" is relative to his independent judgment, nobody has a need to defend any argument, and we find a paralysis of conscience in every component of society.

CATHOLIC TIP

Relativism is the scourge of our age, and every Catholic must be able to talk about it when evangelizing. To counter relativism, we can first point out its absurdity. Relativism says there are no absolute truths, but this statement automatically contradicts itself by resting on an absolute truth. Addressing relativism requires tactful correction, patience, prayer, forgiveness, and yes, even comfort. It's important to point out the flaw in relativistic arguments, yet we must subscribe to the truth with generosity and serenity. Offer a counter argument that is enriched with authenticity, love, and compassion. You might not get the response you want, but planting seeds of doubt with charity will help.

Cardinal Joseph Ratzinger, before he became Pope Benedict XVI, expressed concern about the cancerous moral principle of relativism. Allowing ourselves to be "tossed here and there, carried about by every wind of doctrine" seems the only attitude that can cope with modern times. As a result, we are building a "dictatorship of relativism," as he called it, that does not recognize anything as definitive—even truth itself—and whose ultimate goal consists solely of one's ego and desires in forming conclusions and moral views.[77]

Relics

Objects kept as a memorial of a holy person, usually remains of a saint.

The word "relic" comes from the Latin word *relictus*, meaning "left behind." Relics include the bodies of saints and holy people, as well as their clothing, other objects they used, and objects that have been touched to them.

There are three classifications of relics. First-class relics are any piece of the body of a saint, such as bones, hair, teeth, hands, flesh, blood, or fractions of any of these physical remains. Second-class relics are any object intimately connected with the saint, especially things of personal use, such as clothing, or items associated with important events in the life of the saint. Third-class relics are items that have been touched to the body of a saint. Usually, these are pieces of cloth, oils known to have been purposely touched to the corpse, and sacramentals such as crucifixes, rosaries, or scapulars touched to a relic. This procedure requires no special permission so long as the owner of the relic has consented to this use.

History has also preserved an array of familiar tools from the suffering and Crucifixion of Christ, known as the relics of the Passion. These include the True Cross, the Shroud of Turin, the Veil of Veronica, the nails used, the crown of thorns, and the lance that pierced His side.

Reliquary containing one of the bones of St. Sebastian

Private and public veneration of relics remains a distinctive part of the pious practice of the Faith in the Catholic Church. The *Catechism* explains: "The religious sense of the Christian people has always found expression in various forms of piety surrounding the Church's sacramental life, such as the veneration of relics" (1674).

When the Church says that a relic is "authentic," the relic comes from credible sources, and diligent efforts have been taken to ensure—not with strict certainty, but with prudent human confidence—that the relic is from the correct body and the correct body part. The local bishop is the principal ward and identifier of relics, overseeing the sealing of reliquaries and corresponding documents with his episcopal stamp in wax, making any tampering immediately evident. Occasionally, a bishop will permit

CATHOLIC TIP

Relics can be a point of confusion for non-Catholics, and even for many well-intentioned Catholics, because the veneration of relics can be confused with idolatry, which is strictly forbidden in the Ten Commandments. St. Jerome wrote in the fourth century, "We do not worship, we do not adore, for fear that we should bow down to the creature rather than to the Creator, but we venerate the relics of the martyrs in order the better to adore Him whose martyrs they are" (St. Jerome, Letter to Riparius [A.D. 404]).

The Catholic Church does not condone or promote the worship of relics; rather, Catholics *venerate* relics. Whether in public or private, the veneration of saints takes form in the recognition of the supernatural excellence of these holy men and women. We venerate them by remembering their lives, imitating their charity, asking for their intercession, and honoring their bodies, through which they gave their lives to the Lord. The saints point us to Christ. It is fitting, then, that Catholics honor the bodies of the members of the Body of Christ: "For just as the body is one and has many members, and all the members of the body, though many, are one body, so it is with Christ" (1 Cor. 12:12). The saints have a right to be venerated, but only God has the right to be adored in worship (see "**Adoration**" for more on this distinction).

a non-invasive investigation to better determine authenticity, though even with modern technologies, complete assurance cannot be achieved—we rely on confidence and knowledge.

The reason Catholics venerate relics lies in the Christian teaching that the bodies of the saints on earth were living members of the Mystical Body of Christ (see Rom. 12:5; 1 Cor. 12:12–27; Eph. 3:6; Col. 1:18), and as such, were temples of the Holy Spirit (see 1 Cor. 3:16–17, 6:19). We believe that through these relics, God bestows many benefits on the faithful. The Church encourages the veneration of relics, but it does not obligate Catholics to do so.

Further reading: My book 20 Answers: Relics and Sacramentals *offers some helpful background on relics.*

Religious Liberty

Freedom to believe in and practice one's religion of preference according to one's conscience.

Religious liberty touches on man's human rights, which should be protected and sanctioned by the state. Man's most fundamental treasure is his freedom. God created us with free will, and He wants us to freely choose to love Him and live in accord with His law. Only when a person is free to act for or against God is he truly responsible for his action. Faith is a supernatural gift we must *choose* to accept. Forcing someone to accept faith or forcibly preventing someone from practicing their faith goes against the Church's teaching and the way of Christ we find in the Bible.

The Catholic Church teaches the importance of religious liberty in the public sphere. This freedom should be understood as freedom *for* religion, not freedom *from* religion. Sadly, too often in Western society, religious liberty is understood as the removal of religious expression from the public square rather than the safeguarding of such expression. Thus, the Church teaches, "But that ominous doctrine which attempts to build a society with no regard whatever for religion, and which attacks and destroys the religious liberty of its citizens, is rightly to be rejected."[78]

Further reading: See the Catechism of the Catholic Church *paragraphs 2104–2109.*

Resurrection of the Dead

The reunion of the body and soul of every person who ever lived, which will take place "at the last day" (CCC 1001).

Catholics throughout the world recite their faith in the resurrection of the dead in the Apostles' Creed: "I believe in ... the resurrection of the body and life everlasting." It is also included in the Nicene Creed: "I look forward to the resurrection of the dead." Christian understanding of the resurrection of the dead is rooted in the Resurrection of Jesus from the dead, for we believe that as members of His Body, we will follow where our Head has gone. In this way, we uphold a double meaning of the resurrection with Christ: at Baptism to our new life in Christ, and at the last day with our new body.

The *Catechism* refers to the resurrection of the dead (or the resurrection of the body) as progressively revealed (992). Not only did God foreshadow the resurrection in certain Old Testament events, but it was also explicitly prophesied (Ps. 16:9–10, Isa. 26:19). The idea of the resurrected body is present in the Old Testament: "Thy dead shall live, their bodies shall rise. O dwellers in the dust, awake and sing for joy!" (Isa. 26:19); "And many of those who sleep in the dust of the earth shall awake, some to everlasting life, and some to shame and everlasting contempt" (Dan. 12:2).

In Jesus' day, belief in the resurrection was widespread among the Jews, though certain sects did not accept it. We see the Jews' desire to understand the resurrection when Jesus had to answer pointed questions from the Sadducees about the impact of a resurrection on marriage (see Mark 12:18–27). The promise of the resurrection was brought to completion by Christ in His death and rising.

It is clear from the New Testament that Christians have always believed in the bodily resurrection of all the dead. For example, in 1 Corinthians 15:1–58, Paul's proclamation unites Christians with the real and visible Resurrection of Christ firstly in Baptism and finally in the resurrection of the body and soul *with* Christ, as Jesus stated: "I am the Resurrection and the life" (John 11:25).

The resurrection of the dead will include all people, not just those in Heaven. In answer to the question "Who will be resurrected?" the Church and the Bible are in one accord: "All the dead." Jesus taught that "those who have done good [will go] to the resurrection of life, and those who have done evil [will go] to the resurrection of judgment" (John 5:29).

Resurrection of Jesus

The rising of Christ from the grave three days after His Crucifixion, death, and burial.

The Resurrection is the bedrock of our Christian faith, and the event is described by all four Gospel narratives (see Matt. 28, Mark 16, Luke 24, and John 20). The word "resurrection" comes from the Latin *resurgere*, meaning "to rise again." Christians believe that Jesus was raised from the dead by His own power, and that by His Resurrection He triumphed over death, which plagues mankind as a result of Original Sin.

We profess our belief in Christ's Resurrection in the Apostles' and Nicene Creeds. The Resurrection of Christ is essential to Christianity. It proves that Jesus is God, since He has power over death. It proves that Jesus is the Messiah who fulfills all the prophecies of the Old Testament. And it proves that Jesus is the Savior of all mankind, as He promises that the just will rise with Him in victory (John 3:16, 11:25). And even more than a proof, He

The Resurrection of Christ, by Maerten de Vos

promises us that His Resurrection is also ours (see "**Baptism**" for more).

Jesus' Resurrection is a critical component of our belief in Jesus Christ because if He did not rise from the dead, He would simply be a moral teacher who died a brutal death. His death would be like any other person in history who died for a good cause, and we would have no reason to believe that Jesus is truly God. And so Paul emphatically argues for the Resurrection as the vital, central tenet of the Christian Faith: "Now if Christ is preached as raised from the dead, how can some of you say that there is no resurrection of the dead? But if there is no resurrection of the dead, then Christ has not been raised; if Christ has not been raised, then our preaching is in vain and your faith is in vain" (1 Cor. 15:12–14). The Resurrection of Christ is therefore the key aspect of our Faith, and all believers must hold it with conviction.

Revelation

God making Himself and His divine will known to man.

Revelation, the process of making known what is unknown, is initiated by God, and we are called to participate in this process. Catholics understand God's revelation as happening gradually, through different modes, and for various purposes. Jesus Christ is the fullness of God's revelation of Himself (and His plan) to man.

God reveals Himself in many different ways. He reveals Himself through the natural world, and human beings can come to know Him through His creation. He further revealed Himself through His covenants with His people, allowing His followers to understand His ways. Then, through the prophets, God revealed His divine will. God's final revelation of Himself came in the Person and teachings of Christ, the mediator and fullness of all revelation (CCC 65): "In many and various ways God spoke of old to our fathers by the prophets; but in these last days he has spoken to us by a Son, whom he appointed the heir of all things, through whom also he created the world" (Heb. 1:1–2).

God's gradual revealing of Himself to man is known as divine revelation, and the sum of the teachings of Christ is known as the deposit of faith (see "**Deposit of Faith**"). This gradual process of God imparting knowledge of Himself to man, also known as "public revelation," ended with the death of the apostle John. The Catholic Church continues to preach, teach, protect, and administer the full deposit of faith.

CATHOLIC TIP

How was the Faith communicated after the apostles? There was a strong spoken tradition among the people of God before Christ, and this tradition continued in the early Church with the apostles. Eventually they were divinely inspired to write down some of their teachings. But we have to remember that a FedEx truck didn't deliver Bibles to the Upper Room; the gospel of salvation through Jesus Christ was transmitted as an oral tradition long before it was written down. Relatedly, it was St. John whose Gospel reminded us that "there are also many other things which Jesus did; were every one of them to be written, I suppose that the world itself could not contain the books that would be written" (John 21:25).

When St. Paul wrote to the Thessalonians, "Brethren, stand firm and hold to the traditions which you were taught by us, either by word of mouth or by letter" (2 Thess. 2:15), he referred not only to the *mode* of the teaching, but to *his authority* as a transmitter of the teachings of Christ. Thus, revelation is cohesive and harmonious, found in Tradition and in Scripture. This is a useful lesson to bring up when sharing the Faith with those who believe Scripture alone is the source of our belief.

In Catholicism, we also recognize private revelation, which is revelation bestowed upon a person or group for some benefit to the individual and the Church as a whole. "It is not [the role of private revelation] to improve or complete Christ's definitive Revelation, but to help live more fully by it in a certain period of history" (CCC 67). We are not required to believe private revelation, but we are encouraged to believe in and participate in those private revelations recognized and approved by the Church, such as the Rosary.

Further reading: Dei Verbum *(the Dogmatic Constitution on Divine Revelation) is the authoritative source on the Church's teaching on revelation.*

Rosary

A sacramental, a pious devotion and prayer in which we meditate on the lives of Jesus and Mary, and the physical sacramental used to say the prayer and other chaplets.

The Rosary is a popular Marian devotion in which we meditate on twenty "mysteries"—events of Jesus' life. Traditionally, there were fifteen mysteries of the Rosary divided into three sets of five:

+ **Joyful Mysteries** (prayed on Mondays and Saturdays)
  The Annunciation
  The Visitation
  The Nativity
  The Presentation of Jesus at the Temple
  The Finding of Jesus in the Temple
+ **Sorrowful Mysteries** (prayed on Tuesdays and Fridays)
  The Agony in the Garden
  The Scourging at the Pillar
  The Crowning with Thorns
  The Carrying of the Cross
  The Crucifixion and Death of our Lord
+ **Glorious Mysteries** (prayed on Sundays and Wednesdays)
  The Resurrection
  The Ascension
  The Descent of the Holy Spirit
  The Assumption of Mary
  The Coronation of the Virgin

CATHOLIC TIP

The Rosary should become an indelible fixture in the spiritual life of every Catholic. The popular method of praying the Rosary is well-known and accessible. Here is a simple "how-to" on praying the Holy Rosary.

1. Make the Sign of the Cross. Pray the Apostles' Creed.
2. On the first bead, pray one Our Father.
3. On the set of three beads, pray three Hail Marys, followed by a Glory Be.
4. Announce the first mystery, then pray one Our Father.
5. On the first set of ten beads, pray ten Hail Marys, followed by a Glory Be and the Fatima Prayer (O my Jesus, forgive us our sins, save us from the fires of Hell, and lead all souls into Heaven, especially those in most need of Thy mercy).
6. For each subsequent decade, announce the mystery, then pray one Our Father, ten Hail Marys, a Glory Be, and the Fatima Prayer.
7. Concluding prayers:

   Hail, Holy Queen, Mother of Mercy! Hail, our Life, our Sweetness and our Hope! To thee do we cry, poor banished children of Eve; to thee do we send up our sighs, mourning and weeping in this valley of tears. Turn, then, most gracious advocate, thine eyes of mercy toward us, and after this, our exile, show unto us the blessed fruit of thy womb, Jesus. O clement, O loving, O sweet Virgin Mary!

V: Pray for us, O holy Mother of God

R: That we may be made worthy of the promises of Christ.

V: May the divine assistance remain always with us;

R: And may the souls of the faithful departed, through the mercy of God, rest in peace. Amen.

Let us pray: O God, whose only begotten Son, by His life, death and Resurrection, has purchased for us the rewards of eternal life, grant we beseech Thee, that meditating on these mysteries of the most holy Rosary of the Blessed Virgin Mary, we may imitate what they contain and obtain what they promise, through the same Christ, Our Lord. Amen.

In 2002, Pope St. John Paul II approved five additional mysteries—the **Luminous Mysteries** (prayed on Thursdays)—in his apostolic letter *Rosarium Virginis Mariae*. They are:

The Baptism of Jesus
The Wedding at Cana
Jesus' Proclamation of the Kingdom of God
The Transfiguration
The Institution of the Eucharist

Saints, popes, theologians, and spiritual directors recommend the Rosary to increase our faith, bring healing, and impart wisdom, hope, charity, and the fruits of the Holy Spirit. The Rosary is believed to have been revealed to St. Dominic by the Blessed Virgin Mary around 1208 to combat heresy and help believers grow closer to God. Dominicans continue to pray a version closest to the oldest observed texts of the prayer.

The rosary as a physical sacramental (see "**Sacramental**") consists of beads (or knots) to help keep track of the prayers.

A rosary

Further reading: Kevin Orlin Johnson's book Rosary: Mysteries, Meditations, and the Telling of the Beads *is a masterwork on the Holy Rosary. Other prodigious sources on the Rosary include the papal encyclicals of Leo XIII* (Supremi Apostolatus Officio *and ten others) and Pius XI* (Ingravescentibus Malis*) and the Apostolic Letter* Rosarium Virginis Mariae *by John Paul II.*

S

Sacrament

An efficacious sign of God's grace by which divine life is dispensed to believers.

The sacraments are concrete, outward signs of spiritual realities. That is, the rites and liturgies that accompany them in celebration both signify and make the graces present. The Church recognizes seven sacraments that were instituted by Christ and entrusted to the Church (CCC 1114, 1131). They are Baptism, Confirmation, the Eucharist, Reconciliation, Anointing of the Sick, Holy Orders, and Holy Matrimony. The first three listed here are also known as the Sacraments of Initiation. Together, they bring one into the fullness of the life of the Church. The Anointing of the Sick and Reconciliation are known as the Sacraments of Healing, and Holy Orders and Matrimony are called the Sacraments of Service.

The word "sacrament" comes from *sacramentum*, a Latin word indicating something's sacredness. Literary evidence suggests that biblical authors understood the word "sacrament" as we apply it today, as it was the Latin word chosen to translate the Greek *mystērion*, the word Paul uses to describe "mysteries" of the Faith, such as Holy Matrimony: "For this reason a man shall leave his father and mother and be joined to his wife, and the two shall become one flesh. This is a great mystery, and I mean in reference to Christ and the church" (Eph. 5:31–32).

That the sacraments are efficacious is a chief teaching in sacramental theology. The sacraments impart grace (see "**Grace**") *ex opere operato*, a Latin phrase meaning "from the work performed." This means that the sacraments derive their efficacy—their ability to effect grace—not from the minister or the recipient but from the sacrament itself, which receives its power from the saving work of Christ and the power of God. While the sacraments impart grace regardless of the merits of the minister or the recipient, their ability to bear fruit may be affected by the recipient's disposition (CCC 1128). Dispositions are required to prepare a person to receive sacramental grace *as a condition*, but they are *not the cause* of the grace conferred.

Sacramental

A sacred sign that bears some resemblance to the seven sacraments and disposes one to receive grace.

The Second Vatican Council's Constitution on the Sacred Liturgy, *Sacrosanctum Concilium*, says that sacramentals "signify effects, particularly of a spiritual nature, which are obtained through the intercession of the Church. By them men are disposed to receive the chief effect of the sacraments, and various occasions in life are rendered holy."[79] The Code of Canon Law states, "The Apostolic See alone can establish new sacramentals, authentically interpret those already received, or abolish or change any of them" (CIC 1167, no. 1). Ordinarily, the minister of sacramentals is a cleric who has been provided with the requisite power (CIC 1168).

The definition of sacramental is broad because "There is hardly any proper use of material things which cannot thus be directed toward the sanctification of men and the praise of God."[80] There are many sacramentals, but the Church must institute them as such. Sacramentals include blessings, objects, and gestures, which is why the Church correctly describes them as "signs." The *Book of Blessings* points out that "Among these signs perceptible to the sense by which human sanctification in Christ and the glorification of God are 'signified

A holy-water font

and brought about in ways proper to each of these signs'" (no. 9). Most Catholics are familiar with sacramentals such as crucifixes, rosaries, candles, scapulars, holy water, anointing oils, and the sign of the cross.

The *Catechism of the Catholic Church* speaks of three kinds of sacramentals—blessings, exorcisms, and forms of popular piety. Among the sacramentals, the Church places priority on blessings. The act of blessing coincides with the Lord's power to "make all things new" and for His purposes. Therefore, when a priest or deacon gives a blessing to people, he is renewing their consecration to God. When a bishop dedicates a new church, or a priest blesses a new chalice for use in the Mass, they are consecrating—reserving—these for liturgical use. Similarly, when a blessing is invoked over a meal, the special intention of praise and thanksgiving to God is reflective of the eucharistic meal and the heavenly banquet. Blessings call to mind that the faithful share in the "cup of blessing" by command (1 Cor. 10:16). The *Book of Blessings* informs us "Through [blessings, the Church] calls us to praise God, encourages us to implore his protection, exhorts us to seek mercy by our holiness of life, and provides us with ways of praying that God will grant the favors we ask" (no. 9).

A scapular

Exorcisms (see "**Exorcism**") are also sacramentals. They are functionally and effectively different from blessings. In an exorcism, "the Church asks publicly and authoritatively in the name of Jesus Christ that a person or object be protected against the power of the Evil One and withdrawn from his dominion" (CCC 1673). A simple exorcism is given with Baptism (three in the Extraordinary Form), and a major exorcism may be administered by a trained priest in strict compliance with the rules of the Church and with the approval of the bishop.

Forms of piety and devotion are tremendously important to the life of a Catholic not because they replace the liturgy but because they extend it. These sacramentals include objects (like rosaries and holy water) and gestures (like the genuflection one makes before the tabernacle).

Sacramentals bear resemblance to the sacraments because they prepare us to receive the fruit of the sacraments and sanctify different circumstances of life.

Further reading on sacramentals: 20 Answers: Sacramentals and Relics *by Shaun McAfee and* The Externals of the Church *by John Francis Sullivan. Every family should own a copy of the USCCB's* Catholic Household Blessings and Prayers *as a guide and aid to daily Catholic living.*

Sacred Art

Artwork that directs the heart and mind to God.

Sacred art can include any art form, from painting and sculpture to music. It is meant to provide inspiration and knowledge: "These arts, by their very nature, are oriented toward the infinite beauty of God which they attempt in some way to portray by

CATHOLIC TIP

Sometimes Catholics, with our love for sacred art, are accused of violating the Second Commandment: "You shall not make for yourself a graven image, or any likeness of anything that is in Heaven above" (Exod. 20:4). Iconoclasm—the destruction of sacred images—has even led to schism in the Church's history. Today, there are Christians who believe that making a painting of Christ would be a sin. How do we answer this?

First, we can show how this interpretation of the Second Commandment conflicts with several other passages in the Bible. God gives detailed instructions for the design of the Ark of the Covenant, which featured two golden cherubim (Exod. 25:17–19). In Numbers 21 and 1 Kings 6, God commands His people to create images of trees, flowers, and a huge serpent. It seems that God wants His people to create images for adoration and other holy purposes.

We can also argue for sacred imagery based on the benefits of religious art. Images of our Lord don't just represent God, they also represent *what God has done*. Catholics kissing their crucifix aren't worshiping an image; they are adoring the God who died on a Cross for their sins.

the work of human hands; they achieve their purpose of redounding to God's praise and glory in proportion as they are directed the more exclusively to the single aim of turning men's minds devoutly toward God."[81]

Sacred art has been employed within the Church since the very beginning of Christianity. The early followers of Christ worked to Christianize the motifs, styles, and techniques of their time, and images adorned altars and the walls of the catacombs. Sacred art developed over time, with Christian artists using the techniques of their time to reveal profound truths of the Faith. Today, artists continue to express the truth and beauty of our Faith using various forms of media.

In every age, sacred art should complement the liturgy and arouse a deeper religious and worshipful experience. The Fathers of the Second Vatican Council wished to promote sacred art, reinvigorating modern Catholics to use their talents to glorify God. The Constitution on Sacred Liturgy says, "Bishops should have a special concern for artists, so as to imbue them with the spirit of sacred art and of the sacred liturgy.... It is also desirable that schools or academies of sacred art should be founded in those parts of the world where they would be useful, so that artists may be trained."[82]

Sacred Heart of Jesus

A special form of devotion to Jesus through the honoring of His heart as a symbol of His love for all mankind.

Devotion to the Sacred Heart derives from a personal faith but also from a theological appreciation for the Incarnation. Jesus, who is perfectly God, also became perfectly man with a perfect human heart. Corporeally, this is true, but the consequence of the Incarnation also preserves the symbolic understanding of the heart as the source of love and goodwill for all persons. If love comes from the heart, then a perfect heart loves perfectly, and this analogy encapsulates the reason devotion to the Sacred Heart is permissible and so popular in the Church today.

The Sacred Heart of Jesus

The devotion is deeply rooted in the Church's tradition as well as Christians' sincere devotion to the Passion and relics of the Passion (see "**Relics**"). As the medieval crusaders brought home relics of the Passion, devotion to Jesus' heart also grew, since His heart is the bodily center of His personhood and the spiritual center of His sufferings for humanity. Various saints, such as Bernard of Clairvaux and Francis of Assisi, carried on this devotion, and in 1353, Pope Innocent VI instituted a Mass honoring the mystery of the Sacred Heart. Later, St. Margaret Mary Alacoque (1647–1690), a French nun, established the norms for devotion to the Sacred Heart after a series of visions she received between 1673 and 1675. Popular imagery of the devotion depicts a human heart wrapped in thorns, with a flame and cross emerging from the top.

The *Catechism* discusses devotion to the Sacred Heart, noting that the Passion of Christ causes all believers to echo the words of St. Paul: "The Son of God ... loved me and gave himself for me" (Gal. 2:20). It continues, "He has loved us all with a human heart. For this reason, the Sacred Heart of Jesus, pierced by our sins and for our salvation, 'is quite rightly considered the chief sign and symbol of that ... love with which the divine Redeemer continually loves the eternal Father and all human beings' without exception" (CCC 478).

Further reading: The Autobiography of St. Margaret Mary *is a popular and fruitful examination of the Sacred Heart devotion.*

Sacrifice

A freewill gift to God in praise and thanksgiving and the summit of worship in a ritual offering to God by a priest.

Almost all world religions include sacrifice, indicating that man has a natural urge to please God in humility of heart and to make atonement for sin.

Sacrifice was a key aspect of the law given to Moses, particularly animal sacrifice, which was not a barbaric slaying of animals to make up for human error but an offering of life as an act of humility and ransom for the guilt of sin. God commanded a bloody sacrifice to atone and to make satisfaction. As the author of the Letter to the Hebrews writes, "Indeed, under the law almost everything is purified with blood, and without the shedding of blood there is no forgiveness of sins" (Heb. 9:22). Throughout the Old Testament, however, God revealed that the sacrifice He truly desired was the self-sacrifice of the human heart: "The sacrifice acceptable to God is a broken spirit; a broken and contrite heart" (Ps. 51:17).

The Jewish people always believed that the blood of the victim was the atoning life-source (Lev. 17:11), and the more perfect the victim, the more perfect (pleasing) the sacrifice. And so we see throughout the Old Testament that the Hebrew people were constantly tempted to join in with pagan worship: they knew that a human's blood was more valuable, since man is a higher being than the other animals. Regardless, the Jews never condoned the sacrifice of humans, although human sacrifice was common in the surrounding pagan tribes.

Jesus Christ, the Son of God, offered Himself as the perfect, universal, and absolute sacrifice for all mankind. Jesus described His sacrifice at the Last Supper: it included the "body which is given for you" (Luke 22:19) and "blood of the covenant, which is poured out for many for the forgiveness of sins" (Matt. 26:28). He commanded the apostles, now priests of the New Covenant, to perform this sacrifice in memory of Him. The sacrifice on the Cross was the bloody sacrifice for atonement and satisfaction (CCC 616), and the sacrifice of the Mass, in which Christ is mysteriously present, is the same unbloody sacrifice.

God taught His people throughout the ages to value sacrifice as the principal method of worship, culminating in Jesus' perfect sacrifice on the Cross, which is re-presented at every Mass. In addition, by virtue of our Baptism, through which we share in Christ's priesthood, each of us is also called to make sacrifices by participating in the Mass and making personal offerings, often by depriving ourselves of certain enjoyments or comforts.

Further reading: St. Robert Bellarmine's famous treatise On the Most Holy Sacrifice of the Mass.

Sacrilege

Abuse against a sacred object or transgression against religious practice and teachings.

The term "sacrilege" receives no shortage of misuse and is often treated in jest, referring to light grievances such as acting up in church, but the true act of sacrilege is a grievous sin. It is the intentional abuse of something holy, such as the mistreatment of a sacramental, the destruction of a grave, the desecration of an altar, or irreverence for God's name.

Theologians place sacrilege into three general categories: personal, local, and real. Violence against a cleric or religious, violation of ecclesial power, and the violation of a vow of chastity are three common examples that constitute personal sacrilege: they are sacrileges against the *person or office*. Local sacrilege regards the maltreatment of a sacred *place* such as a cemetery, a chapel, or a monastery. The category of a real sacrilege is directed to sacred *things*, such as vessels and materials used for Mass, rosaries, or the Holy Bible.

Sacrilege is more common in the modern world than most would realize, and it takes an observant and considerate eye to avoid such violations. Ensuring clergy are treated with the dignity of their office, avoiding misuse of the sacred space in churches, and keeping safe and secure the sacramentals used in prayer, the liturgy, and worship are all practical means of avoiding sacrilege.

Saints

Faithful men and women who have died and, after intense scrutiny and verification of miracles, are declared by the Church to be in Heaven.

The term "saint" comes from the Latin *sancti* meaning "holy ones," and its earliest usage among Christians applied not only to the dead but to living Christians as well (see "**Communion of Saints**" for more). In the New Testament, the word "saint" refers to all those who are part of the Christian community (1 Cor. 1:2). Over time, the term "saint" came to refer to those who were the most exemplary of the Christians or those who were martyred. Eventually, the word was limited to those who had completed their earthly pilgrimage in death and were believed to be in Heaven.

In the early centuries of the Church, there was no formal process for declaring a person a saint or declaring patrons of specific places and causes (see "**Patron Saints**"). But gradually, as early as the eighth and ninth centuries, as persecutions had generally died down and the Church became more complex administratively, the faithful began to appeal to the pope for recognition of certain people's holiness of life, and there developed a clear process

Relief of the saints in Heaven, abbey church of Saint Foy, France

CATHOLIC TIP

Personally speaking, I recall that in the initial years after my conversion, I wasn't very interested in the saints. I had a patron saint from Confirmation, and I was generally attracted to several of the saints' theological works, but I found the saints intimidating in their absolute perfection of virtue and knowledge.

I more enjoyed Augustine's *De Trinitate* or the *Summa Contra Gentiles* of Aquinas before I read Antonio Gallonio's volume on Philip Neri. But when I picked up that world-famous biography and got to the first hilarious story of Neri and the ox, I had to keep reading. And after discovering his sidesplitting letter to Charles Borromeo, I had to read Borromeo's life too. I then discovered that the Lombardian Cardinal gave first communion to Aloysius Gonzaga, so I had to read his life. And while reading his life, I learned that the young man chose Robert Bellarmine as his spiritual director and confessor.

One saint after another—they all knew each other and formed this family—and through this experience, I became an avid friend of the saints. I appreciated Aquinas's academic work more after discovering his classmates thought him not very bright; and learning about Augustine's conversion highlighted his intense love of truth and God, which made his theological works shine brighter. Now, I love to read about the saints, from the most familiar to the more obscure. It started with one good book. If the reader is at all sensing a lack of appreciation for the saints, I recommend just diving into one good biography or collection of stories—the saints are truly our witnesses and friends!

for recognizing saints (see "**Canonization**" for more on this process).

Saints are venerated with the observance of feasts to commemorate their life in the General Calendar, as determined by the Church. In most cases, a saint's feast day is the day of his or her death, but not always.

Catholics pray, asking the saints for their intercession. This is because Catholics believe that those in Heaven are nearest to God and thus are the best equipped to pray for us and intercede on our behalf. We do *not* worship the saints, but we pray *with* them and ask them to *pray for us*: "Christian intercession participates in Christ's, as an expression of the communion of saints. In intercession, he who prays looks 'not only to his own interests, but also to the interests of others,' even to the point of praying for those who do him harm" (CCC 2635).

Further reading: Alban Butler's Lives of the Saints *is the most thorough collection of saints, their stories, and their patronages.*

Salvation

Our liberation from sin and its consequences, brought about by Jesus' life, death, and Resurrection.

The term "salvation" comes from the Greek *sōteria*, literally meaning an act of rescuing from grave danger. The study of the doctrine of salvation is thus called soteriology.

The Christian doctrine of salvation states that God rescues His people from sin and delivers them to eternal life with Him. This rescuing is a near-constant theme throughout the Old Testament, beginning with the various covenants God made with Noah, Abraham, and Israel, and seen most intensely in the rescue of God's people from slavery in Egypt. The prophets also wrote of the salvation of God's people. Isaiah, for instance, prophesied that such salvation would come from a "suffering servant" (Isa. 52:13–15) who would be "wounded for our transgressions ... bruised for our iniquities" (Isa. 53:5). In the New Testament, we find the fulfillment of Isaiah's words with Jesus' salvific act of freely dying in our stead: "All this is from God, who through Christ reconciled us to himself.... For our sake he made him to be sin who knew no sin, so that in him we might become the righteousness of God" (2 Cor. 5:18–21).

Believing in Jesus Christ and in the One who sent Him for our salvation is necessary for obtaining salvation: "For God so loved the world that he gave his only Son, that whoever believes in him should not perish but have eternal life. For God sent the Son into the world, not to condemn the world, but that the world might be saved through him" (John 3:16–17). This belief is crucial to our salvation: "Since 'without faith it is impossible to please [God]' and to attain to the fellowship of his sons, therefore without faith no one has ever attained justification, nor will anyone obtain eternal life 'but he who endures to the end'" (CCC 161).

Yet the concept of salvation is much more complex than a simple statement of belief. The Church writes of an "economy" of salvation, affirming that salvation is a product of sanctification, which is a process: "Work out your own salvation with fear and trembling; for God is at work in you" (Phil. 2:12–13). This economy of salvation is found in Baptism (John 3:5), faith (Mark 16:16, Rom. 10:9), and the observance of God's commandments (James 2:14–26). The clear evidence found in the Bible and the teaching of the Church suggests, then, that salvation is an "already but not yet" scenario.

Further reading: Jimmy Akin's The Drama of Salvation *is an exhaustive study of salvation from a biblical and magisterial perspective.*

Salvation History

A theological approach to human history that shows how events contributed to God's overall plan for the salvation of mankind.

Salvation history brings together the events of human history into one story of salvation from God's perspective: past, present, and future. God is meticulously interested in human beings and involved in each phase of human history. The study of salvation history reveals God's plan and man's involvement in it.

Passages in the Bible indicate that this method of understanding God's involvement in human history is a longstanding tradition. The Psalms, for example, recall the events of the Exodus and various covenants and so witness to God's continuous call for the conversion of each generation of His people. St. Stephen, the Church's first martyr, details the story of salvation beginning with Abraham in Acts chapter 7. And the opening chapters of the Letter to the Hebrews review the narrative of God's plan as it unfolded, pointing to Jesus as the messianic fulfillment of the entire drama.

In the Catholic Church, salvation history is also recounted in the liturgy—its main and proper setting. The Mass readings often demonstrate a theme of the fulfillment of God's plan and man's anticipation of Christ. The Divine Office follows this same theme, expanding on the liturgical seasons with supplementary readings from Scripture, the saints, popes, and other figures who illustrated well the significance of moments in salvation history. Feast days throughout the liturgical year also recount the story of salvation, especially concerning the life of Jesus.

Further reading: Salvation is from the Jews *by* Roy *Schoeman.*

Scandal

A grave sin by which a person deliberately leads someone else into sin, either by an act or omission.

The *Catechism of the Catholic Church* explains, "Scandal is an attitude or behavior which leads another to do evil" (2284). Scandal is a topic brought up in the teachings of Christ. After laying out the hypocrisy of the pharisees, Jesus delivers a sharp warning: "Whoever causes one of these little ones who believe in me to sin, it would be better for him to have a great millstone fastened round his neck and to be drowned in the depth of the sea" (Matt. 18:6). The severity of the grave offense is worse for those

CATHOLIC TIP

The Church teaches that there is "no salvation outside the church" (CCC 846). This seems to be a harsh statement, but the teaching is centered on Christ as the Head of the Church, which is His Body (Rom. 12:5, Col. 1:18). Christ told us that all salvation is through Him (John 14:6). The Church is the Body of Christ, which is why she is bold enough to proclaim these words, since there is no salvation outside of Christ's salvific work.

Catholics speak of the Church as the "Barque of Peter." Paintings from the early centuries through the modern day depict the Church as a great ship, captained by a pope who is Christ's vicar on earth (Matt. 16:18). This is beautiful when we recall that the word "salvation" means "to rescue," as souls are rescued from the tempestuous waves and brought onto the safety of the ship.

who knowingly lead others into sin: "Temptations to sin are sure to come; but woe to him by whom they come!" (Luke 17:1).

Common scandals include abuse of office, sexual crimes, and simony (the selling of Church offices or sacred things), among others. But an often-overlooked scandal is the willful teaching of heresy or any teaching (or teaching by example) that is contrary to good morals or religious practice. Examples might be notable Catholics teaching that abortion is acceptable, or priests inserting novel words and phrases into the consecration at Mass, not following the liturgical formulas.

Our modern society generally defines scandal as a morally illicit act, creation of circumstances, or event that causes public outrage. The Church's definition is not exactly the same, but the two are related. What happens when a true scandal occurs is not just that people are led into sin but that the faithful lose trust in the hierarchy, the authority, and eventually the teachings of the Catholic Church or Christianity altogether. The weight of scandal, then, should cause clergy, teachers, parents, politicians, and authorities of all kinds to consider seriously the effects of their decisions, lifestyle, teachings, and example. "Every one to whom much is given, of him will much be required" (Luke 12:48).

Science

The systematic study of the world, encompassing a wide range of disciplines.

Most science revolves around the systematic study of the world through natural experiments that lead from hypotheses and theories to discoveries of laws. Of course, among these studies are those that cannot be observed or interpreted under a microscope, such as those experiments that involve logic, behavior, data, and so on.

Theology is a legitimate science because it encompasses a thorough appreciation of the natural world while considering the impacts of revelation, leading man to knowledge of the highest things. If natural science aims to understand the natural world in order to help man discover *where he is*, then theology studies religion to help man understand *who he is* (see "**Theology**" for more).

Backers of scientific discovery and those of religious authority have clashed from time to time throughout history, not because one is any more or less legitimate or necessary then the other but because authorities in each area often overstep their own disciplines. Natural scientists have infringed upon theological certainties, and theologians have stubbornly applied personal interpretations to limit authentic discovery.

Despite this conflict, the Church preaches a consistent message that faith and science are not opposed but complement each other when applied with due diligence. The *Catechism* clearly defends this sage position: "There can never be any real discrepancy between faith and reason. Since the same God who reveals mysteries and infuses faith has bestowed the light of reason on the human mind, God cannot deny himself, nor can truth ever contradict truth" (159). It would be folly to proclaim a God who created a natural world with contradicting truths.

But the Church teaches also that faith is above reason. Faith exists so that we may know things that are not apparent to reason: hope, love, mercy, virtue, compassion, and more. Thus, the products of faith—the imperative questions about life and existence—are beyond the skill and limitations of the natural sciences.

Further reading: Stacy Trasancos's Particles of Faith: A Catholic Guide to Navigating Science.

Separation of Church and State

The philosophical concept that separates religious and secular authorities with the goal of giving neither one control over the other.

In medieval thought and civil policy, there was little separation between the Church and civil authority, largely because Church and state authorities were united and shared in the belief that power comes from God. The modern world, however, observes a stricter divergence of the powers of the state from the powers of the Church. The Founding Fathers of the United States, for example, so valued the idea of the separation of Church and state that it is written into the Constitution as an immutable rule.

The separation of Church and state means that the government as a civil authority cannot establish a statewide religion, and all citizens have freedom of conscience to follow the religion of their choosing. The goal is mutual cooperation, and the state is responsible for creating and sustaining an atmosphere in which citizens can choose their religion and work out their eternal welfare without harm or disruption.

Sin

Any deliberate act, word, thought, or omission in defiance of God's law.

God's law encompasses truth, commandments, reason, and our conscience (CCC 1849). The root of all sin is Original Sin (see "**Original Sin**"), man's fallen nature inherited as a result of the sin of Adam and Eve, who first revolted against God. The sins we ourselves commit, which are known as "personal" sin, come from disobedience that results from our self-love, which says deep inside us "I know better" and "I'll do things my way." The biblical meaning of the word we translate as "sin" is "wrongdoing" or "to miss the mark," because all things are measured against God's perfect ways.

The result of sin is death (Rom. 6:23), and all humans have sinned (Rom. 3:23), except for Mary, who was preserved from Original Sin (see "**Immaculate Conception**"), and Jesus, who is God. Consistent with the Bible, the Church teaches that the first remedy for sin is Jesus' atoning death (Heb. 10:3–10). Sacramentally, the remedy for sin is Confession: "If we say we have no sin, we deceive ourselves, and the truth is not in us. If we confess our sins, he is faithful and just, and will forgive our sins and cleanse us from all unrighteousness" (1 John 1:8–9; see also "**Reconciliation**").

Sins are generally divided into two categories: mortal and venial. A mortal sin is a serious sin that kills the life of grace in our soul. It consists of grave matter and must be committed with full knowledge and deliberate consent. If one of these conditions is not fully present, while the sin may still be substantial, the person is not guilty of a mortal sin. All mortal sin presupposes understanding of the character of the sin: *I knew it was wrong, and I did it anyway.*

Venial sins require a similar level of examination. "One commits *venial sin* when, in a less serious matter, he does not observe the standard prescribed by the moral law, or when he disobeys the moral law in a grave matter, but without full knowledge or without complete consent" (CCC 1862). Frequent, persistent, unresolved venial sins *may* constitute a grave object.

The moral weight of a sin can be judged by examining the object, the intent, and the circumstance (see "**Concupiscence**" and "**Morality**"). These elements elucidate important truths about sin. All acts are committed for a perceived good, including sins. Sin is an evil wrongly perceived as a good, and all sins are offenses against God because He is perfect goodness. As St. Thomas Aquinas puts it, "sin consists in turning away from the immutable good."[83] This concept of a corrupted good also extends to one's perception of sin. If a person engages in an act that he believes to be a sin, even if

CATHOLIC TIP

Each person is called to answer for his sins, but it's easy to get caught up in the act of judging others, even though we are expressly commanded by Christ, "Judge not, that you be not judged" (Matt. 7:1). This command is often misappropriated by the world, even by many Christians. Oftentimes, it is used as an excuse to clear a person's conscience when someone else points out a fault: "Don't judge me!" or "Only God can judge me." Thus, many Christians are scared to speak up out of fear of being criticized or being labeled as a hypocrite.

But this clearly twists the Christian message proclaimed by Jesus:

> When you see a cloud rising in the west, you say at once, "A shower is coming"; and so it happens. And when you see the south wind blowing, you say, "There will be scorching heat"; and it happens. You hypocrites! You know how to interpret the appearance of earth and sky; but why do you not know how to interpret the present time? (Luke 12:54–56)

The same message is echoed by Paul: "Do you not know that the saints will judge the world? And if the world is to be judged by you, are you incompetent to try trivial cases? Do you not know that we are to judge angels? How much more, matters pertaining to this life!" (1 Cor. 6:2–3).

With a history of prophets and patriarchs issuing warnings and shaking the dust off their feet in response to the immorality of the peoples they preached to, the consistent message we see in the Bible is that Christians are unambiguously called to judge—to judge the acts and measures of sin. Yet Jesus warns us, "Judge not," meaning we are not to adjudicate the condemnation and punishment inflicted on someone as a result of their sin. These things are left to God alone, not any man. Christians are called to bring lost sheep back into the fold and to drive away evil. This act of love is the proper context of judgment in the work of evangelization.

the act is not sinful in itself, the person is still guilty of sin because of his willful intent to offend God. The same is also true of sins of omission: "Whoever knows what is right to do and fails to do it, for him it is sin" (James 4:17).

Soul

The animating principle of the body.

Nearly every culture has some concept of the soul. The ancient Greek philosophers Plato and Aristotle developed an articulation of the soul that is highly influential to Catholic thought, particularly in the synthesis of St. Thomas Aquinas, who articulates that the soul is the "form" of the body and is what gives a creature "movement" or life. All living creatures have a soul to varying degrees of superiority: plants, animals, and humans. The human soul is the source of our thinking and passions (see "**Passions**") and is the spiritual and immaterial part of a person. The human soul is also immortal, meaning it will never cease to exist.

The Bible uses many different words to describe aspects of the immaterial reality of man's existence, such as life, emotions, and thinking. The first mention of the soul in the Bible is in the Creation narrative, when God gives the "breath of life" to Adam (Gen. 2:7). In the New Testament, which was written in Greek, the soul is often expressed as *psychē*, which means "life," but Paul utilizes the word *pneuma*, literally meaning "breath," to contrast the soul or spirit with the flesh (*sarx*).

The Catholic Church teaches that the soul is immediately created by God. This soul remains as the form of the body until death, when the soul and body are separated. At the end of the world, each soul will be reunited with its body (CCC 366) (see "**Resurrection of the Dead**").

Stations of the Cross

A special form of private devotion and a sacramental that follows and contemplates the path of Jesus from His condemnation to Calvary.

Christ declared to His disciples, "If any man would come after me, let him deny himself and take up his cross and follow me" (Matt. 16:24). This is discipleship summarized, the Christian standard: imitate Christ by accepting suffering and working through the trials of life with patience and perseverance.

For hundreds of years, the early Christians took these words both figuratively—an acceptance of the sufferings of life and imminent persecutions—and literally by traveling to the city of Jerusalem to see and follow Christ's path from His condemnation in the home of Pilate to His execution on Golgotha. This route became known as the *Via Dolorosa* (Way of Sorrows), and it is still marked with precision for pilgrims to Jerusalem to follow. Over time, as borders became impassible or the journey itself became more treacherous, the Church approved the prayers and devotion.

Christians have faithfully kept this tradition, and today, those wishing to follow in the footsteps of Christ are offered a wonderful sacramental in the Stations of the Cross as they call to mind the events of the Passion narrative. There are fourteen stations in the traditional Stations of the Cross:

1st Station: Jesus is condemned to death
2nd Station: Jesus carries His Cross
3rd Station: Jesus falls the first time
4th Station: Jesus meets His Mother
5th Station: Simon of Cyrene helps Jesus to carry His Cross
6th Station: Veronica wipes the face of Jesus
7th Station: Jesus falls the second time
8th Station: Jesus meets the women of Jerusalem
9th Station: Jesus falls a third time
10th Station: Jesus' clothes are taken away
11th Station: Jesus is nailed to the Cross
12th Station: Jesus dies on the Cross
13th Station: The Body of Jesus is taken down from the Cross
14th Station: Jesus is laid in the tomb

The Stations of the Cross as a sacramental is twofold: the physical sacramental is the individual

Sixth Station: Veronica wipes the face of Jesus

CATHOLIC TIP

When Jesus told His followers that they must take up their crosses—a barbaric tool of Roman execution so familiar to that generation—it must have come as tremorous news to them, as they had often grumbled among themselves as to who would be the greatest in Heaven. It is no different in our time: the age of comfort, ease, convenience, lavish vacations, and fast cars beckons us to have more and live an easy life. The world provides several such lies to excuse us from following His example. The world tells us that if we suffer, we must be doing something wrong because "that's just bad karma." Conversely the world tells us that to be happy we must, "live our best life." Such philosophies are oxymorons for the Christian. Jesus' Cross, as St. Paul reminds us, is a contradiction to the world (1 Cor. 1:20–25). And we haven't come much further in two thousand years. The Stations of the Cross offer an abiding way to reflect on the Passion and to inspire Christians today to carry their crosses.

fourteen crosses that line Catholic churches, and the pious devotion is the readings, reflections, and prayers at each individual station. Hence, the Stations are not the individual pictures or scenes from the Passion, rather they are composed of the individual crosses. Catholic churches throughout the world display the Stations along their walls or on pillars. In some small chapels, the Stations are as simple as a set of small crosses with Roman numerals, and in others, they are made of precious materials, ornate, and crafted by the best artists available.

There are many variations of the Stations. Some follow the meditations of certain saints and others offer reflections of popes. Pope St. John Paul II offered and promoted a Scriptural Way of the Cross that he led many times during his pontificate.

Whatever the form of the physical stations—whether in a church, or outside on a path, or in the familiarity of one's home—the recitation of the Stations of the Cross comes from a published booklet. These should always be approved by a bishop with an *Imprimatur* and checked for doctrinal consistency with a *Nihil Obstat* by an authorized censor (normally included in the front with the publication and copyright information). These particular devotions are titled and are most often known as the *Way of the Cross.*

Stewardship

Wise and caring enjoyment over the gifts, power, and resources God affords to each individual.

The Christian view of stewardship is that all possessions—including land, animals, wealth, power, goods, and services given to a person—are God's first and are entrusted to men to be used to sustain life, bless others, and glorify God. What stewardship implies is that each man is given what God has deemed fit and necessary for work and leisure. Note that these gifts are not equal from one person to the next—some receive more, others less. "The goods of creation are destined for the whole human race. However, the earth is divided up among men to assure the security of their lives" (CCC 2402). The teaching of Christ also enhances our understanding that stewardship over belongings has an end in giving back to God, as we learn in the parable of talents (Matt. 25:14–30).

Stewardship as a teaching is always associated with the social doctrine of the Church (see "**Catholic Social Teaching**"), touching on important areas such as the environment (see "**Environment**"), parenting, economics, and private property (see "**Private Property**"). The Church has a legitimate place in these discussions since she is concerned with true happiness and peace for all people (see "**Happiness**"). Therefore, a constant topic of discourse for popes and bishops is the promotion and understanding of laws that govern social living. The primary guidance to the faithful, as Christian stewards, is to receive God's gifts with gratitude, to cultivate them responsibly, to share them lovingly in justice with others, and to return them with increase to the Lord. Reflecting the reality that responsibility will be given even in Heaven, Christ reveals that stewardship on earth plays a direct role in this division in eternity: "For to every one who has will more be given, and he will have abundance; but from him who has not, even what he has will be taken away" (Matt. 25:29).

St. Francis Receives the Stigmata, by Ambrogio Bergognone

Stigmata

The miraculous appearance of the wounds of Christ on a person.

"Stigmata" comes from the Greek word *stigma* that means "marks." The stigmata can include any of the wounds of Christ's Passion, particularly nail marks on hands and feet, a wound on the abdomen, or wounds on the head. A person with the stigmata is known as a stigmatist. A common sign of the stigmata is when physicians are unable to cure the wound or determine its spontaneous source.

Famous stigmatists include St. Francis of Assisi and, much more recently, St. Padre Pio of Pietrelcina. These saints endured the full stigmata until their death. Partial stigmatists are also documented, such as St. Rita of Cascia, who received a wound on her forehead in honor of Jesus' crown of thorns. St. Catherine of Siena endured the stigmata as well, as confirmed by her contemporaries, but it was invisible.

The stigmata is not a punishment from God but rather a gift given to certain souls of deep sharing in the suffering of Christ.

Further reading: The stigmatist saints record some of the most interesting stories and present evocative wisdom to readers. The lives and diaries of St. Gemma Galgani, St. Padre Pio, St. Rita of Cascia, St. Catherine of Siena, and St. Francis of Assisi are among the most popular.

Suffering

The state of pain, hardship, or torment experienced by all human persons.

Prior to the Fall, humans enjoyed pure happiness in the sight of God and in a state of paradise. Theologically, suffering is a result of sin—both Original Sin (see "**Original Sin**"), as explained by God to Adam and Eve (Gen. 3:14–19; cf. Rom. 5:12–14, 8:18–25), and actual sin (John 5:14; see "**Sin**" for more). Suffering may be brought about through our own actions, through the acts of another person (intentional or unintentional), or naturally and through no person's fault, such as in a natural disaster.

The New Testament assures us that all persons will suffer, as human experience confirms. We are asked to respond to this suffering with faith and virtue: "Count it all joy, my brethren, when you meet various trials, for you know that the testing of your faith produces steadfastness" (James 1:2). The Church does not necessarily teach that we should enjoy suffering or create suffering, but when it comes, we should look at suffering positively, as an opportunity to grow in virtue.

Jesus confirms that suffering is a particular aspect of the Christian life, especially in the form of persecution. "If the world hates you, know that it has hated me before it hated you" (John 15:18). Such persecutions range from antagonism or violent hate for Christian beliefs, to public policy that allows for morally evil acts to persist or laws that violate the conscience of believers. The Christian response, St. Peter writes, is to be accepting of these sufferings as a mark of our identity with Christ: "For to this you have been called, because Christ also suffered for you, leaving you an example, that you should follow in his steps" (1 Pet. 2:21).

The Church teaches that any suffering accepted and offered up to God is a participation in the redemptive work of Christ on the Cross and can remit temporal punishments due to sin. Following Jesus' example, we can also apply the merits of our sufferings to other souls, whether on earth or in Purgatory. This idea is known as redemptive suffering, and biblical evidence strongly supports the teaching: "Now I rejoice in my sufferings for your sake, and in my flesh I complete what is lacking in Christ's afflictions for the sake of his body, that is, the church" (Col. 1:24). "If we are afflicted, it is for your comfort and *salvation*; and if we are comforted, it is for your comfort, which you experience when you patiently endure the same sufferings that we suffer" (2 Cor. 1:6, emphasis added).

Suicide

The deliberate taking of one's own life.

Suicide may be performed as an end (when one desires to end his own life), or as a means to an end (for example, to end suffering). The Catholic teaching on suicide is that it is a mortal sin, "seriously contrary to justice, hope, and charity. It is forbidden by the fifth commandment" (CCC 2325). This includes assisted suicide or euthanasia, which is also a grave sin (see "**Euthanasia**").

While the Church's stance on suicide is strong, applying the natural law (see "**Natural Law**") and morality found in God's commandments, the Church is also sensitive to the extreme events that may lead one to commit suicide. The responsibility for suicide may be diminished by one's mental state or other circumstances: "Grave psychological disturbances, anguish, or grave fear of hardship, suffering, or torture can diminish the responsibility of the one committing suicide" (2282).

Indirect suicide occurs when one's death comes as an unintended consequence of another action. For example, when St. Aloysius Gonzaga ministered to plague victims, he contracted the plague and died. His self-sacrifice was highly meritorious: "Greater love has no man than this, that a man lay down his life for his friends" (John 15:13).

The suicide of a loved one is a tremendously painful event, and we worry for the souls of those who have died to suicide. The Church offers a tender and intelligent sign of hope to encourage those whose loved ones have taken their own lives: "We should not despair of the eternal salvation of persons who have taken their own lives. By ways known to him alone, God can provide the opportunity for salutary repentance. The Church prays for persons who have taken their own lives" (CCC 2283).

Summa Theologiae

St. Thomas Aquinas's main theological work and crowning achievement.

The *Summa*, as it is often called, is a thorough treatise on the Catholic Faith intended to be a "summary" (*summa*) of the Christian Faith. Written in the second half of the thirteenth century, the work is a synthesis of philosophical influences on Christian thinking, biblical teaching and divine revelation, and the theological contributions of the Church Fathers and other theologians. It is considered not just to be Thomas Aquinas's greatest work, but the most important, influential, and profitable theological work ever written.

The *Summa Theologiae* is logically constructed using the Scholastic method, dividing subjects into questions and answers in a succession that builds from broad inquiries to specific difficulties about the Catholic Faith. The style is suitable to those looking for basic answers to questions ranging from "Does God exist?" to "Is he who raises someone from the Baptismal font required to instruct him?"

Pope Leo XIII called for a return to Thomas Aquinas as the source of renewed philosophical and theological thought and conversation in his encyclical *Aeterni Patris* (1879). Since then, the Church sees St. Thomas's work as especially valuable in addressing the challenges of our present age. Indeed, the *Summa* is more important now than ever before to reform and address our age so riddled with confusing and militant philosophies that oppose Catholic teaching.

The *Summa Theologiae* is a massive work, indispensable to all Catholics for its sweeping arguments across every subject of Christianity. But print editions are also quite expensive for the average budget. Thankfully, the whole *Summa* is available online at newadvent.com.

Synod

A general meeting of bishops and other clergy to discuss matters pertaining to theology, discipline, liturgy, or other topics important to the Church.

Synods are normally conducted within a diocese (see "**Diocese**") but may also be made up of more than one diocese. They can even be national or international depending on the topic or topics under consideration. Regular synods occur in Rome—such as the Synod on the Family in 2014—where the pope, bishops, canon lawyers, other clergy, and authoritative experts gather to remark on current events such as the family, abortion and contraception, or the environment. These synods and the resulting documents do not exceed the authority of the ordinary (bishops) but are highly consultative and purposed to provide resolution to problems.

An emerging topic of interest among synod bishops, as well as some laypeople and academic Catholics, is the concept of *synodality*, which is a word used to describe the way in which the Church collegially gathers its authorities and experts for the purpose of advising and informing the pope and other Curia offices. The practice is nothing novel to the modern synod, but some fear that taking synodality to an extreme may produce a democratic approach to Church discipline and the formation of teaching—a practice that encroaches on the authority of bishops and the continuity of Catholic Tradition.

CATHOLIC TIP

When our bishops gather in synods, it is always a momentous occasion. We must remember that they are mortal, imperfect men who need the prayers of the faithful as they help advise the pope and shepherd the flock. As our leaders gather, and throughout the synodal process, Catholics do well to keep themselves informed through trustworthy news outlets and with consideration of the facts from insightful and reliable voices. But most importantly, the faithful must practice prayer and fasting for these synods to prosperously guide the Church through the grit of modern challenges.

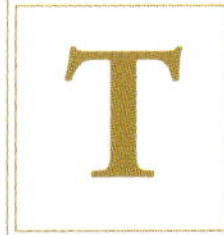

Tabernacle

The vessel in which consecrated hosts are reserved.

The word "tabernacle" comes from the Latin *tabernaculum*, meaning "tent," directly pointing to the Old Covenant tabernacle tent in which the Ark of the Covenant was housed (Exod. 25–40). This tabernacle and the Ark are where God dwelt among His people, and likewise, the tabernacle in a Catholic church achieves the same purpose. Because Jesus is truly present in the tabernacle, a sanctuary lamp, usually red, remains lit next to the tabernacle to indicate the Real Presence of Christ in the Eucharist (see "**Eucharist**").

Many tabernacles also contain a lunette, which is a small encasing used to display a host in a monstrance or ostensorium for benedictions and adoration. The tabernacle is usually decorated in an ornate fashion, appropriate to the high value of its contents, and is normally located in the sanctuary of the church.

While the tabernacle is a distinctive part of Christianity's roots in the Old Testament Law, it is also a wonderful source of devotion. As we are beckoned to spend time with Jesus, truly present

A tabernacle

CATHOLIC TIP

Roman and Eastern Catholics alike refer to the Blessed Virgin Mary as the Ark of the Covenant and as the tabernacle. The reason for this practice is that just as God chose to dwell and be carried among His people in a sacred tent and perfect vessel, so the womb of Mary was the perfect and sacred vessel in which God chose to dwell and be carried among His people. Referring to Mary in such a way gives great glory to God and shows the bridge between the foreshadowing of God's plan in the Old Testament and its fulfillment in the New Testament.

in the exposition of the Eucharist, we are likewise called to spend time with Him in the tabernacle.

Ten Commandments

The commands God gave the people of Israel on Mount Sinai through Moses. Also known as the Decalogue.

The Ten Commandments are apodictic, meaning they obligate a person directly: "You shall" and "You shall not" direct the behavior of God's people as desirable or harmful. Monuments to the Ten Commandments adorn the entrance to many Catholic parishes and are also often seen in courthouses.

The Ten Commandments appear in multiple places in the Pentateuch, the first five books of the Old Testament. Most commonly, we refer to Exodus 20:3–17 and Deuteronomy 5:7–21 for the list of the commandments, but forms of the list of commandments also appear on other occasions (Exod. 34:14–26, Lev. 19:3–4), although there are not ten commandments in the latter lists. Even in Exodus 20 and Deuteronomy 5, there are multiple commands combined into one, which are counted differently by Jews, Catholics, and Protestants (for example, "You shall have no other gods before me. You shall not make for yourself a graven image" in Exodus 20 is counted as one commandment by Catholics but two by most Protestants). Hence, when discussing the Ten Commandments among different religious groups, the organization will be different.

Through the commandments, God revealed Himself to His people. After delivering the Israelites from slavery and giving them shelter, He understood the people were still rebellious at heart and lacked understanding of God's holiness and moral standards. God directed these commandments to the people, but He used Moses as an intermediary since the people feared God after the violent storm and events of Exodus 19. God Himself wrote the commandments on stone tablets (Exod. 32:16), and Moses delivered them. But when Moses came down

Moses Presenting the Tablets of the Law, by Philippe de Champaigne

from Mount Sinai and saw the people worshipping a golden calf, he became so angry that he smashed the tablets. God, undeterred in His love for the Israelites, gave the commandments to Moses again to be chiseled on new tablets (Exod. 34:1, 28).

The Ten Commandments are broken up and structured thematically. The first three refer to the love of God, and the final seven to the love of one's neighbor. The traditional Catholic numbering of the commandments is as follows:

1. You shall worship the Lord your God, and only Him shall you serve.
2. You shall not take the name of the Lord your God in vain.
3. Remember the sabbath day, to keep it holy.
4. Honor your father and mother.
5. You shall not kill.

6. You shall not commit adultery.
7. You shall not steal.
8. You shall not bear false witness against your neighbor.
9. You shall not covet your neighbor's wife.
10. You shall not covet your neighbor's goods.

These commandments are later interpreted by Christ in the Sermon on the Mount (Matt. 5).

The Council of Trent teaches that the Ten Commandments are obligatory for Christians and that the justified man is still bound to keep them. The Second Vatican Council confirms: "The bishops, successors of the apostles, receive from the Lord ... the mission of teaching all peoples, and of preaching the Gospel to every creature, so that all men may attain salvation through faith, Baptism, and the observance of the Commandments."[84]

Depiction of the theological virtue of hope

Further reading: Written in Stone: How the Ten Commandments Strengthen and Heal Our World, *by Fr. P.J. Gannon, S.J.*

Theological Virtues

The infused virtues that are the foundation of the spiritual life and unite us to God through Jesus Christ (CCC 1812).

The three theological virtues are faith, hope, and love (or charity), as illuminated throughout the Gospels and confirmed by Paul (1 Cor. 13:13). All virtues help man to be happy, but these three help the faithful to act as children of God and to merit eternal life. They are known as the "theological" virtues because they have God for their immediate and proper object, they are divinely infused as gifts, and they are known only through divine revelation. All other Christian virtues are rooted in these three, which are the very foundation of Christian activity (CCC 1813).

Faith (see "**Faith**") is the infused supernatural virtue that moves the will to assent to the truths of Revelation. Hope (see "**Hope**") takes that faith and builds upon it so one trusts with unshakable confidence that God will give him all he needs to attain everlasting life. Charity (or love—see "**Love**") is the ultimate end, the evidence and substantial emanation of faith and hope. St. Paul points to charity as the highest virtue, illustrating that if our faith and hope do not result in charity, then they are empty and dead (1 Cor. 13:1–3).

The theological virtue of charity is not simply the act of giving, such as giving away one's used clothes to charity each Christmas. Rather, it is the burning love of God that causes us to love all men for the sake of God. Charity is a love that compels one's will to act on behalf of others even if it comes

CATHOLIC TIP

The thing about the theological virtues is that they are gifts from God, free gifts that require no merit of our own. But there is one important principle: we must remain in a state of grace for theological faith, hope, and love to exist within us. That formula is not too difficult to comprehend or agree with, since we cannot have these theological virtues, by means of our love of God, if we are not in a state of grace. That is, we cannot do the work of these virtues if we don't actually derive them from a true love for God.

And so we must pray for graces. Habitual grace is the permanent disposition to live and act in keeping with God's will. Sanctifying grace, a stable and supernatural disposition that perfects the soul itself to enable it to live with God and to act by His love, is a habitual grace (CCC 2000). All Christians should pray continuously for sanctifying grace. And we receive the most efficacious sanctifying grace when we visit the sacraments.

But we should not stop there: we need to pray also for the graces to pray, and even the graces to pray for graces. This practice is unnatural for us, because unlike hunger appetite, which is instinctive, the instincts to pray must be developed and become habitual—which is why it is known as "habitual" grace and not "instinctive" grace!

at a cost to oneself. The end goal is not because it is good to be charitable, as if the good in charity was the goal. The object, motive, and end goal of charity is directed to God, informed by faith, and composed by hope.

Paul speaks of these theological virtues as threefold and elucidates that faith and hope are enduring but neither persists in the heavenly realm more than love (1 Cor. 13:8–12). This is because in Heaven, we will see clearly what we accept in faith while on earth, and we will have no need for hope since we are among the blessed. But charity will remain because in Heaven we will live through, with, and in God.

Theology

The sacred science that studies God and things of God.

The word "theology" comes from the Greek words *theos* and *logos*. *Theos* means "god" or "divine," and the *logos* indicates "discourse." Together, these words form "theology," or "to talk of the divine." Like any of the sciences—the "ology" discourses—theology is an intentional study aimed at discovering the divine and understanding revealed truth. The goal of theology is to understand and articulate what we can know of God through reason (see "**Reason**") and revelation (see "**Revelation**").

Theology seeks to know who God is. Knowing who God is also allows us to entertain and answer the deepest questions: *What is the purpose of life? Why is there pain? Who made the universe? Why is there something rather than nothing? Why do good people suffer? What is good and evil?*

Although early Christians *did* theology, they did not *define* theology in any certain terms. St. Anselm of Canterbury (1033–1109) provided a universal definition for Christian theology as "faith seeking understanding." Anselm's idea of theology presumes that one will believe before he understands.

Today, the vast majority of thinkers and natural scientists would submit that one must understand before believing, a product of Enlightenment philosophies. This concept divides theologians today. Yet faith does not preclude rational human knowledge but agrees with it, and good theology must be developed through careful reasoning and consideration of natural facts and supernatural beliefs.

There are several branches of theology, primarily fundamental theology, systematic theology, and pastoral theology. Fundamental theology broadly covers topics that pertain to divine revelation, God, and man's relationship with Him. Systematic theology, also known as dogmatic theology, investigates all aspects of faith and the hierarchy of truths in an orderly study. Pastoral theology (also called practical theology) seeks to take the truths of theology and apply them to the life of believers to deepen faith and help people seek God in a personal relationship.

More theological disciplines have grown in prominence to add to the understanding of the spiritual life. Mystical theology takes on the questions pertaining to contemplation, prayer, and the interior life. Ascetical theology studies Christian perfection. And one of the most important theological genera is the study of moral theology, which addresses moral dilemmas through the lens of divine revelation, Sacred Scripture, and the wisdom of the Church's moral tradition.

Further reading: Joseph Ratzinger's Principles of Catholic Theology.

Theology of the Body

A Catholic vision of the human person articulated by Pope St. John Paul II.

Pope St. John Paul II laid out a cohesive understanding of the human person during his Wednesday audiences from 1979 to 1984. The collection of 129 addresses is now known as the Theology of the Body. It is a structured analysis of the human person that addresses the modern world while offering a holistic and Catholic approach to issues surrounding human sexuality.

John Paul II's critical work came at a high point in the sexual revolution. He was already writing and teaching on human sexuality in the 1960s, and his thought matured through his pontificate. He contributed groundbreaking insights on sexuality and the right relationship between a man and a woman as he reflected on our creation, the deepest desires of the human heart, and the meaning of life. His work still offers hope and healing in the modern world, as popular notions of sexuality are still more greatly confused.

The Theology of the Body is divided into two parts. The first part is "The Words of Christ," which investigates the human person "in the beginning," then after Original Sin, and finally at the end of time and the Parousia (see "**Parousia**"). The second part is titled "The Sacrament" and discusses marriage and responsible sexuality.

Further reading: Catholic Answers' Inseparable: Five Perspectives on Sex, Life, and Love *provides a well-organized take on conjugal love, natural law, and the "language of the body." Readers wanting to discover the fullness of the Theology of the Body would do well to pick up* Man and Woman He Created Them *by Pope St. John Paul II.*

Theotokos

A name traditionally given to the Virgin Mary, meaning "God bearer."

The name *Theotokos* is used to identify the Blessed Virgin Mary in theological, liturgical, and supplicative prayer contexts. The word is weighty in Catholic theology (both Eastern and Roman) because it evidences Mary's divine maternity. The name "God bearer" expresses that she is the mother of Jesus, who is God.

Theotokos is first found in a text from A.D. 325 (possibly earlier), written by Alexander of

Mosaic of Mary as *Theotokos*

Alexandria. The use of the term increases in the writings of several Church Fathers after this (see "**Fathers of the Church**"). The title came under fire in the fifth century, though, particularly due to the teachings of Bishop Nestorius of Constantinople, who taught that Mary could only be called *Christotokos* (Christ bearer). This disagreement sparked the Council of Ephesus in 431.

Nestorius's schismatic theology held more substance than words when describing the maternal relationship between Mary and Jesus. He claimed that there are two separate persons in Christ, and hence, a separate nature belonging to each, and that Mary could only be the mother of one. By the end of the Council of Ephesis, however, Cyril of Alexandria overcame Nestorius's arguments, Nestorius was removed from his see in Constantinople, and the Council confirmed the original Nicene Creed.

The Catholic Church teaches that Jesus is one person—the Son of God, the second Person of the Trinity—with two natures: one human, the other divine. Hence, the Incarnation was the moment in which the two natures were together united in the person of Christ (see "**Incarnation**"). This union of the two natures in the person of Christ is also known as the Hypostatic Union, a term defined in the Council of Ephesus by Cyril of Alexandria (see "**Hypostatic Union**").

As we can see, *Theotokos* is an honorable title for Mary, but it actually says appreciably more about the person of Christ.

Further reading: The collection of Cyril of Jerusalem's Catechetical Lectures.

Thomas Aquinas

Saint, Doctor of the Church, and patron of apologists, philosophers, and educational institutions.

Thomas Aquinas (1225–1274) was canonized within fifty years of his death (in 1323) and is celebrated for his mastery of Catholic theology and for synthesizing the Faith in his numerous documents, chiefly his *Summa Contra Gentiles* and the *Summa Theologiae*.

Thomas was born to a noble family near Aquino in the Lazio region of Italy (hence the name "Aquinas"). His parents' wish was for him to become an abbot in a Benedictine monastery. He initially pursued this vocation, but he was drawn to the intellectual might and preaching mission of the recently formed Dominican order, which he eventually joined against the wishes of his family. He became the pupil of Albertus Magnus (St. Albert the Great), a celebrated scholar, and later became a professor at the University of Paris.

His scholarly approach is emphasized in today's theological colleges and seminaries and is known as

Thomism, which aims to understand, apply, and recreate Thomas's intellectual approach. Thomas's work has provided theologians with solid definitions and philosophical arguments, including rational proofs for the existence of God and understanding of the human person.

St. Thomas Aquinas, Fountain of Wisdom, by Antoine Nicolas

Because of the merits of his theology, methods, doctrine, and principles, popes and Canon Law urge that his works be used in theological institutions and seminaries. "We exhort you, venerable brethren, in all earnestness to restore the golden wisdom of St. Thomas, and to spread it far and wide for the defense and beauty of the Catholic faith, for the good of society, and for the advantage of all the sciences."[85]

As with any other saint, Thomas's merits were not only found in his unquestionable mastery of Catholic theology but also in his holiness. From an early time in his studies, he was called the "Dumb Ox" for his corpulence and his slow speech. Yet his love for God drove him to become a leading professor and orator, even being summoned by Pope Urban IV to compose the liturgy for the new Feast of Corpus Christi. At the end of his life, he humbly described all of his work as "straw" compared to the magnificence of what had been revealed to him.

Further reading: Dr. Kevin Vost's One-Minute Aquinas *and* How to Think Like Aquinas.

Tithing

The giving of a portion of the fruit of one's monetary earnings to support the Church.

Tithing was an item of significant importance in the Old Testament. For the Israelites, the established requirement was a tenth of the fruits of labor or income. Abraham was the first to give a tenth in offering after his meeting with Melchizedek (Gen. 14:19–20). Jacob also gave a tenth of everything he had to God (Gen. 28:20–22). The tithe was written into the letter of the law given to Moses: "All the tithe of the land, whether of the seed of the land or of the fruit of the trees, is the Lord's; it is holy to the Lord" (Lev. 27:30). This tenth was understood as one's lot, either produce or livestock or something else with physical value. And if the entire lot (including the tenth) was needed, the person could offer a monetary value equal to the value of the goods. The law of Moses also stipulated tithing laws for festivals, orphans, and other occasions.

Christians maintained the practice of tithing. Yet for the first Christians, the tithe was seen not as a tax—a set amount to give as a matter of obligation—but as a freewill offering. Imbued with the teachings of Christ, the understanding of tithing among Christians was to give in secret (Matt. 6:1–4), to give appropriately (Matt. 23:23), to give generously according to one's ability (Mark 12:41–44), and to give with humility (Luke 18:9–14). Christians also consider one's time as a worthy tithe. Offering one's services to the parish or a special event can often have as good an effect as a monetary tithe.

CATHOLIC TIP

Tithing enables a parish to accomplish several aspects of its mission, more than just feeding priests and keeping the lights on. Tithes provide a budget for missionary sponsorship, direct help to the poor, the procurement of sacred art, funding for study materials for groups, and payroll for church staff, and they also allow the parish to remain independent of financial burdens and avoid lending streams. All Catholics should tithe according to their means. Without being scrupulous, it is generally appropriate to give between five and ten percent of one's gross income or revenue (personal or business). Consider your personal and family needs, along with the vast good that your giving will accomplish.

Tradition

The "living transmission" (CCC 2650) of divine revelation that, together with Sacred Scripture, comprises the deposit of faith entrusted to the apostles.

Sacred Tradition encompasses those truths of the Faith that are implicitly present in the Bible but not explicitly explained. Tradition comes to us from the authority of the bishops with the help of the Holy Spirit (John 14:26). Tradition also encompasses the transmission of sacred knowledge, passed from generation to generation in the succession of bishops. Sacred Tradition differs from customs that have been present in the Church for a long time.

The concept of Tradition through Apostolic Succession is well laid out in the Bible. Paul's letters contained heavy emphasis on the fact that his preaching message was associated with his preaching authority: "And what you have heard from me before many witnesses entrust to faithful men who will be able to teach others also" (2 Tim. 2:2); "So then, brethren, stand firm and hold to the traditions which you were taught by us, either by word of mouth or by letter" (2 Thess. 2:15); "And how can men preach unless they are sent?... So faith comes from what is heard, and what is heard comes by the preaching of Christ" (Rom. 10:15, 17).

Jesus, too, ensured the apostles that the succession of their message would come with special authority: "He who hears you hears me, and he who rejects you rejects me, and he who rejects me rejects him who sent me" (Luke 10:16). This is why Paul calls himself an ambassador, not a messenger, of Christ (2 Cor. 5:20).

Dei Verbum, the Dogmatic Constitution on Divine Revelation from the Second Vatican Council, contains a wealth of insight on the powerful relationship between Sacred Scripture and Sacred Tradition. Indeed, the two go hand in hand (see CCC 78):

> For both [Scripture and Tradition], flowing from the same divine wellspring, in a certain way merge into a unity and tend toward the same end. For Sacred Scripture is the word of God inasmuch as it is consigned to writing under the inspiration of the divine Spirit, while sacred tradition takes the word of God entrusted by Christ the Lord and the Holy Spirit to the apostles, and hands it on to their successors in its full purity.... Therefore both sacred tradition and Sacred Scripture are to be accepted and venerated with the same sense of loyalty and reverence.[86]

Further reading: The Meaning of Tradition *by Yves Congar.*

CATHOLIC TIP

Tradition is such an integral part of Catholic theology, and it is a touchpoint on seemingly everything we do. Therefore, it comes up often when discussing the Catholic Faith with our separated brethren. There are many tactics to employ to make an effective presentation of why Catholic theology makes use of Sacred Tradition. Firstly, Catholics do well to recognize that Protestants have their own tradition as well, but they approach it differently than the Catholic Church. Protestants might not use the word "tradition," but they do recognize theological principles that are not explicitly found in the Bible. The difference is, Protestants use their understanding of tradition so long as it is consistent with what can be interpreted in Sacred Scripture, and their tradition is binding only by the degree to which it can be justified by what is found in the Bible. Catholics find more flexibility, observing the Bible as an authority with consideration given to what we find in the historical testimony and practices of the Church. Understanding this difference greatly aids in having productive conversations with Protestants.

Transgenderism

The subjective identification of one's gender as one that differs from the objective sex identified at birth.

Practically speaking, a person's transgenderism may be permanent, habitual, or temporary. Some with transgenderism undergo surgery to change their genital physiology, which is known as gender reassignment.

Transgenderism is not compatible with Catholic teaching because it contradicts the understanding of the human person, who is created by God as either male or female. "So God created man in his own image, in the image of God he created him; male and female he created them" (Gen. 1:26). The Christian vision of sexuality stems from personhood, where identity is a witness of the biological, physiological, and spiritual realities present in each person. According to the Sacred Congregation for Catholic Education, "Sexuality, oriented, elevated and integrated by love acquires truly human quality. Prepared by biological and psychological development, it grows harmoniously and is achieved in the full sense only with the realization of affective maturity, which manifests itself in unselfish love and in the total gift of self."[87]

A person's sex is unchangeable, regardless of how one feels about his image or his physical appearance. This applies even to intersex people or those with sexual development disorders, since their overall genetic makeup is either male or female and may never be changed by any alteration of mindset or physical arrangement.

The Church has much to say about and *to* those who struggle with gender dysphoria. First, these people are loved by God and have inherent dignity. Transgenderism is against the natural law (see "**Natural Law**"), however, and so the Church asks that transgender people remain mindful of their call to holiness and chastity as applicable to their situation.

Further reading: Made This Way *by Leila Miller and Trent Horn.*

Transubstantiation

A theological term employed by the Catholic Church to describe the change in substance of the species of Holy Communion at the time of consecration.

The two parts of the term "transubstantiation" enhance our grasp of the meaning. *Trans* indicates a change, and *substance* indicates the nature of something. Specifically, the species of bread and wine change substantially into the Body and Blood of Christ, although they maintain the appearances (known as "accidents" in philosophical terms) of ordinary bread and wine. "There is no deception in this sacrament; for the accidents which are discerned by the senses are truly present. But the intellect, whose proper object is substance, is preserved by faith from deception."[88] Aquinas further explains, "This is not a formal, but a substantial conversion; nor is it a kind of natural movement: but, with a name of its own, it can be called 'transubstantiation.' … He is invisibly under the species of this sacrament, wherever this sacrament is performed."[89]

The Virgin Adoring the Host, by Jean Auguste Dominique Ingres

Catholics have long professed the doctrine of transubstantiation, though the specific term came about as the theologians of the Middle Ages realized they needed more scientific precision to explain and define Catholic beliefs. The term "transubstantiation" appears as early as the writings of Hildebert of Tours (ca. 1055–1133), and it was used with significant solemnity and expression in the Fourth Lateran Council (1215). We also find the word in St. Thomas's *Summa Theologiae* (see "**Summa Theologiae**"), written around the year 1265. Therefore, by the time of the Protestant Reformation, the principle was well-established and seldom questioned.

Still, the doctrine was debated by many of the earliest Protestant revolutionaries. Martin Luther defended resolutely the Real Presence of Jesus in the consecrated bread and wine, though his beliefs can be defined by the term *con*substantiation rather than *tran*substantiation, as he taught that the substance of the bread and wine remains present alongside the substance of the newly present Body and Blood of Jesus at the consecration (the prefix *con-* means "together, with" in Latin). Luther also taught that the words of consecration, not the priest, held the power to make the bread and wine the Body and Blood of Christ, and he denied any sacrificial significance of the Lord's Supper; though it was, he maintained, a sacrament.

Other Protestant Reformers, however, known as Sacramentarians, such as Ulrich Zwingli, held the position that the presence of Christ in Holy Communion was purely spiritual and that the Lord's Supper was merely a memorial of the original Last Supper event rather than a re-presentation of the Passion. Eventually, each reformer began to define the Lord's Supper in his own way, and there is no common consensus today among the various Protestant denominational groups; many do not even consider Communion to be a sacrament.

The Catholic Church's response to Luther, Zwingli, and other so-called reformers was the Ecumenical Council of Trent (1545–1563), which issued a bold statement: "In the sacred sacrament of the holy Eucharist, after the consecration of the bread and wine, our Lord Jesus Christ, true God and man, is truly, really, and substantially contained under the species of those sensible things."[90]

Trinity

A theological term used to describe the Catholic doctrine of three divine persons – the Father, the Son, and the Holy Spirit – subsisting in one God.

The Blessed Trinity is a central doctrine of the Christian Faith, yet since its truths cannot be fully comprehended, it is also a great mystery. The Catholic Church professes that the Godhead, another name for the Holy Trinity, is comprised of three distinct Persons who are all equally God with all perfections from all eternity. God the Father is the first Person of the Trinity. The Son is the second Person of the Trinity and proceeds from the Father by generation. The Holy Spirit is the third Person of the Trinity, and He proceeds from the Father and the Son by way of spiration.

Christian scholars have long held the position that there are signs of the Trinity present not only in the New Testament but also in the Old Testament. The three angelic visitors who visit Abraham in Genesis 18 are often regarded in the commentary of the Church Fathers to witness the reality of the Trinity. Augustine remarks: "But since three men appeared, and no one of them is said to be greater than the rest either in form, or age, or power, why should we not here understand, as visibly intimated by the visible creature, the equality

The Baptism of Jesus was a manifestation of the Trinity: the Holy Spirit, in the form of a dove, appeared with Jesus, and the voice of God the Father was heard.

CATHOLIC TIP

Devotion to the Trinity takes a supreme leap when we devoutly sing and pray the *Gloria* at Mass. It is the chief means of honoring the Blessed Trinity and establishing our assent to the divine mystery. The *Gloria* may also be said in private, but in keeping with the omission from the Masses during Advent and Lent, we would also do well to omit it at these times and yearn more anxiously to one day understand the fullness of the Trinity in Heaven.

of the Trinity, and one and the same substance in three persons?"[91]

The greatest theological proponent of the Trinity is the Church Father Athanasius of Alexandria. He was a staunch defender of Catholic doctrine both before and during the Council of Nicaea (AD 325), and he especially sought to end the heresy of Arianism, which taught that Christ was not divine but a created being. The Athanasian Creed, not directly attributed to Athanasius, itemizes and defines the trinitarian formula in its first stanza:

> Whosoever will be saved, before all things it is necessary that he hold the Catholic Faith. Which Faith except everyone do keep whole and undefiled, without doubt he shall perish everlastingly. And the Catholic Faith is this, that we worship one God in Trinity and Trinity in Unity. Neither confounding the Persons, nor dividing the Substance. For there is one Person of the Father, another of the Son, and another of the Holy Ghost. But the Godhead of the Father, of the Son and of the Holy Ghost is all One, the Glory Equal, the Majesty Co-Eternal. Such as the Father is, such is the Son, and such is the Holy Ghost. The Father Uncreate, the Son Uncreate, and the Holy Ghost Uncreate. The Father Incomprehensible, the Son Incomprehensible, and the Holy Ghost Incomprehensible. The Father Eternal, the Son Eternal, and the Holy Ghost Eternal and yet they are not Three Eternals but One Eternal. As also there are not Three Uncreated, nor Three Incomprehensibles, but One Uncreated, and One Incomprehensible. So likewise the Father is Almighty, the Son Almighty, and the Holy Ghost Almighty. And yet they are not Three Almighties but One Almighty.

What the Trinity represents, aside from incomprehensible glory and mysteriousness, is the mutual love and unity that subsists within this threefold Godhead. The love and unity in the Trinity is so complete and undividable that none of the Persons exists except in relation to the others.

Truth

The agreement of the mind with reality.

A classic theological (and practical) definition of truth comes from St. Thomas Aquinas, who argued based on the teachings of St. Augustine that truth is the conformance of the intellect with an object.[92] In other words, truth exists when one's mind agrees with what something actually is. Thomas's argument for this definition is preferred by Catholic philosophers for its efficient pattern of logic.

Truth in knowledge is man's ultimate goal, the object and source of his happiness (CCC 2002). The discovery of truth leads us to a moral and

CATHOLIC TIP

Truth is a very divisive topic in today's relativist society (see "**Relativism**"). Truth is immutable, meaning that if something is true, it is always true and cannot be changed. If something is true, the implication is always that the opposite must not be true. If God exists, no other truth can contradict that. Or if euthanasia is immoral, no circumstance or intention can alter that truth.

Our society has bought into the philosophy of relativism because it offers convenience and significantly reduces personal responsibility. Relativism eases the rational process required to solve complicated social and moral dilemmas, removes the necessary conflict to correct a person or situation, and reduces the footprint of guilt on a person's conscience. The "It's okay for you, but not for me" mentality removes a person from a dilemma but does so falsely. What's wrong in the light of truth is always wrong, and it deserves correction.

Catholics today must also be vigilant not to overapply absolutes when there is room for preference, nor operate with personal preferences when an object involves an absolute.

upright life and to union with God through Jesus, who is truth itself: "I am the way, and the truth, and the life; no one comes to the Father, but by me" (John 14:6).

Truth has caught the interest of nearly every philosopher. At the trial of Jesus, Pontius Pilate asked Jesus, "What is truth?" (John 18:38). Truth is often fit into two different but intersecting philosophies. *Ontological truth* is concerned with things we presume to be true. Good ontology causes us to seek truth by asking questions such as, "Why is there a God?" or "What is the purpose of life?" and seeks answers that help determine the integrity of an idea. *Epistemological truth* is concerned with methods of determining truth. Good epistemology uses logic as a mechanism of deduction in deriving truths and truthful conclusions. Christians need to use both wisely in order to answer life's toughest and most pressing questions.

Further reading: Ralph McInerny's book A First Glance at St. Thomas Aquinas *offers great counsel on understanding and investigating the subject of truth.*

U

Unity

Oneness or lack of division.

Unity refers to God Himself and to the Church. Unity in God refers to God's simplicity, a theological doctrine that His perfection constitutes no division of parts. God is His divine nature and "comprehends in Himself the whole perfection of being."[93] He is infinite, which means He cannot be divided, and because He cannot be divided, there are not many gods but one God (see "**God**").

That the Catholic Church exhibits unity is one of the four marks of the true Church (see "**Four Marks of the Church**"), as stated in the Apostles' Creed: "I believe in one, holy, catholic, and apostolic church." This unity in the Church means her members testify to the same doctrine, worship together as one, and accept the authority of the pope as the visible head of the Church on earth. Unity, however, does not indicate or promise uniformity in nonessentials, as there are differences unique to cultures, rites, and religious orders.

This universal Church—the Body of Christ composed of all believers—is one in identity, but this oneness is not the unity conceptualized in the Four Marks of the Church. Christians, then, must continue to work toward an ever-improving unity. This work, which is known as ecumenism (see "**Ecumenism**"), is necessary because the Christian mission is built on Jesus' desire that we may be one, as the Father and the Son are one (John 17:20–24). In short, the unity of Christians should directly reflect the unity we find in the Godhead, and not merely as a platitude or nicety but because the Christian church will truly operate and perfect its mission if it works in harmony and unison rather than discord and division.

United States Conference of Catholic Bishops (USCCB)

The episcopal conference of the Catholic Church in the United States.

The USCCB is the governing body of bishops for the United States and the U.S. Virgin Islands.

At the Last Supper, Jesus prayed for unity among His followers.

CATHOLIC TIP

The USCCB has religious and political authority for Catholics in the United States. The Catholic faithful ought to pay considerable attention to the statements, letters, assessments, and norms forthcoming from the USCCB to stay up to date regarding changes in liturgy, education, and positions potentially affecting voting and rights. The episcopal body also produces numerous resources to help Catholics live their faith in light of current events. Following the USCCB on social media or on their website is a helpful way to stay current on topics vital to the spiritual health of the faithful.

(Other countries or regions have their own episcopal conferences.) The hierarchical leadership of the USCCB has included active and retired bishops. The conference is composed of regions and various offices of special interest, and at its head is an elected president. The group meets regularly to discuss issues pertaining to or affecting the Church in the United States. They vote to enact norms to enforce within the USCCB's jurisdiction or subject to the approval of the Vatican (see "**Vatican**"). Modern issues of particular interest for the USCCB include the defense of conscience, immigration policy, catechetical standards, and attempts to resolve moral issues affecting the faithful.

Vatican

An independent territory ruled by the Supreme Pontiff and free from overt interference; officially the Vatican City State since 1929.

While most of the Vatican's territory is located within the city of Rome, it also has extraterritorial rights to the four major basilicas in Rome and the apostolic palace in the village of Castel Gandolfo. Its various offices of delegation assist with the administration activities and are composed of clergy, laity, the Swiss Guard, and security agreements with local paramilitary forces.

The Vatican is situated on what was in ancient times known as Vatican Hill, which was probably home to an Etruscan settlement before the Romans settled there. Roman Emperors Caligula and Nero later built circuses for huge chariot races there.

The Vatican coat of arms

Tradition records that St. Peter was crucified upside down (at his own request, seeing himself unworthy to suffer in the same manner as his Savior) in one of these circuses on Vatican Hill. The burial place of St. Peter was adorned with a massive basilica built by Constantine in the fourth century, which was replaced in the Renaissance with the current basilica of St. Peter. Other notable sites at the Vatican include the enormous Musei Vaticani (Vatican Museum), the papal gardens and palace, and the Vatican Radio station designed by Marconi, the inventor of the radio. Papal Masses, canonizations, audiences, and the pope's Wednesday Angelus prayer and address take place in St. Peter's Square, the large plaza outside of the basilica.

The Vatican City State has endured many changes in presence and structure since ancient times, but a general ruling of sovereign land has been a practice of the Church since the fourth century, when the Edict of Milan offered Christianity full legalization throughout the Roman Empire. The Church's lands then grew from a small site in Rome to the Papal States that covered almost a quarter of the Italian peninsula, but that land then was given over to the newly-unified Italy in 1871. Regardless of the size of its borders, however, the Vatican City State is well-situated to secure the Church's political needs and links it appropriately with its historic heritage.

Vatican II

The colloquial name given to the Catholic Church's twenty-first ecumenical council, which was the second council held at the Vatican.

The Second Ecumenical Council of the Vatican, colloquially known as Vatican II, was called by Pope

Vatican II in session

St. John XXIII shortly after he was elected in 1958. It took three years to plan, and it finally started in 1962. It was completed in 1965 by Pope St. Paul VI. The council is observed by historians and theologians of the time to have brought an end to the Counter-Reformation, which had begun with the Council of Trent (1545–1563), and it produced several documents that are pertinent to understanding the Church in the modern world.

John XXIII's announcement of the council was a shock to many in the Roman Curia and the college of cardinals, the majority of whom expected him to have a brief pontificate with little to no change. What prompted the pope's desire for a general council was the need to address matters pressing to the Church in modern times. He wanted an "update" (*aggiornamento* in Italian) so the Church could thrive in her mission. The preparatory years leading up to the council were spent gathering and evaluating topics and forming documents to be discussed at the council. In the council sessions, the topics would be briefed, studied, and criticized or defended with the goal of producing a document to guide the Church as a whole. The *aggiornamento* was met with resistance, but support grew over the course of the council, which promulgated sixteen documents:

1. *Sacrosanctum Concilium*: The Constitution on the Sacred Liturgy discusses the Church's treatment of worship, particularly in the Mass and other liturgies.
2. *Dei Verbum*: The Dogmatic Constitution on Divine Revelation sets forth authentic doctrine on divine revelation—Scripture and Tradition—and how it is handed on.
3. *Lumen Gentium*: The Dogmatic Constitution on the Church communicates how the faithful share in the Church's nature and universal mission.
4. *Gaudium et Spes*: The Pastoral Constitution on the Church in the Modern World discusses numerous topics, including politics, war, social justice, and the dignity of the human person.
5. *Gravissimum Educationis*: The Declaration on Christian Education clarifies what the Church thinks about the importance of education.
6. *Nostra Aetate*: The Declaration on the Relation of the Church to Non-Christian Religions sheds light on how the Church understands and treats non-Christian religions.
7. *Dignitatis Humanae*: The Declaration on Religious Freedom is a straightforward treatise on religious freedom in the modern world.
8. *Ad Gentes*: The Decree on the Mission Activity of the Church assesses, directs, and promotes missionary work in the Church.
9. *Presbyterorum Ordinis*: The Decree on the Ministry and Life of Priests addresses and guides priests, both pastoral and religious.
10. *Apostolicam Actuositatem*: The Decree of the Apostolate of the Laity is full of information

CATHOLIC TIP

The documents of the Second Vatican Council are not just for bishops, seminarians, and those seeking an advanced degree; they are for all the faithful. They are some of the most informative and readable Church documents available, and they are among the most essential for Catholics. I particularly recommend reading the four major documents: *Lumen Gentium*, *Gaudium et Spes*, *Sacrosanctum Concilium*, and *Dei Verbum*. All Catholics should also understand the particular mission of the laity presented in *Apostolicam Actuositatem*, while thumbing through others at a leisurely pace.

on the expectations and special standing of the laity in spreading the gospel in the world.

11. *Optatam Totius*: The Decree on Priestly Training is essential reading for seminarians, priests, rectors, and bishops.
12. *Perfectae Caritatis*: The Decree on the Adaptation and Renewal of Religious Life was meant to "treat of the life and discipline of those institutes whose members make profession of chastity, poverty, and obedience and to provide for their needs in our time."[94]
13. *Christus Dominus*: This document provides a charter for the role of the bishops in the Universal Church.
14. *Unitatis Redintegratio*: The Decree on Ecumenism aims at the restoration of unity among all Christians.
15. *Orientalium Ecclesiarum*: The Decree on the Catholic Churches of the Eastern Rite explains the Church's relations with and esteem for the Catholic Churches of the East.
16. *Inter Mirifica*: The Decree on the Media of Social Communications examines how man is called to communicate, discussing the importance of quality communication with the new media.

Much consternation still exists amongst Catholics as to the proper handling of the decrees and interpretations of the text in the documents of Vatican II. Such "shake ups" are common after ecumenical councils. Regardless, the documents contain no new dogmas, although they do affirm previously defined dogmas of the Faith—an important concept to acknowledge. These require the assent of faith for all Catholics. Even if the documents are not affirming infallible dogma, the Second Vatican Council presents the teachings of the ordinary and universal Magisterium through an ecumenical council of the Church, and the teachings are guarded from doctrinal error and are binding on all Catholics—they are not optional.

Further reading: Ralph McInerny's book What Went Wrong with Vatican II *is a fine offering to those wishing to understand better the controversy surrounding the Second Vatican Council. The journal of Henri de Lubac, who had a great influence on the entire council, is also available and sheds much needed light on the events as they occurred.*

Vestments

Garments used by clergy and assistants during liturgies and sacred ceremonies, particularly the Sacrifice of the Mass.

Liturgical vestments are often ornate to represent the beauty and divine function of the liturgy. They are also designed in such a way, layer upon layer, to

A chasuble

reflect the armor of a warrior headed into battle, reminiscent of Ephesians 6:10–20. (This armor-like quality was especially obvious of the vestments used prior to the Second Vatican Council.)

Priests and deacons in the early Church wore garments in keeping with the style of the times: alb, cincture, robe, and an over-the-head vestment. As times and fashions changed, the clergy nevertheless retained the look that they viewed as a connection to the apostles. This look gradually became distinctive in the Church. Hence, the vestments of modern clergy are impressively like those of clergy in the earliest liturgies.

Today, Latin Rite priests often wear the amice, alb, cincture, stole, and chasuble. Deacons retain much of the same but wear the stole across the body as well as a dalmatic to distinguish them from priests. A bishop is often distinguished by wearing a miter as a headpiece and a pallium over his chasuble.

Corresponding to the feast and season, vestments, most notably the chasuble, change in color. Green is used for Ordinary Time (see "**Ordinary Time**") in order to represent eternal life, hope, and growth in the Holy Spirit. Violet is worn during the seasons of Advent and Lent, when the Church focuses on prayer and fasting, as it represents penance and humility. Black may be used on All Souls' Day and requiem Masses (Masses for the dead), as it represents mourning and death. Rose, which is worn on Gaudete Sunday (the Third Sunday of Advent) and Laetare Sunday (the Fourth Sunday of Lent), represents joy. Red signifies the Lord's Passion, blood, fire, God's Love, and especially martyrdom, and so it is worn on feasts of the Lord's Passion, feasts of the martyrs, Palm Sunday, and Pentecost. White is worn during the seasons of Christmas and Easter, feasts of the Lord (other than of His Passion), and feasts of Mary (such as the Assumption or the Immaculate Conception), the angels, and saints who were not martyrs. It is also worn on All Saints Day (November 1), feasts of the apostles, nuptial Masses, and funeral Masses. Gold may replace white, red, or green (but not violet or black).

Virgin Birth

The dogma that Jesus Christ, Son of God, was born of Mary through the Holy Spirit with no biological father.

Christian teaching, as expressed in the *Catechism*, has always included the belief of Christ's virgin birth. "From the first formulations of her faith, the Church has confessed that Jesus was conceived solely by the power of the Holy Spirit in the womb of the Virgin Mary, affirming also the corporeal aspect of this event: Jesus was conceived 'by the Holy Spirit without human seed'" (496). This belief naturally coincides with the Catholic teaching of Mary's perpetual virginity, which states that Mary remained a virgin her entire life, conceiving no other children. This is why the Church Fathers continuously include the two teachings in unison:

> Hippolytus of Rome (A.D. 210): "But the pious confession of the believer is that ... the Creator of all things incorporated with Himself a rational soul and a sensible body from the all-holy Mary, ever-virgin, by an undefiled conception."[95]

> Athanasius (A.D. 360): "Let those who deny that the Son is by nature from the Father and proper to His essence deny also that He took true human flesh from the ever-virgin Mary."[96]

Catholics affirm the virgin birth in both the Apostles' and Nicene Creeds. Sacred Scripture attests to this fact when the Angel Gabriel appears to Mary and informs her of God's plan (Luke 1:26–38), which is fulfilled a full term later (Luke 2:1–7). The virgin birth also reflects the messianic prophecy foretold by Isaiah: "Therefore the Lord himself will give you a sign. Behold, a young woman shall conceive and bear a son, and shall call his name Immanuel" (Isa. 7:14). *Lumen Gentium*, the Second Vatican Council's Dogmatic Constitution on the Church, discloses perfect wisdom on the subject of the virgin birth: "This union of the mother with the Son in the work of salvation is made manifest from the time of Christ's virginal conception up to His death.... This union is manifest also at the birth of Our Lord, who did not diminish His mother's virginal integrity but sanctified it."[97]

Virginity

The intentional state of abstaining from sexual activity.

Virginity in the context of religious vow or state of life does not require physiological integrity, since surgeries or certain attacks may unintentionally defile a person's bodily integrity. The concept of virginity is also distinct from that of the discipline of celibacy (see "**Celibacy**").

The vow of virginity, most outstandingly observed by the Virgin Mary as a perpetual virgin (see "**Virgin Birth**"), is among the most excellent imitations of virtue in the spiritual life. Consecrated virgins are still an acceptable and laudable state. Historically, virginity was an "order" in the early Church (such as St. Mary of Egypt), and it exists as a vocational state of life today.

The Rite of Consecration to a Life of Virginity found in the Roman Pontifical may be used by nuns, religious sisters, or women living within the world who make the act of consecration and agree to live under the authority of the bishop, who decides the particular conditions. This specific rite is solely applicable to women. The merit of virginity is multifold. Sexual acts belong to marriage, and, analogous to priestly celibacy, consecrated virginity allows a woman to follow and imitate Christ more perfectly (CCC 923). Virginity also permits a more practical benefit, namely, the ability to form and live the consecrated life more faithfully (CCC 924).

Virginity before marriage is praised by the Scriptures: "Let marriage be held in honor among all, and let the marriage bed be undefiled; for God will judge the immoral and adulterous" (Heb. 13:4). It is still lauded by the Church today.

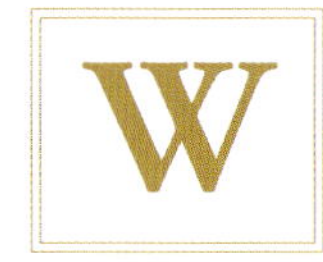

Wisdom

The gift of the Holy Spirit that disposes a person to appreciate truth and divine things.

The Bible tells us that "God loves nothing so much as the man who lives with wisdom" (Wisd. 7:28). Wisdom as a gift of the Holy Spirit comes from the teaching of Isaiah: "And the Spirit of the Lord shall rest upon him, the spirit of wisdom" (Isa. 11:2). Indeed, the prophet describes wisdom as a characteristic of the Christ, who will be the "shoot of Jesse" (Isa. 11:1). Thus, when a person actively participates in the gift of wisdom, he is participating in the life of Christ, who promised to send the Advocate (the Holy Spirit) to bear witness to Him (John 15:26), and he is demonstrating evidence of Christ's work inside him.

St. Thomas Aquinas and several other theologians (and even the pagan Greek philosopher Aristotle) placed wisdom as the highest of the gifts necessary for salvation.[98] Aquinas argued this idea from many points of view, but in summary, the gift of wisdom aids a person in committing to acts of charity, which is the highest of the theological virtues (see "**Theological Virtues**"). Without the God-inspired wisdom of choosing meritorious acts out of love for God and neighbor (as opposed to self-centered accomplishments), acts cannot be truly from a theological charity, since they do not have God as their final intent and end.

From another more luminous perspective, Holy Wisdom is associated with the person of Jesus Christ, the Son of God. The Evangelist Luke explains that Jesus was "filled with wisdom" (Luke 2:40), a continuation of the personification of wisdom often interpreted in the Old Testament with passages like Proverbs 8 and Baruch 3, which place God on earth among men—Jesus Christ incarnate. For this reason, Mary is also portrayed in tradition as the "Seat of Wisdom," since she was so completely receptive to Holy Wisdom that she was chosen from all women to bear and mother the Christ Child.

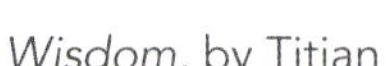

Wisdom, by Titian

Works

The redemptive labors undertaken to reestablish order after Original Sin in order to obtain merit and satisfaction for actual sin in the temporal sphere.

Work has many meanings to a Christian. From a biblical perspective, man was given work to do in the Garden of Eden, but this work was changed to drudgery as a punishment for Original Sin (see "**Original**

The Holy Family at work

Sin"). Nevertheless, work is a human right, since the human being created in the image of God has a natural propensity to work and to create as a participant in God's plan.

From a theological perspective, works are observed as a product, or evidence, of one's justification through faith. The Christian perspective accounts for an economy of merit in which work can be offered up as redemptive. This idea helps us to restore order in the temporal world by making sense and value of our labors. Moreover, if one suffers in labor and offers it up, the pains are a participation in the life of the Suffering Servant, Jesus Christ. As Paul writes, "Now I rejoice in my sufferings *for your sake*, and in my flesh I complete what is lacking in Christ's afflictions *for the sake of his body*, that is, the church" (Col. 1:24, emphases added).

The theological value of works in the economy of salvation affects justification (see "**Justification**") and is observed most prominently in the letter of James: "What does it profit, my brethren, if a man says he has faith but has not works?... So faith by itself, if it has no works, is dead" (James 2:14, 17). As proof of this idea, the New Testament writer recalls the sacrifice of Abraham, who was justified by his works: "For as the body apart from the spirit is dead, so faith apart from works is dead" (James 2:26).

James's teaching is in line with the longstanding and unchanged teaching of the Catholic Church that faith and works flow together from life in Christ and from His free gift of grace.

Works of Mercy

Selfless acts of love by which Christians serve others out of love for Christ.

The Church breaks down the chief works of mercy a Christian can perform into seven corporal (bodily) works and seven spiritual works.

Corporal works (from the Latin *corpus*, meaning "body") affect the physical well-being and dignity of man. The seven corporal works of mercy are: feed the hungry, give drink to the thirsty, clothe the naked, shelter the homeless, visit the sick and imprisoned, and bury the dead.

Spiritual works of mercy are acts of charity for the spiritual needs of others. They are: instruct the ignorant, counsel those who doubt, admonish sinners, be patient with offenders, forgive transgressions, comfort the afflicted, and pray for the living and the dead (see "**Death and Burial**").

Further reading: Pope Francis's The Name of God Is Mercy *was written for his Extraordinary Jubilee Year of Mercy. It has become a central teaching of his papacy and a worthwhile read.*

World Religions

The body of beliefs pertaining to each faith system and manner of acknowledging and worshiping God throughout the world.

The word "religion" comes from the Latin *religio*, which means "reverence." Religion is part of the natural law (see "**Natural Law**"), and it commands us to acknowledge God in prayer, moral living, worship, and sacrifice. Man is innately religious, desirous of experience and knowledge that transcends himself.

Aside from Christianity, there are two other major monotheistic religions in the world: Judaism and Islam (see "**Judaism**" and "**Islam**"). These three are the Abrahamic religions, as they worship the God of Abraham as the only God. Judaism is the most ancient of these three religions, and it was revealed by God Himself to Abraham and his descendants. Christianity centers on the belief that Jesus is the Son of God sent to redeem mankind. Christians follow Jesus' teachings and promote the importance of love and concern for all humanity. Of the three monotheistic religions, only Christianity teaches that God is three Persons in one God, which we call the Holy Trinity (see "**Trinity**"). Islam was founded by the prophet Muhammed in the seventh century. Islam means "submission," as the religion teaches submission to the will of God.

Other major western religions include the Church of Jesus Christ of Latter-Day Saints and Jehovah's Witnesses. These claim the title "Christian" but do not acknowledge the divinity of Jesus Christ, and they confound and oppose numerous Christian teachings. Mormonism is essentially polytheistic (see "**Mormonism**" and "**Jehovah's Witnesses**").

Belief systems generally classified as "Eastern religions" include Buddhism, Sikhism, Hinduism, Jainism, Shinto, and other smaller but related religions. Buddhism is generally non-theistic, though some sects worship the Buddha as a divine figure. It is more a system of spiritual philosophy than a religion, and it promotes detachment as a main tenet. Sikhism is monotheistic and worships a formless and omnipresent god who is often defined as *Waheguru*, "Wonderful Lord." Hinduism is pantheistic: they worship many gods, but all gods—indeed, all life—are simply expressions of the divine, all-encompassing life force known as Brahman. All three religions believe in reincarnation and the immortality of the soul and have "enlightenment" as their final goals, although they disagree on the manner, means, and expression of this enlightenment.

Further reading: To learn more about the Church's teaching on non-Christian religions, read Nostra Aetate *(The Declaration on the Relation of the Church to Non-Christian Religions).*

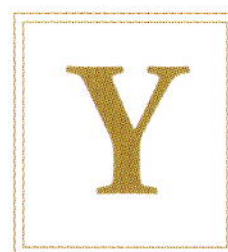

Yahweh

The primary transcription of the Hebrew name of God as He revealed Himself to Moses and thus to all His people.

God addresses Moses from the burning bush.

After Moses fled the land of Egypt (Exodus 3), he met God on Mount Horeb (also called Mount Sinai). There, God instructed Moses regarding his divine mission to emancipate the Israelites from slavery. In fear, Moses asked for God's name in case the Israelites should ask him who had sent him. God responded from the burning bush, "I am who I AM": in Hebrew, הוהי, or YHWH. These four letters, known as the tetragrammaton, are most frequently

CATHOLIC TIP

Did Jesus really say He is God? Many people are skeptical that Jesus ever explicitly stated that He is God. The prophet Isaiah proclaimed, "Truly, thou art a God who hidest thyself" (Isa. 45:15). Jesus intentionally steered away from shouting "I'm God! I'm here! Come follow me!" Instead, the Savior, understanding the heart of man perfectly, allowed the conviction of conscience and the inspiration of belief to come together as faith, a theological virtue (see "**Faith**" and "**Theological Virtues**"). Thus, He ordered demons and instructed people not to reveal who they knew Him to be (Matt. 8:4, 16:20; Mark 3:12).

Jesus taught people as they could best understand, even if it made them uncomfortable. The names "I am" and YHWH became almost unspeakable for common society in the time of Jesus, not just because the name of God is not to be used in vain according to the Second Commandment but because the meaning of the name indicates a self-existence, uncreated, a being that always existed with no beginning: God. No comparison could be made with such a being. Yet when some of the Jews wished to know with what authority Jesus spoke, He replied, "Before Abraham was, I am" (John 8:58). At that moment, the onlookers wanted to stone Him to death (the lawful penalty for blasphemy) because Jesus so directly identified Himself with Yahweh. This event underscores Jesus' highly vocal but also highly subtle means of announcing the gospel and ushering forth the reality of His divinity.

transcribed in modern languages as "Yahweh," since there are no vowels in the Hebrew alphabet.

This "I am" is more literally translated as "to be," and although the exact meaning is not understood, scholars agree that it is meant as a continuous act: is, was, and always will be. Given the circumstances, "Yahweh" is better understood to mean "He who causes to be."

Yoga

A method of physical, mental, and spiritual discipline developed in India and increasingly popular in the Western world.

Yoga formally belongs to the Hindu religion as a means of using bodily positions of strain mixed with relaxation to grow in spiritual "mindfulness." Various yoga disciplines help the Hindu achieve *moksha*, or union with the divine, all-encompassing life force known as Brahman. There are many different types of yoga: those interested in knowledge choose Jnana yoga; deeply pious people choose Bhakti or Raja yoga; and those who are action-oriented are devoted to Karma yoga. In the West, however, yoga is primarily used as a posture-based fitness routine that broadens endurance, strengthens core muscles, and promotes breathing techniques, mindfulness, and relaxation.

The Church has no specific teachings on yoga, but many modern voices have commented on the subject. Pope Francis, for example, warned in 2015 about yoga, reminding Catholics worldwide that it is the Holy Spirit that works in us to raise our hearts and minds to God, not our own efforts. When we cooperate with the Gifts of the Holy Spirit (see "**Gifts of the Holy Spirit**"), fruits of the Holy Spirit become apparent in us (see "**Fruits of the Holy Spirit**"). These "first fruits" are what lead Christians deeper into communion with the divine and in greater beatitude reflective of Christ (CCC 1830–1832).

CATHOLIC TIP

Can a Catholic do yoga? Many Catholics argue that yoga is an efficient athletic training regimen, since its formidable style greatly increases health, healing, and power. But yoga, especially as a spiritual device, is incompatible with the Catholic Faith for many reasons. At its core, the purpose of yoga is certainly spiritual and is used to help a person reach a different type of consciousness, a "Universal Consciousness," which through its stretches, poses, breathing techniques, and its utterances, is to be the vehicle to the divine—a person's true self. Catholics, instead, profess that the "divinity inside us" is solely derived from the presence of Christ in our souls—that when we may cooperate with His grace and follow His commands.

Although the basic forms of stretching and straining have legitimate fitness benefits, even akin to an ascetic discipline, many experts on demonology and pastoral care do not recommend the practice of yoga. Catholics searching for alternatives may enjoy Pietra Fitness routines, and many others available with a quick Internet search.

Z

Zeal

Intense love for God that moves the will of a believer to act.

The word "zeal" comes from the Greek word *zēlos* meaning "a noble passion," which is also related to the Greek verb *zeō*, meaning "to boil over." In theological terms, "zeal" refers to the burning love for the Lord given by the Holy Spirit.

We find an example of this fiery love in the reaction of the disciples on the road to Emmaus after the appearance of the risen Jesus: "Did not our hearts burn within us while he talked to us on the road, while he opened to us the scriptures?" (Luke 24:32). It is also the reaction Jesus had when He chased the money changers from the Temple: "For zeal for thy house has consumed me" (Ps. 69:9).

The *Catechism* reminds us that zeal is an outstanding trait for believers. It moves us to act morally, to desire the Kingdom of God here on earth (2750), and to give in love to those who need most (2004). But zeal is also a term that comes with a tinge of negativity. The Zealots of the Bible were a political offspring of those inspired by the Maccabean revolt: "Let everyone who is zealous for the law and supports the covenant come out with me!" (1 Macc. 2:27). A "zealous" Catholic could refer to someone who is a pious believer, active in the parish, but it can also refer to one who gets too caught up in emotions or causes, hindering his complete and authentic living of the gospel.

A healthy sense of self-awareness helps the Catholic to develop the right perception, although it is not always guaranteed.

The Supper at Emmaus, by Jean Baptiste de Champaigne

Acknowledgments

It's common for pure joy to sweep over me as I finish a book. Ordinarily, I breathe a sigh of relief and wonder, "What's next?" But this book was a little bit different because the writing process received so many unexpected interruptions. And for it to become a completed project—especially as well as I feel it has turned out—there are a few people to acknowledge.

I wrote more than half of this from the walls of Italy's greatest monasteries, refectories of monks, and in the great library of St. Dominic's basilica in Bologna. In a small cell of the Sant'Agostino monastery of San Gimignano, I received several books owned by the recently deceased Fr. Brian Lowery—a good friend I had made just two years before—that greatly aided me in the writing of this book. I went on several retreats to Varese, Norcia, and Montepulciano, prayerfully trying to get many of these words right for the reader and to escape the busyness of home life. I'm grateful also to Dom Cassian, OSB, and the prior of the Benedictines of Norcia, Dom Benedict Nivakoff, OSB, for allowing me to stay with them so many times to retreat from the world and focus on this writing.

It was a special privilege to live in Italy, but I made the decision to move back to the United States and chose New Orleans as our new home. Immediately after arriving, I wasn't even sure I could finish this book, as I was searching for time amid the panic of returning to our home after Hurricane Ida and managing a complete rebuild. To all the donors, neighbors, and volunteers who helped make that difficult experience one of faith, hope, and charity, I am ever grateful.

I really want to thank my wife for her undying support—I never had to wonder if I could escape to get a few thousand words in. Special thanks to the priests—particularly the two in the dedication—who helped me better understand more than one of these very difficult topics, and to the apologists at Catholic Answers who double-checked some facts with me. It all comes down to the editor, though: Mary Beth Giltner, I am so impressed with your skill and leadership style—thank you for this special opportunity and for the endless hours spent bringing out the best in me.

Now, reader, thank *you* for reading this book. I pray you will find it useful in your walk with Christ.

Endnotes

1. Pope St. Paul VI, apostolic exhortation *Evangelii Nuntiandi* (December 8, 1975), no. 13.
2. St. Thomas Aquinas, *Summa Theologiae* II–II, q. 64, art. 6.
3. USCCB Marriage and Family Life Ministries, "Annulment," accessed August 25, 2022, https://www.usccb.org/topics/marriage-and-family-life-ministries/annulment#tab--what-is-an-annulment.
4. *Pastoral Care of the Sick: Rites of Anointing and Viaticum*, no. 98.
5. St. Ignatius of Antioch, "Epistle to the Smyrnaeans," no. 8.
6. Pope St. Clement I, "Letter to the Corinthians," no. 44.
7. Pope Pius XII, apostolic constitution *Munificentissimus Deus* (November 1, 1950), no. 44.
8. *Dei Verbum* (Dogmatic Constitution on Divine Revelation) (November 18, 1965), no. 11.
9. Ibid., no. 21.
10. St. Thomas Aquinas, *Summa Theologiae* II–II, q. 64, art. 2.
11. Ibid., q. 108, art. 1.
12. Pope St. John Paul II, apostolic exhortation *Catechesi Tradendae* (October 16, 1979), no. 18.
13. Pope St. Paul VI, *Gravissimum Educationis* (Declaration on Christian Education) (October 28, 1965), no. 3.
14. *Lumen Gentium* (Dogmatic Constitution on the Church) (November 21, 1964), no. 12.
15. Karol Wojtyla, *Love and Responsibility*, trans. Grzegorz Ignatik (Pauline Books & Media: 2001), p. 159.
16. Tertullian, *On Idolatry*, no. 15.
17. *Lumen Gentium*, no. 40.
18. Council of Trent, Session 14.
19. *Dei Verbum*, no. 4.
20. "Apostles' Creed," *Catholic Encyclopedia*, New Advent, 2022, https://www.newadvent.org/cathen/01629a.htm.
21. *Dei Verbum*, no. 10.
22. St. Thomas Aquinas, *Summa Theologiae* II–II, q. 30, art. 4.
23. Ibid.
24. St. Faustina, *Diary*, trans. Teresa Bałuk-Ulewiczowa (Krakow: Misericordia Publications, 2020), 300. A full text of this book is available on the website for the Congregation of the Sisters of Our Lady of Mercy, https://www.saint-faustina.org/diary-full-text/.

25. *Sacrosanctum Concilium* (The Constitution on Sacred Liturgy) (December 4, 1963), no. 100.
26. Pope Pius IX, apostolic constitution *Ineffabilis Deus* (December 8, 1854).
27. *Lumen Gentium*, no. 11.
28. Pope St. John Paul II, Message for the 1990 World Day of Peace, no. 6.
29. Pope Benedict XVI, remarks after Angelus address, August 27, 2006.
30. Pope Francis, encyclical letter *Laudato Si'* (May 24, 2015), no. 50.
31. Pope St. Paul VI, apostolic exhortation *Evangelii Nuntiandi* (December 8, 1975), nos. 26–28.
32. St. Thomas Aquinas, *Summa Theologiae* I, q. 48, art. 1.
33. Pius XII, papal encyclical *Humani Generis* (August 12, 1950), no. 37.
34. St. Thomas Aquinas, *Summa Theologiae* II–II, q. 2, art. 9.
35. *Dei Verbum*, no. 5.
36. Pope St. Paul VI, *Gravissimum Educationis*, no. 3.
37. USCCB, "Lenten Fasting & Abstinence," 2021, https://www.usccb.org/resources/Fasting-Lent-Info.pdf.
38. Fr. Reginald Garrigou-Lagrange, *Providence: God's Loving Care for Men and the Need for Confidence in Almighty God* (Gastonia, NC: TAN Books, 1998).
39. Pope St. John Paul II, General Audience (July 28, 1999), no. 4.
40. Sacred Congregation for the Doctrine of the Faith, *Persona Humana* (December 29, 1975), no. 8.
41. *Gaudium et Spes* (Pastoral Constitution on the Church in the Modern World) (December 7, 1965), no. 27.
42. Pope St. Paul VI, apostolic constitution *Indulgentiarum Doctrina* (January 1, 1967), "Norms," no. 1.
43. *Enchiridion of Indulgences*, no. 2.
44. *Pastor Aeternus* (Dogmatic Constitution on the Church of Christ) (July 18, 1870), ch. 4 no. 93.
45. Pope St. Paul VI, *Nostra Aetate* (Declaration on the Relation of the Church with Non-Christian Religions) (October 28, 1965), no. 3.
46. "Do Jehovah's Witnesses Shun Those Who Used to Belong to Their Religion?," JW.org, https://www.jw.org/en/jehovahs-witnesses/faq/shunning/.
47. *Lumen Gentium*, no. 31.
48. Pope St. Paul VI, *Apostolicam Actuositatem* (Decree on the Apostolate of the Laity) (November 18, 1965), no. 1.
49. *Sacrosanctum Concilium*, no. 2.
50. Pope Francis, papal bull *Misericordiae Vultus* (April 11, 2015), no. 20.
51. St. Thomas Aquinas, *Summa Theologiae* III, q. 46, art. 2, 3.
52. *Ad Gentes* (Decree on the Mission Activity of the Church), no. 6.
53. Ibid., no. 2.

54. *Gaudium et Spes*, no. 58.
55. *Ad Gentes*, no. 6.
56. Ibid., nos. 11–12.
57. Pope Pius X, encyclical letter *Pascendi Dominici Gregis* (September 8, 1907), no. 40.
58. First Vatican Council, Dogmatic Constitution on the Catholic Faith, "Of Faith and Reason," no. 1.
59. Pope Pius XII, encyclical letter *Mystici Corporis* (June 29, 1943), no. 30.
60. Council of Trent, Session 5, articles 1–2.
61. Joint Catholic-Orthodox Declaration of His Holiness Pope Paul VI and the Ecumenical Patriarch Athenagoras I, December 7, 1965.
62. Pope St. John Paul II, *Ut Unum Sint* (May 25, 1995), no. 54.
63. St. Thomas Aquinas, *Summa Theologiae* II–II, q. 83, art. 9 (as quoted in the *Catechism of the Catholic Church*, no. 2763).
64. *Lumen Gentium*, no. 57.
65. St. Thomas Aquinas, *Summa Theologiae* II–II, q. 152, art. 3.
66. Pope St. Paul VI, encyclical letter *Humanae Vitae* (July 25, 1968), no. 23
67. Ibid.
68. St. John Damascene, quoted in the *Catechism of the Catholic Church*, no. 2559.
69. *Dei Verbum*, no. 7.
70. Pope St. John Paul II, encyclical letter *Laborem Exercens* (September 14, 1981), no. 8.
71. See Pope St. John XXIII, encyclical letter *Mater et Magistra* (May 15, 1961), no. 19.
72. Pope Pius XI, encyclical letter *Quadragesimo Anno* (May 15, 1931), no. 49.
73. St. John Chrysostom, "Homily on 1 Corinthians."
74. Pontifical Commission for Justice and Peace, "The Church and Racism: Towards a More Fraternal Society" (November 3, 1988), no. 24.
75. *Didache*, no. 14.
76. United States Conference of Catholic Bishops, "Guidelines for the Reception of Communion" (November 14, 1996).
77. Cardinal Joseph Ratzinger, Homily for April 18, 2005.
78. *Lumen Gentium*, no. 36.
79. *Sacrosanctum Concilium*, no. 60.
80. Ibid., no. 61.
81. Ibid., no. 122.
82. Ibid., no. 127.
83. St. Thomas Aquinas, *Summa Theologiae* II–II, q. 118, art. 2.
84. *Lumen Gentium*, no. 24.
85. Pope Leo XIII, encyclical letter *Aeterni Patris* (August 4, 1879), no. 31.
86. *Dei Verbum*, no. 9.
87. Sacred Congregation for Catholic Education, "Educational Guidance in Human Love: Outlines for Sex Education" (1983).

88. St. Thomas Aquinas, *Summa Theologiae* III, q. 75, art. 5.
89. Ibid., q. 75, arts. 4, 1
90. Council of Trent, Session 13, ch. 1.
91. St. Augustine, *De Trinitate*, bk. 2, ch. 11.
92. St. Thomas Aquinas, *Summa Theologiae* I, q. 16, art. 1.
93. Ibid., q. 11, art. 3.
94. Pope St. Paul VI, Decree on the Adaptation and Renewal of Religious Life *Perfectae Caritatis* (October 28, 1965), no. 1.
95. Hippolytus of Rome, *Against Beron and Helix*, fragment 8.
96. Athanasius of Alexandria, *Discourses Against the Arians*, 2, no. 70.
97. *Lumen Gentium*, no. 57.
98. See St. Thomas Aquinas, *Summa Theologiae* I–II, q. 68, art. 2

Image Credits

4. Confessional in the Church of St. Alphonsus, Salta, Argentina, Wikimedia Commons, public domain.
5. *Adoration of the Magi*, by Giotto, Scrovegni Chapel, Padua, Wikimedia Commons, public domain.
6. Advent wreath, photo by Grant Whitty on Unsplash.
7. *Tobias and the Archangel Raphael*, by Davide Ghirlandaio, Wikimedia Commons, public domain.
9. Detail of a stained-glass window showing St. Malachy receiving the sacrament of Anointing, St. Patrick's Cathedral, Armagh, Northern Ireland, photo by Andreas F. Borchert, CC BY-SA 4.0, https://commons.wikimedia.org/w/index.php?curid=81359308.
10. *St. Catherine among the Philosophers*, by Scarsellino (Ippolito Scarsella), Wikimedia Commons, public domain.
11. *Christ and the Twelve Apostles*, by Taddeo di Bartolo, Wikimedia Commons, public domain.
12. *Our Lady of Lourdes*, by Virgilio Tojetti, Wikimedia Commons, public domain.
13. Altarpiece depicting the Ascension of Christ, by Martin Schongauer, photo by TxllxT TxllxT—own work, CC BY-SA 4.0, https://commons.wikimedia.org/w/index.php?curid=132608599.
15. *The Assumption of Mary*, by Guido Reni, photo by GoldenArtists—Own work, CC BY 4.0, https://commons.wikimedia.org/w/index.php?curid=141428127.
17. Baptismal font in the baptistery of San Giovanni Battista, Volterra, Italy (318677271), giadophoto/Adobe Stock.
18. *The Sermon on the Mount*, by Ivan Makarov, Wikimedia Commons, public domain.
19. Rosary on an open Bible, Wikimedia Commons/Pixabay, public domain.
21. *Head of a Bishop* (ca. 1770), by Gaetano Gandolfi, Wikimedia Commons, public domain.
24. Canonization of Bl. Pope John XXIII and Bl. Pope John Paul II, April 27, 2014, photo by Jeffrey Bruno from New York City, United, CC BY-SA 2.0, https://commons.wikimedia.org/w/index.php?curid=32427709.
26. Wrath and Sloth, in *Les Péchées Capitaux* (The deadly sins; ca. 1620), illustration by Jacques Callot, Wikimedia Commons, public domain.
27. Illustration of the four cardinal virtues in *La Somme le roi*, by Dominican Laurent d'Orléans (ca. 1290–1300), Wikimedia Commons, public domain.

28. *The Catechism Lesson* (1890), by Jules-Alexis Muenier, Wikimedia Commons, public domain.
29. Pope Leo XIII (ca. 1878), who wrote *Rerum Novarum*, one of the most famous Church documents related to social issues, Wikimedia Commons, public domain.
31. Vessel, called "Alabaster" (see Matt. 26:7), for sacred chrism, Patriarchal Residence, Moscow, photo by Shakko—own work, CC BY-SA 3.0, https://commons.wikimedia.org/w/index.php?curid=4618735.
31. Nativity Scene, altarpiece in the church of Saint Matthew in Stitar, Croatia (256042880), photo by zatletic / Adobe Photo Stock.
33. *The Forerunners of Christ with Saints and Martyrs*, by Bl. Fra Angelico, photo by Sailko, own work, photo taken on March 1, 2017, CC BY 3.0, https://commons.wikimedia.org/w/index.php?curid=67529402.
34. *The Sacrament of Confirmation* (after 1757), by Pietro Longhi, Wikimedia Commons, public domain.
36. *The Conversion of St. Paul*, by Spinello Aretino, Wikimedia Commons, public domain.
37. *Agnus Dei* (Lamb of God), by Francisco de Zurbarán, Wikimedia Commons, public domain.
39. *St. Lawrence Enthroned with Saints and Donors*, by Fra Filippo Lippi, Wikimedia Commons, public domain.
40. Silhouette of a person standing near a cross, photo by Soroush Alavi on Unsplash.
42. The fall of Lucifer, illustration by Gustave Doré in John Milton's *Paradise Lost* (1866), Wikimedia Commons, public domain.
43. Military man praying the Rosary (191804646), photo by Yakobchuk Olena / Adobe Stock Photo.
44. Drawing of St. Ignatius of Loyola (1703), by Nicolas Bazin, Wikimedia Commons, public domain.
46. Divine Mercy image (1934), by Eugeniusz Kazimirowski, Divine Mercy Sanctuary in Vilnius, Wikimedia Commons, public domain.
49. *The Four Doctors of the Western Church: St. Augustine of Hippo*, attributed to Gerard Seghers, Wikimedia Commons, public domain.
50. Home oratory, photo by Leila Marie Lawler, author, *The Little Oratory: A Beginner's Guide to Praying in the Home*.
51. Stained-glass window depicting the Resurrection of Christ, St. Patrick Church, Troy, Ohio, photo by Nheyob—own work, CC BY 4.0, https://commons.wikimedia.org/w/index.php?curid=143288526.
52. Holy Resurrection Melkite Church, Columbus, Ohio, photo by Nheyob—own work, CC BY-SA 4.0, https://commons.wikimedia.org/w/index.php?curid=48322846.
55. Road in between brown wooden fences, Photo by Werner Sevenster on Unsplash.
57. *Disputation of the Holy Sacrament*, by Raphael, Wikimedia Commons, public domain.

59. Eucharistic miracle of Lanciano, by AFC photo—own work, CC BY-SA 3.0, https://commons.wikimedia.org/w/index.php?curid=31362184.
60. *St. Francis of Assisi*, by Franciso Pacheco, photo by Jl FilpoC—own work, CC BY-SA 4.0, https://commons.wikimedia.org/w/index.php?curid=100559815
62. Fr. Gregor Mendel, Wikimedia Commons, public domain.
63. Fr. Gabriele Amorth, photo by Angela Musolesi—own work, CC BY-SA 4.0, https://commons.wikimedia.org/w/index.php?curid=129111867.
65. Martin Family, by Gérard—own work, CC BY-SA 4.0, https://commons.wikimedia.org/w/index.php?curid=86472399.
67. Corpus Christi procession in Bielso-Biała 2023, photo by Silar—own work, CC BY-SA 4.0, https://commons.wikimedia.org/w/index.php?curid=132800686.
68. Stained-glass window of Christ revealing His Sacred Heart to St. Margaret Mary, St. Margaret Mary Alacoque Church, Woodbridge, Ontario, photo by Nheyob—own work, CC BY-SA 4.0, https://commons.wikimedia.org/w/index.php?curid=125072725.
69. *The Return of the Prodigal Son*, by Bartolomé Esteban Murillo, Wikimedia Commons, public domain.
70. *The Last Judgment*, by Fra Angelico, photo by Richard Mortel from Riyadh, Saudi Arabia, CC BY 2.0, https://commons.wikimedia.org/w/index.php?curid=69729875.
71. Freemasons' Hall, London, photo by Eluveitie—own work, CC BY-SA 3.0, https://commons.wikimedia.org/w/index.php?curid=19119013.
73. Stained-glass window depicting the Holy Spirit in the form of a dove, Church of St. Pothin, Lyon, France, photo by Thaï Ch. Hamelin / ChokdiDesign on Unsplash.
74. *The Nativity with God the Father and the Holy Ghost*, by Giambattista Pittoni, Wikimedia Commons, public domain.
77. Angel statue, Castelo Sant'Angelo, Rome, Italy,_photo by Antônia Felipe on Unsplash.
80. *Christ in Limbo* (1441–1442), by Fra Angelico, Wikimedia Commons, public domain.
81. *Luther Burns the Papal Bull in the Square of Wittenberg*, by Karl Aspelin, Wikimedia Commons, public domain.
83. *Mary and Joseph with the Infant Jesus*, by Julius Frank, Wikimedia Commons, public domain, PD-US.
85. Statue depicting the virtue of hope, Cathedral of the Assumption of Mary, Guadalajara, Mexico, photo by Nheyob—own work, CC BY-SA 4.0, https://commons.wikimedia.org/w/index.php?curid=39308446.
87. Statue of the Immaculate Conception, Malalos City, Bulacan, Wikimedia Commons, public domain.
88. Photo of immigrants on a ferry boat near Ellis Island (1920), Wikimedia Commons, public domain.
89. *Baby Jesus with St. John the Baptist*, by Felicián Moczik, Wikimedia Commons, public domain.

91. Mosque illustration, Archives of Pearson Scott Foresman, Wikimedia Commons, public domain.
92. Portrait of Cornelius Jansen (seventeenth century), by Jean Morin, Wikimedia Commons, public domain.
93. Charles Taze Russell, Wikimedia Commons, public domain.
94. *The Good Shepherd*, by Philippe de Champaigne, photo Yelkrokoyade—own work (date: 2014-12-30 10:46:40), CC BY-SA 4.0, https://commons.wikimedia.org/w/index.php?curid=37811320.
95. *St. Joseph Carrying the Child Jesus on the Left Arm*, by Pieter van Lint, Wikimedia Commons, public domain.
96. Central panel of *The Last Judgment* triptych by Hans Memling, Wikimedia Commons, public domain.
99. *The Sermon on the Mount*, detail of altarpiece by Henrik Olrik in St. Matthew Church, Copenhagen, Denmark, Wikimedia Commons, public domain.
102. Priest administering ashes on Ash Wednesday, photo by Thays Orrico on Unsplash.
103. Easter Vigil liturgy, collegiate church of Gdańsk-Wrzeszcz, 2013, photo by Michał Winiarski (Winiar)—own work, CC BY-SA 3.0, https://commons.wikimedia.org/w/index.php?curid=25400890.
107. *The Wedding at Cana*, by Bernardino Poccetti (1604), photo by Sailko, CC BY-SA 3.0, https://commons.wikimedia.org/w/index.php?curid=39619707.
108. *The Stoning of St. Stephen* (1863), by Gabriel-Jules Thomas, lunette of the main gate of the church Saint-Etienne du Mont, Paris, Wikimedia Commons, public domain.
109. Statue of the Blessed Virgin Mary and the Christ Child, St. Bernard Catholic Church, Burkettsville, Ohio, photo by Nheyob—own work, CC BY-SA 3.0, https://commons.wikimedia.org/w/index.php?curid=26884969.
111. *Jesus Healing the Sick*, by Heinrich Hofmann, Wikimedia Commons, public domain.
113. Statue of St. Francis Xavier, St. Francis Xavier Catholic Church, Superior, Wisconsin, photo by Billertl—Own work, CC BY-SA 4.0, https://commons.wikimedia.org/w/index.php?curid=39707891.
115. Monastery of Subiaco, photo by Simone Frignani—own work, CC BY-SA 4.0, https://commons.wikimedia.org/w/index.php?curid=90448520.
118. Joseph Smith (ca. 1842), painter unknown, Wikimedia Commons, public domain.
120. *St. Teresa in Ecstasy*, by Giovanni Battista Piazzetta, Wikimedia Commons, public domain.
123. Rose quartz, Wikimedia Commons, public domain.
124. Depiction of the Descent of the Holy Spirit on Pentecost, in the Vaux Passional illuminated manuscript, Wikimedia Commons, public domain.
126. Pope Francis wearing green vestments, Philadelphia, 2015, photo by Governor Tom Wolf—https://www.flickr.com/photos/governortomwolf/21153126323/, CC BY 2.0, https://commons.wikimedia.org/w/index.php?curid=43773836.

128. Iconostasis in Russian Orthodox Church, Deventer, the Netherlands, Wikimedia Commons, public domain.
129. *Benediction of God the Father* (1565), by Luca Cambiaso, Wikimedia Commons, public domain.
131. Stained-glass window depicting St. Peter, St. Raphael Church, Springfield, Ohio, photo by Nheyob—own work, CC BY-SA 4.0, https://commons.wikimedia.org/w/index.php?curid=37373595.
133. Center panel of the triptych *The Crucifixion* (1482–1485), attributed to Pietro Perugino, Wikimedia Commons, public domain.
135. Statue of St. Anthony of Padua and the Christ Child, St. Anthony of Padua Church, Morris, Indiana, photo by Nheyob—own work, CC BY 4.0, https://commons.wikimedia.org/w/index.php?curid=141404367.
137. Stained-glass window (1895) depicting Pentecost, Church of the Assumption of Mary, Mittich, Lower Bavaria, photo by Wolfgang Sauber—own work, CC BY-SA 4.0, https://commons.wikimedia.org/w/index.php?curid=121603750.
139. Pilgrims in Fátima, photo by Beltranlazaga own work, CC BY-SA 4.0, https://commons.wikimedia.org/w/index.php?curid=127829574.
140. Person praying (307645925), photo by Tinnakorn / Adobe Stock Photo.
142. *St. Anthony Preaching before the Fishes*, by Gerard David, photo by Sailko—own work, CC BY 3.0, https://commons.wikimedia.org/w/index.php?curid=64515965.
144. Priestly ordinations of members of the Institute of the Incarnate Word held at the Basilica Shrine of the Immaculate Conception, Washington, D.C., 2015, photo by Institute of the Incarnate Word—own work, CC BY-SA 4.0, https://commons.wikimedia.org/w/index.php?curid=46419111.
147. *Madonna and Child with Souls in Purgatory*, by Luca Giordano, Wikimedia Commons, public domain.
150. *The Last Communion of St. Mary of Egypt*, by Marcantonio Franceschini, Wikimedia Commons, public domain.
154. Reliquary containing one of the bones of St. Sebastian, Wikimedia Commons, public domain.
157. *The Resurrection of Christ* (ca. 1564), by Maerten de Vos, Wikimedia Commons, public domain.
160. Rosary, photo by James Coleman on Unsplash.
162. Holy-water font, Wikimedia Commons, public domain.
162. Scapular, photo by Sarah sofía at English Wikipedia, CC BY-SA 3.0, https://commons.wikimedia.org/w/index.php?curid=5105605.
164. Statue of the Sacred Heart, photo by Jonathan Dick, O.S.F.S., on Unsplash.
166. *The Blessed in Heaven* (1096–1107), abbey church of Saint Foy, France, Wikimedia Commons, public domain.
169. Microscope illustration by Gordon Johnson / Pixabay.

172. Sixth Station of the Cross, Wikimedia Commons, public domain.
174. *St. Francis Receives the Stigmata*, by Ambrogio Borgognone, photo by Crijam—own work, CC BY-SA 4.0, https://commons.wikimedia.org/w/index.php?curid=80805899.
178. Tabernacle in the Church of Virgen de los Remedios (Our Lady of Good Remedy), San Fernando, Pampanga, Wikimedia Commons, public domain.
179. *Moses Presenting the Tablets of the Law* (ca. 1648), by Philippe de Champaigne, Wikimedia Commons, public domain.
180. Depiction of Hope in *The Theological Virtues: Faith, Charity, Hope* (1495–1505), by an anonymous artist, Wikimedia Commons, public domain.
183. The Blessed Virgin Mary as *Theotokos*, apse mosaic in Hagia Sophia in Turkey, Wikimedia Commons, public domain.
184. *St. Thomas Aquinas, Fountain of Wisdom* (1648), by Antoine Nicolas, Wikimedia Commons, public domain.
187. *The Virgin Adoring the Host*, by Jean Auguste Dominique Ingres, Wikimedia Commons, public domain.
188. *The Baptism of Christ*, by Antoine Coypel, Wikimedia Commons, public domain.
191. *The Last Supper* (1389–1390), by Lorenzo Monaco—DSVTP1176, CC BY-SA 4.0, https://commons.wikimedia.org/w/index.php?curid=103375924.
193. Emblem of the Vatican, Wikimedia Commons, public domain.
194. Vatican II in session, Wikimedia Commons, public domain.
196. Green chasuble, photo by Ji-Elle—own work, CC BY-SA 3.0, https://commons.wikimedia.org/w/index.php?curid=15158674.
198. *Wisdom*, by Titian, Wikimedia Commons, public domain.
199. *House of Nazareth*, predella relief by Theodor Schnell the Younger, photo by Andreas Praefcke, Wikimedia Commons, CC BY 3.0, https://commons.wikimedia.org/w/index.php?curid=11870007.
201. *Landscape with Moses and the Burning Bush*, by Domenichino, Wikimedia Commons, public domain.
203. *The Supper at Emmaus* (1664), by Jean Baptiste de Champaigne, Wikimedia Commons, public domain.

About the Author

Shaun McAfee is a convert to the Catholic Faith and a Lay Dominican with the Central Province of St. Albert the Great. He served in the Air Force before earning a bachelor's degree in Aeronautics at the University of North Dakota, and later resumed his work for the U.S. Army as a Civilian, serving in Afghanistan, Japan, and Italy. He holds a Master of Business Administration from Liberty University and a Master of Dogmatic Theology from Holy Apostles College and Seminary. He currently lives in New Orleans, Louisiana, with his wife, Jessica, and their six kids. Shaun McAfee is the founder and editor of EpicPew.com and writes at the *National Catholic Register* and for numerous other Catholic publications and resources. His books include:

Compendium of Sacramentals: Encyclopedia of the Church's Blessings, Signs, and Devotions (TAN Books, 2023)
20 Answers: Sacramentals and Relics (Catholic Answers Press, 2021)
Epic Saints: Wild, Wonderful, and Weird Stories of God's Heroes (TAN Books, 2020)
I'm Catholic. Now What? (Our Sunday Visitor, 2019)
20 Answers: Conversion (Catholic Answers, 2019)
Inseparable: Five Perspectives on Sex, Life, and Love in Defense of Humanae Vitae (Catholic Answers, 2018)
Social Media Magisterium (En Route, 2018)
Reform Yourself! (Catholic Answers Press, 2017)
St. Robert Bellarmine (En Route, 2016)
Filling Our Father's House (Sophia Institute Press, 2015)

Sophia Institute

Sophia Institute is a nonprofit institution that seeks to nurture the spiritual, moral, and cultural life of souls and to spread the gospel of Christ in conformity with the authentic teachings of the Roman Catholic Church.

Sophia Institute Press fulfills this mission by offering translations, reprints, and new publications that afford readers a rich source of the enduring wisdom of mankind.

Sophia Institute also operates the popular online resource CatholicExchange.com. *Catholic Exchange* provides world news from a Catholic perspective as well as daily devotionals and articles that will help readers to grow in holiness and live a life consistent with the teachings of the Church.

In 2013, Sophia Institute launched Sophia Institute for Teachers to renew and rebuild Catholic culture through service to Catholic education. With the goal of nurturing the spiritual, moral, and cultural life of souls, and an abiding respect for the role and work of teachers, we strive to provide materials and programs that are at once enlightening to the mind and ennobling to the heart; faithful and complete, as well as useful and practical.

Sophia Institute gratefully recognizes the Solidarity Association for preserving and encouraging the growth of our apostolate over the course of many years. Without their generous and timely support, this book would not be in your hands.

www.SophiaInstitute.com
www.CatholicExchange.com
www.SophiaInstituteforTeachers.org